THE SUBWAY DIARIES

HEIDI KOLE

"The Subway Diaries"
Copyright © 2009 Heidi Kole

All rights reserved under International and Pan-American Copyright Conventions.

Published in the United States by Bohemiantherapy Publishing LLC 2009.

The Library of Congress has cataloged this edition as follows:

Kole, Heidi

The Subway Diaries / Heidi Kole - 1st American ed.

p cm.

ISBN 978-0-9819700-0-4

1 Title
Cover photography:
Henning Peter Fischer Photography
www.hpfphotography.com
Cover design: Max Shuppert
http://maxshuppert.com

www.bohemiantherapypublishing.com

Acknowledgements

Antonia Kasper – Editor

I want to acknowledge with special thanks, Antonia Kasper. Over a span of a few months she pushed me to literary and creative limits I'd never imagined, and tirelessly encouraged me to discover my true voice. Her out of the box thinking has been an inspiration. For that, I'm grateful. All this she accomplished with a four-month-old baby daughter. To me, thats the definition of a "super woman." Thank you, Toni, for accompanying me on this journey.

Veronica Smith – Copy editor

A special thank you to the ever talented Veronica Smith for catching all we missed, despite drenching rainstorms ruining entire weeks of work and a stomach flu laying you flat; all with such grace, lightheartedness, and enthusiasm. You'll go far in this business, I feel it.

Those who allowed The Diaries to come through me to life

Dirk Kennedy for working his magic on all the random & crazy sounds I brought up from the underground. Max Shuppert for his tireless artistry in designing the covers, typesetting, exceptional professionalism & makin' me giggle. Til Turner for expert input on grammar & style and being a joy to work with. Hennig Fischer for braving the underground with me to shoot the cover. Henry Picado for sharing his immense talent as a clothing designer. Tyrone Smith for his coaching talent and musical contributions that often mirrored my musical journey underground. To Pete Bennett for his unwavering support. To Veronica Smith for her expert final proof. To all the photographers who contributed their talent, passion and love of their art to the Diaries: Tolga Adanali, Paul Stetzer, Diana Mejia, Jennifer Thomas, and Harvey Manger-Weil. Jason Hee for his web design. Damian Schoefield for his support and stellar input throughout the entire birthing of The Diaries. Michelle Hotaling and Pete Kennedy for their creative and constructive read-throughs. Susan Gordon-Clark for her phenomenal cold reading skills. Kitty Werner for sharing her business savvy, Hector Rodriguez, Jr. for his support and artistic and professional guidance throughout this entire process. Poet Minor for her talent as a videographer and support as a friend. Lyle Puente, Johnny Becker, Kathy Lynn Wood, Erin O'Reily, and Edie Collins at Dig This Real for believing in me. And to Celene Dutzman for her endless support over the past years, always bringing me back to earth when I momentarily bounce off, with friendship and wisdom.

Dedication

This book is dedicated to the artists of the New York City subways.
It's because of you, your kindness, generosity, and love that I have learned what the journey called life is all about.
If life is the dance, you are all the dancers.

This book is for you.

Table of Contents

Strength & Metamorphosis	1
Courage & Angels	5
Tunnel Vision & Keeping a Straight Face	11
Cops & Candy	16
The Search for a Spot & the African Queen	20
Sleight of Hand, Flowerpots, and Saxophones	26
Clean Sweep	31
A Bit More Music, One Less Saxophonist	36
That Touch	40
"I'm a Producer"	46
A Still Silent City	53
Settin' Up on Me & Tag Teamin' the Sweet Spot	55
Heartbeat of New York	61
East Side Them—West Side Me	70
Danny Boy	73
Projectile Pennies	78
What Ya Can't Buy	83
Duck 'n' Run	87
Mad Man of the NRW	91
"Ampaphobia" & Acts of Kindness	95
Izzy	99
Tell Me Off	102
Bohemian Nights	104
MUNY	109
Madness & Marley	112
Listen Closely	116
One	118
Ron's Way	121
I Travel	126
Le Volume	129
Harmony & Subcultures	131
In The Studio	135
The System	136
Gimme A Break!	142
Lowdown from Annette & Saturday with Simon	145
MUNY, Take Two	151
Dimitri & Breath of Life	153

Table of Contents

Remind Me...	157
The Sticks	161
Stand By Me	163
The Drunken Prophet	167
Miranda	172
Reunions	177
Journeys	183
Let's Be Candid	185
Rental Fee on the ACE	194
The Powers That Be	200
Abraham, The Peace of Time	203
Connections & Candy Apples	209
That Subway Face	212
Truth	214
Tryin' Out My Train Legs	220
The Cold & Cracks in the Economy	225
Rockin' The Port	234
MUNY, Take Three	245
Changes & That Pursuit of Happiness	248
Thinking Back, Looking Forward	254

Friday, December 30th, 2005

Strength & Metamorphosis

It's funny how when you least expect it, life throws you a curve—a curve that pulls out a strength you never knew you had, a strength that changes you forever.

"Ow! That hurt like hell!" Man, one minute you're nonchalantly ice-skating around in circles, just mindin' your own business, then BAM: you open your eyes with a big ol' lump on your head and a headache of all headaches. It was one of those "hit your head, out for a sec, think you're okay, but you're really not" kind of accidents.

I came to New York City as an artist from Washington, D.C. in 2004, wondering if I'd be working primarily in the stunt or the music industry. Up until my move, I'd been a performer: working as a singer, dancer, and actress in musicals, TV, and film, as a voice-over artist, as well as a stunt person for film and TV. The latter, along with voice-over work, had been my bread and butter for the past three to four years. In addition to all of this, during the last few years prior to my move to New York, I'd also begun writing music, beginning with two musicals and quickly moving to stand-alone songs. Although I felt after all my adventures within the entertainment industry, I'd found—or rather, gone back to—my calling as a singer/songwriter, I knew that the stunt business paid. It was unionized and not only paid well for each job, but also provided me with continuous residuals for airings on television, cable, and DVD. When I arrived in New York City, I figured I'd accept work as it came. As life would have it, stunts came my way and the music took a back seat.

Life was moving forward in my new city. I was getting work, I had an apartment (which is no small feat in The Big Apple), and was beginning to make friends in this fast paced city. Then I had that stupid accident: And no matter how I tried to ignore it, the accident laid me up for quite a while. Caught in a relatively helpless state of pain, I was subjected to a barrage of tests, injections, and drug experiments, all in the hopes that the intense pain would eventually end.

I found the accident physically tough, but nothing compared to the emotional pain I felt being alone with the recovery process in a brand new city like New York. I'd come from a family of supreme denial and complete absence from as far back as I could remember when it came to my well-being in times of pain or crisis. Other things my family was good at: emotionally being there—not so much. This fact made me both extremely independent and resourceful from a very early age. I'm sure they were doing the best they knew how at the time, and I firmly believe that people can and do change, but it didn't make the experience any easier. Even with those highly honed coping skills, this was a test I felt completely unprepared for.

Since I wasn't able to work, I found it lonely and tough to keep my head above water both financially and emotionally. Now, without a career, I tried to rekindle my self-worth. I found myself getting lost in my music, delving deeper and deeper into my creativity every day, writing more and more. At times I would venture out to try and play open mics at local bars and clubs. I often left, though, before I even went onstage because, like clockwork, after an hour or so, the pain would return. But I kept focusing on my music.

Luckily, after almost a year of what seemed like a slew of inept doctors poking and prodding me with no positive results, I was drawn to someone I now believe to be a healer, Alex. She and I became fast friends. Remarkably, Alex had started out as a professional guitar player, worked at numerous record labels in Nashville and New York City, and was now a practitioner of Feldenkrais, a specified branch within physical therapy focusing on retraining the body, in midtown Manhattan. Her story is also one of perseverance, much like many of her clients. Having battled rheumatoid all her life, she found Feldenkrais to be the only thing that allowed her to function pain-free. I believe now that's what makes her such a master of healing, because she's been there herself. Those who are in the healing arts and have actually, personally "been there" in one way or another have a special power, a gift that allows them to reach deep inside another and actually repair damage that even the most complex and advanced medical techniques could not even begin to touch. To that I can attest.

Alex is a tiny woman, with a unique combination of nurturing and feistiness in her spirit. She has shiny, bright white hair, cut to her shoulders, while her wrinkle-free face is practically flawless, giving her an elusive ageless look and energy. She's almost elf-like with twinkly blue eyes. You'd think her former career might have been that of a nymph-like dancer rather than a concert guitarist, the way she darts about the physical therapy office, rarely staying in one place for more than a second when she's not working on a patient.

One day, while in physical therapy, I remember mentioning to her that, since my first day in New York, I'd been curious about performing in the New York City subways, but had always been too scared to do so. I'd always been curious, even before the accident, but I was now taking the thought seriously. I was now entertaining the thought of singing in the subways to actually bring in some cash. "Yeah, but still, I'm really scared," I'd repeat to Alex over and over while lying on the Feldenkrais table.

"You should do it. What do you have to lose?" she assured me. I assumed her encouragement stemmed from her own inner strength and experience.

For almost three weeks, I'd ask myself the question, then Alex, and myself again: "Should I go? Should I do this?" Each time, I'd hem and haw and Alex would answer with conviction, "You should do it, Heidi. What do you have to lose?" For those three weeks I thought about what might be a logical answer to her question—what do I have to lose? I thought about this so I'd have a reason, a valid excuse *not* to go, since I was really timid at the concept of singing in the trains. And having put this quandary out to Alex and the universe, that dark and dirty place that felt so awfully intimidating and frightening, somehow still pulled at me.

At every session, I'd lie there thinking to myself about logical answers that could keep me from having to try this seemingly bizarre concept that somehow kept on tugging at me. It seemed so very foreign to everything I'd experienced and was trained to do up to this point and yet, despite what seemed to be the obvious oxymoron, I couldn't seem to come up with any reason not to go. I finally mumbled to Alex during a session, "Probably nothing. I probably have nothing to lose by, you know, at least trying. At least trying it once." And, who knows, maybe there's actually something there for me. *Something I don't know about yet*, I thought to myself, working hard at keeping the positive in the forefront. The truth is, I knew that by the end of those three weeks my entire savings would be gone and I was going to be trapped in a financial corner. New York City isn't a place where one can even remotely survive without money. In that respect, trying out the "subway busker" thing (an artist who entertains people for money, usually by singing or dancing) grew more appealing every passing day.

I'd thought of multiple more run-of-the-mill type options for income, but I'm an artist: that's where my heart was, what I'd been trained in, and what I do. I was still in too much pain to sit for hours in audition lines for musicals and operas. I could still only be up and out for about one to five hours at a stretch before I'd have to go home. I didn't have the income to promote myself in the voice-over industry, which can cost thousands to get restarted in. So music, on my own, seemed to be my most ready and flexible option.

The accident drove home in a way I hadn't really wanted to digest, the reality of how solo I was now in this huge bustling city. I don't think anyone wants to digest that kind of stuff, but it forced me to "deal," whether I liked it or not. In that context, Alex's encouraging words and nudging to sing the trains meant more to me than she will probably ever know. She was truly the only one who knew what I was contemplating. She was the only one who I felt accountable to. So I latched onto her support and encouragement, finally allowing it to carry me underground.

Once I decided that I was going underground, I knew I'd have to plan. I'd have to pick the right day to enter, the one day I felt strong enough both physically and emotionally to venture into the subways and take whatever they dealt.

Monday, January 16th, 2006

Courage & Angels

"Brighter Day"

Give me somethin' I can breathe with
Somethin' I believe in
So I can see
There's a brighter day
There's a brighter day

Today, Monday, I brought my guitar to physical therapy. I figured that it would be easier to enter the trains from there with Alex's encouragement behind me than alone from my apartment. I held tightly onto Alex's words, "Good luck and be careful." I needed to make sure someone knew I was going to do this. It was important for someone to know how much courage and strength it took me to go underground. It was cold, half snowing, half sleeting, and even though the physical therapy office is only one block from the subway entrance, I can't tell you how many times I had to fight the urge to turn around and go back home. But with my guitar on my back, I swiped my MetroCard, went through the turnstile, and entered the subway station.

I had no idea where to go (or really what to do, for that matter). It's a huge place. The New York City subways have over a hundred stations and carry over five million people a day. It's a maze of moving humanity. The subways hold the heat of the summer in the fall for about a week, but once it turns chilly they suddenly become as icy as the outdoors, sometimes worse. It was cold outside and we were far enough into winter that the subways were freezing as well. I was shivering, afraid, confused, and wondering how on earth I'd talked myself into coming down here to begin with. I kept searching to ground myself down there. I'd performed all my life and pretty much know the ropes of performing on stages, cruise ships, movie sets, television shows, bars, clubs, and adapt easily to each and every one. But this subway thing was different. For one thing, there's very little light underground. That fact I found both intimidating and a bit reassuring since I kept thinking maybe no one would even notice me and I could scoot out of there unobserved. Yet, somehow I remained. Despite the unlikely surroundings I didn't leave instead I felt compelled to stay. At the time, I couldn't tell you why I felt compelled to stay. I can only say I felt this odd tug-of-war going on. I felt both over prepared from my years of training as a musician, and yet under prepared as a human being to be in this cavernous, dark environment that was now my stage.

Those feelings of over- and under-preparedness most probably came from my background. Inherently I was a happy kid: upbeat, giggly, and creative, always searching for and/or creating my next adventure. From the get-go I'd known who I was: an artist. I'd been both musical and creative from birth, although the restrictions put on expressing that creativity growing up were stringent. As I was growing up, I was exposed to only a small fragment of the musical universe— that fragment being classical music and musical theater...the end. When I brought up really studying and pursuing anything artistic for life, I was reprimanded; when I pushed the subject, I was punished. So, though I'd done my best to be true to my heart amidst these strict controls; despite my "out of the box" nature, everything I'd done up to this point in my life as an artist had somehow remained safely within the confines of those rules. Although I didn't really know exactly what was missing—you never really do as a kid because what is, is—I always felt as if I were in a "box" of sorts, wearing someone else's shoes, shoes that were somehow the wrong size. I see now, in retrospect, how the threat of force inflicted against a soul can shape or constrict a life without one even realizing it.

As I stood on the platform, my mind raced. The past, present, and future all jumbled together. Am I crazy to even contemplate this? How did I get here? Maybe no one would even notice me here. Maybe no one would even be on the platform today and I'd have a valid excuse to just go home. The thoughts continued to race. My small, five foot one stature somehow felt extra tiny surrounded by the cold steel tracks and endless cement tunnels of the subways. It was dirty, very dirty, and dark. The kind of dark one might imagine right before the last shovel full of dirt was piled onto you in a grave. There are things in the city subways you sometimes wish you hadn't encountered: rats, garbage, an array of the foulest of smells, even human excrement in the most unusual of places. The smell stuns the senses. And yet, I still didn't turn back.

I got to the bottom of the stairs to the platform. As I stood on the cement, the cold bleeding up through my shoes, I suddenly had a change of heart and felt sad that there were no people anywhere to be seen. I had gotten brave enough to get all the way down there and logically I knew— more people meant more money. *I mean, if I'm going to do this, I want it to be worth it,* I thought. But at the same time, I was somewhat relieved because I was still feeling completely intimidated by this unimaginable performance space I was about to sing in. When I got to the bottom of the steps to the subway platform, I just stood there. If anyone was watching, I must have looked rather silly as I kept taking very small steps forward, then back, sideways, then back again, trying to figure out where to land, still too afraid to unzip my guitar case. I was just about to leave, just about to give in to my fear, when I saw two violinists coming down the opposite staircase. They were heading toward me. In an instant, all the fear that had been clutching me was replaced by an overwhelming sense of competition. If these two musicians were headed toward where I was standing, there must be a reason. Now I wanted this spot to play in. I unpacked my guitar. I laid my case on the platform floor with one dollar strategically placed inside. With my now frigid fingers, I kneeled down to check the tuning, stood up, and began to sing a song I'd just finished writing:

> *Give me somethin' I can walk with*
> *That you and I can talk with*
> *And we won't stop 'cause*
> *There's a brighter day*
> *There's a brighter day*

After two or three tunes, I felt braver and wiser: braver because I realized that I would prefer to have people around than not if I'm going to put all this effort into performing, and wiser knowing that the two girls were probably not headed to perform where I was standing, especially since there were no people around to listen. But I was grateful for that illusion, as it got me singing. However, the lack of an audience and the cold was taking its toll. I decided to see if there were any waiting passengers on the uptown side of the tracks.

As I knelt down on the cement platform to pack up, I heard a voice say, "Are you leaving?"

I looked up to see a middle-aged, Hispanic man, perhaps a blue-collar worker, in dark green pants and a light green shirt that was hidden by a large brown overcoat.

"No," I said, startled that this random person seemed to appear out of thin air. "No, I'm just... I'm just moving to the other side where there are more people."

As I zipped up my guitar case, he stared down at me and said, "Come with me. Come with me," he urgently bragged, "and I'll show you 'the spot.'"

I cautiously followed him. I was preoccupied, wondering what exactly he was talking about and whether following a stranger to this supposed "spot" was a good or bad idea, given that we were in the middle of New York City and it was the subways. He encouraged me to continue following him with a hand gesture. I wondered what he was all about. How had he even seen me on that platform? How did he know I needed some help? Had he done this before with random virgin subway musicians? I took a few skips to catch up, because I hadn't come up with any valid reason not to at least see what this "spot" thing was all about.

As we walked, I asked, "So, you're a musician as well?" I figured anyone who would have "spot" information must be a musician. I also thought I'd prefer him to answer in the affirmative to that question, as I'd feel a whole lot better about this whole random "spot" adventure if he were. "No," he said, "but I've been riding this train for fourteen years and I've seen people play here. I *know* this is the 'spot'." He turned and smiled at me. "You can make money... here!" Suddenly, the man pointed to the empty area at the top of the staircase where the platform became very large and wide resembling a small stage. It had a wall as a backdrop, bordered by a small newsstand built right into the wall, and then flowing out from the wall was this big, open space. "This is it. This is where they *all* play." He smiled, "Good luck." Then he turned around and walked toward the subway's exit. As he disappeared through the turnstile, it was almost as if this random angel had simply appeared out of nowhere. I say out of nowhere because the whole time I had been performing on the platform, not one person had passed. Yet he somehow, mysteriously, had found me. It was all very magical and somewhat surreal. I shook myself out of my semi-stunned stupor and started to set up again, this time feeling far more confident knowing I was in "the spot." The platform was still dark but there was a large overhead light above me, which gave the space a stage-like feel. As I knelt down and unpacked my guitar for the second time, I looked across the three subway tracks to the downtown side. There I noticed a small figure, completely covered head to toe all in black, wearing sunglasses, methodically stacking large white buckets one inside the other. Curious as to what he was doing, I continued to watch, when a minute later the express train ruined my view, so I went back to setting up.

I played, this time to a rush of bustling commuters coming and going, off and on the 1 train. I watched as dollars landed into my guitar case, accompanied by nods and smiles of approval. *This is more like it.* As I was singing, trying to gauge the noise of the trains (which, by the way, is deafening at times), I felt a transformation taking place. I got that "singing in the shower" feeling. That feeling you get when you're singing all by yourself without a care in the world. It's a feeling that you're completely free when no one is listening. But I had this feeling there, right there, smack in the middle of New York City. I was performing on one of the busiest subway platforms in the city and yet that same, uninhibited feeling washed right over me. Despite the cold numbing my fingers, the noise, pigeon feathers, pigeon poop, rats, garbage, and hordes of people rushing by at breakneck speed, I actually felt a sense of contentment there. I felt a sense of freedom that I had rarely experienced performing anywhere else. Then my voice went. It's happened only once in my life. But, there it was again. My voice was backing out. Darn it. This was just getting good.

Reluctantly, I packed up my guitar, wishing I could stay just a little while longer. But competing with three parallel lines of trains for the first time in my life proved too much for my voice this first day. Something left me, something dropped away underground today. I can't say exactly yet what that "thing" was that left me, but whatever it was, its absence allowed me to be completely free and one hundred percent present in the music. I didn't know what it was. All I knew was I'd be returning.

Monday, January 23rd, 2006

Tunnel Vision & Keeping a Straight Face

It took a while for my voice to return. Days, actually. But when it did, I got right back to the underground.

I was still pretty clueless on where to go to sing, so it was half random and "creatively calculated" where I'd perform today. I decided on 34th Street. I had no idea what I'd find performance space-wise, or even if I could play there, but the amount of traffic that I know flows through that area made the choice worth the risk. For one thing: Madison Square Garden looms over an entire city block at 34th Street and is where most major sporting events and large musical events in Manhattan occur. To play Madison Square Garden as a musician, is an honour and carries status. Once you've played "The Garden" as a musical act, you pretty much know you've "made it." Also at 34th Street are Penn Station, Amtrak, and the convergence of all the west side subway lines. So, I figured it was worth at least a try.

Once done with physical therapy, I had relayed to Alex the adventures of the week before, and had gotten my perfunctory "Good luck and be careful, Chickee." Alex often calls me "Chickee" as a sign of endearment that never fails to make me feel safe and welcome, two sentiments that were much needed as I headed back underground to my destination d'jour.

I ended up at 34th Street station and looked around the platforms. There was sound, but no musicians. As I walked back and forth on the train platform, I heard an odd, high-pitched sound. I couldn't figure out where the eerie, "Tweety Bird" sound was coming from. Then I noticed that the sound coincided with me walking under long blue metal boxes that were hanging from ceiling. They looked like pieces of bright blue metallic art, with speaker holes in them. And every time some movement would happen underneath these pieces of musical artwork, an eerie songbird like whistle would happen. It sounded like a family of mechanical birds was trapped inside. It reminded me of an audio flytrap or something for subway performers. Needless to say, that explained why there were no musicians on that platform and I walked down the stairs to see what else I could discover. At the bottom of the staircase, to my left was a walkway. It was inviting. And at first glance, it seemed void of musical flycatchers. The walkway wasn't enormously long. During the breaks in foot traffic I could see both ends when I stood in the middle. And, unlike some of the tile work in other New York City subway tunnels I'd seen, these walls were covered with plain, large, shiny white tiles, their glossiness glowing back against the fluorescent lights shining down on them twenty four seven. I realized the breaks in foot traffic happen after each train drops off their passengers. Then the masses flow through the tunnel and exit the station, thereby leaving it empty for a minute before the next train pulls in; thus starting the cycle all over again. It was just too insane to even think about setting up in the midst of the moving masses, so I waited for one of those breaks.

I quickly set up my guitar case, wondering if it, and I, for that matter, would survive the next onslaught of people and not get trampled. Even though the rush hadn't yet begun, just to get a sense of the space, I started to sing:

"Down For The Count"

So you come up to me
You talk real nice and you look so fine and you're
Smilin' sweetly
Every word is so refined, you know

Tunnel Vision & Keeping a Straight Face

> *I'm not easily*
> *Moved by a man's clever advances but*
> *Somehow you got to me*
> *Losin' my head and takin' my chances and*

Oh, my God. I'd never heard acoustics like that in my life. I kept singing, eyes closed, absorbing the stellar acoustics as they bounced off the walls, floor and ceiling of the tunnel, soaking up each note as it left my guitar and voice and bounced back, clear as day. *This is heaven.*

> *Now I'm sittin'*
> *Wonderin' is it all a game*
> *'Cause now you're missin'*
> *Without explanation*
> *It's leavin' me pain*

Suddenly, I heard a rumble, like a small earthquake. I figured it was just the train upstairs. But then, like a knife, the brilliant-sounding echo got cut and I could barely hear myself. I opened my eyes, and saw a stampede of people rushing towards me. Despite my very real fear of being trampled to death, I kept on singing, and amazingly the sea of people nodded, smiled, as my case filled up with money.

I kept singing, but as the crowd advanced and began to pass, I noticed an empty circle that was really not empty at all, but contained seven teenagers each with a basketball, all dribbling, and all seven keeping perfect pace with the sea of traffic. *That's some kind of multi-tasking.* Was this some kind of Harlem Globetrotters wannabes? I mean, who takes their game to the New York City subway tunnels? Unless they're trying to create some kind of new Olympic Sport— Tunnel Surfing. Wouldn't surprise me at all in Manhattan. I continued on.

Chorus

You've got me down for the count
Sittin' on the sidelines
Sittin' on the side lookin' outside in
You got me walkin' about
Not knowin' where my heart should lie
On my sleeve, or should I keep it in

The fabulous acoustics were mine again. By the time the sixth or seventh herd of humanity had poured through the tunnel, I'd lost track of time. At this point, the rolling show was getting pretty entertaining. As I heard the rumble, I once again opened my eyes to the sea of people coming quickly toward me, and once again I saw that space in the crowd.

I sang, nodded in acknowledgment to donations given, and tried my best to keep my focus on the music as the "empty circle" approached me. In this particular space was a fifty-something, tall, lanky, black man. He had a slightly thinning beard, wearing jeans, hiking boots, and a bulky winter coat. Though he was a mature man, he passed me, riding a toddler's bike with empty training wheel brackets hanging from each side. There he was, keeping perfect pace with the crowd. Just as the dribblers had done before him, he kept his eyes straight ahead, with not a hint of self-consciousness in his body. He just pedaled calmly and with complete composure. He pedaled as if everyone were on a toddler's bike with empty training wheel braces.

I noticed the crowd was completely immune to the show, as he pedaled past, looking like a clown in a circus act. I mean, after the urban globetrotters and this guy on a clown bike, I seriously wondered if a pack of elephants was going to follow this three-ringed circus. I could just imagine them squeezing through those turnstiles. Don't know how the bike even got through. Darn, a single human being can barely get through those iron maidens. Although my mind was off in a million directions, the seemingly single-minded crowd of lemmings didn't notice or care at all about any of what was passing. But various members of the crowd did seem to notice that I was having difficulty keeping my composure from busting out laughing. *That* they seemed to notice. Go figure.

Then I got another break, and I went back to fully absorbing the echo. The break was followed by the cyclical muffled rumble of the crowd. Once again, there was a small break in the moving mass of commuters. In this space there was a man, a regal old soul, moving a little bit slower than the masses. He looked grandfatherly, perhaps in his sixties, walking with a limp and pushing a personal, oversized, shopping cart filled to the brim with what looked like multiple music speakers. His walk had a definite rhythm, half-speed to the crowd, and he seemed to be using his cart as a walker. The space people gave him was fascinating and made it seem as if royalty was passing in front of me. As I watched him pass, I wondered with all that gear what he was about? Was he selling the stuff in his cart? Was he moving somewhere? Maybe he too was a subway musician. The regal soul and his kingdom of commuters passed and then I had to call it quits. Between the circus act, the bellyache laughter it had put me through, and the sheer act of digesting everything that had gone on that day, I was spent. I packed my gear, actively anticipating my next adventure in my newfound playground.

Monday, February 6th, 2006

Cops & Candy

The injury has been challenging over this past week. The pain sometimes allows me out only a few hours a day before I have to go back inside and lie down. So I've had to pace myself to re-enter the subways again. I chose a Monday again, so I could go straight from physical therapy to the underground, and that way I'd avoid the "thinking trap." Today was that Monday. Although it was super cold, I had vowed to return to play as long as my head would allow.

I headed from PT to the Times Square station. I live near there, so during my two years in New York, I knew there were various passageways in that station where I'd seen random musicians before. I rode the subway straight from 59th Street to Times Square and hopped off the ACE line. Walking up the stairs from the platforms to the landing, I started to peruse the station for a welcoming spot to play in. Even though I'd played a few times already, and wasn't as timid as day one, every time I changed locations it felt like I was starting all over in the nerves department. I needed to find a spot that felt somewhat inviting in this new huge arena. Times Square is the convergence of most west side subway lines in New York City and the shuttle to the East Side and those lines. It has at least four entrances, with huge neon signs announcing its existence outside each one; stairs; tunnels; passageways; twists and turns; four-story tall escalators; three-story elevators; a police headquarters; a multitude of newsstands, flower stands, and actual stores—right there, underground. If you've never been there before, it's pretty easy to get confused. I had lived in New York just long enough to be able to explore the station without getting lost. I located a passageway adjacent to the largest mezzanine of the Times Square Station, although far enough away as to not to interfere or compete with the other musicians performing on the mezzanine itself.

This passageway had some brilliant tile work. Unlike the plain white of the 34th Street Station, the walkway to 42nd Street was lined in medium-sized light green tiles from top to bottom. Set right into the walls, on both sides of the tunnel, there were miniature shadow boxes, filled with intricate artwork. Each shadow box housed a mini ceramic world inside, with its own unique theme and tone. The brightly coloured plastered Pop Art housed inside the boxes ranged thematically from theater to New Year's Eve (depicted by confetti and balloons and the numbers "2007") to urban street scenes of the city (such as ceramic break-dancers performing in front of high-rise buildings) and fit perfectly into a seven inch symmetrical box, covered with a glass front. After losing myself in the artwork for a few moments, I unpacked my guitar. I felt that jittery "Am I insane to be here again?" feeling and laid my case down on the cement floor. As I placed my guitar strap across my shoulder, and began to tune up, the feeling started to fade.

I began to sing. The acoustics were marvelous. They were different than 34th Street, as it was a much more open space, but remarkable nonetheless.

Forty-five minutes into my set, a pair of cops slowly wandered by and for some unknown reason, dropped candy—two packs of Smarties and a Hot Ball—into my case. I finished a song and opened my eyes just in time to see them donating the sweets. Somewhat confused, I gathered up my courage, smiled, and coyly said, "Ummmmm...you know I don't take candy from strangers."

"Really?" one of the two cops answered, slightly sarcastic.

There was a small break of silence and, not wanting to get on the wrong side of the men in blue, I decided to oblige them. "Okay, thanks," and accepted the donation. *What was that all about? Do subway cops always carry candy? What's up with the sweets in the sub-*

way? I thought to myself. Completely opposite to what I'd expect out of a Transit cop. Two more cops passed by, but this time, no candy. I sang on. Then just about ten minutes later, the two candy-less cops walked back towards me.

"We've been instructed to tell you to move. We honestly don't know why we've been instructed to tell you to move, but we got a call..."

The second cop leaned in and added, "Yeah, we got a call about a musician in the tunnel and since you're the only one here, we figured it had to be you. We really don't know why they need you to move, but ya gotta move. Sorry."

"But, I'm not doing anything wrong, I'm just singing." I made just one attempt at convincing them to let me stay and who knows, perhaps they'd be toting some sweets along with those billy clubs.

"You know, the two cops before you gave me candy." I pointed to my case.

They both jumped in, talking at the same time, their gaze switching back and forth from the candy in my case to their feet to me in embarrassment, "I know, we..." "Yeah, we don't...." "But, ya gotta move...we got word from the supervisor..."

At this point, I had gotten the picture. It made no sense, obviously to them or me, and though I had tried to reason with them...I had to go.

As I packed up my gear and the cops sauntered away, I was interrupted by a voice: "You get moved, too?" I looked up to see an elderly woman, not very tall, a bit hunched over, lowering a guitar that had been formerly slung on her back. She was wearing a beret on her head and sporting a thick, almost-in-the-lip-line layer of bright red lipstick. A large metal harmonica holder that looked like an orthopedic brace dangled from her neck.

"Yeah, kinda odd. The first two gave me candy," I replied as I pointed to my case.

"It's happenin'. You probably gotta move to the platforms...that's where I'm headed, that's where you make all the money anyways," she said as she adjusted her beret and applied another thick layer of bright red lipstick to way more than just her lips.

"Really? Yeah?" I hesitated, "Folks have told me the platforms are better but I'm really new at this and they kinda intimidate me. The dark and the noise and all."

"Oh, you'll be okay, sweetie," she reassured. "I gotta go. I gotta go find a spot." And she hoisted her guitar back onto her hunched shoulder. "Maybe you'll be one of the keepers. Might pass you again."

"Bye," I replied, now curious about this spry, yet, elderly woman. These random folks who keep appearing seemed sort of magical to me. They seemed to appear out of nowhere, always when I'd least expect it. Characters I'd never anticipated would start out as a voice, and then turn into guides of sorts. Where had this woman, like my friend from my first day at 59th Street come from? How did she, like the man, know exactly what I needed? I wondered about this woman, if she plays the trains for her living and whether she's alone or has family. I picked up my guitar and walked away from the "eviction spot." But it's odd, even with today's eviction I was now more determined than ever to return. I think I'm getting hooked to this underground thing, especially with my newfound and ever growing collection of angel-guides.

Tuesday, February 14th, 2006

The Search for a Spot & the African Queen

It's Valentine's Day and I decided that, yes, I would try playing a holiday. I figured Valentine's Day might hold the opportunity to make some dollars since at least a portion of the population would be in an unusually good mood. Plus, I had a bunch of time to kill before going out on this crazy Hallmark holiday with a guy I'd just started seeing. Never knowing what an early relationship holds, I was grateful to have my music with which to get my footing before the night's date. Also, I was able to get back underground a bit sooner than normal this time. Alex's work on me is allowing me to finally make some notable progress physically. I'm feeling hopeful for the first time in over a year that I'm actually going to be okay. I'd been able to boldly play a few more times over the past few days at that same spot at 42nd Street, I suppose, just to hold my newfound territory. No one bothered me this time, so I'm guessing both the candy and the eviction had been random occurrences. The latter probably just a station manager in a really bad mood, instructing his "winged monkeys" to do his evil deeds by eliminating the music.

Alex and I had been brainstorming while I was on the physical therapy table over the past weeks about good spots to play in. Sometimes I think she's getting into this subway thing even more than me. Maybe that's because she's a kindred musical spirit and therefore she knows the inexplicable need to have to play, or maybe it's because she'd secretly wondered about playing the trains just once like me. Whatever the reason, she was committed to helping me plan each day's route. I had told her that I really liked the whole tunnel gig for many reasons: the warmth, the acoustics. So I thought I'd scope out more similar locations. Alex had mentioned a tunnel that was a passageway farther east than I had yet ventured, near a park that bordered both the east and west sides of midtown Manhattan called Bryant Park.

"I think it's near the BD lines," Alex said. "You'll see it when you get over there; you can't miss it and there are always musicians there. If I were playing, I'd go there." I took her advice, swiped my MetroCard, and entered the train.

The Bryant Park station is a relatively civilized stop compared to others in Manhattan. Bryant Park itself sits above the train station. It went from drug haven in the seventies to its now beautiful regal self in the early nineties. Today it's got a huge ice-skating rink in the winter and fantastic concerts in the summer. And of course, it's known for the ever popular and trendy New York City Fashion Week with its high fashion and hoopla, which is held every year in the park. I'm beginning to see that the vibe of the stations mirrors that of what lies above. And in this case, the vibe is a "new and improved" Bryant Park.

It's cleaner and although a transfer station where many lines converge, seems to have a rare order about it for a city subway station. Of course, there are tons of people running here and there, and crisscrossing at various points throughout the terminal. But despite all the movement, it still has a slight air of conformity to it. I guessed it was partly due to being positioned on the line between the east and west sides of Manhattan. The east side is known for being far less rambunctious than the west in this part of town. Well, that is my personal analysis anyway.

In Manhattan, there is a stark difference between the vibe on the east side and that of the west side. The dividing line is actually Fifth Avenue but feels like it starts to differ at Central Park and Broadway. The west side of Manhattan is greatly influenced by Broadway and the large arts communities that surround the theaters. It has a fun, vibrant, trendy, neon, and very up-all-night kind of energy to it. You see every person, costume, and craziness that you can imagine. The east side of Manhattan is far more conservative, often times more moneyed and less "artsy" than the neighborhoods across the park. The sidewalks are filled with nannies pushing strollers holding babies of the rich families, men and women in business suits, and wealthy couples walking their miniature dogs with the utmost composure. There is no neon, no bounce, and no random insanity meandering on the east side as on the west. There are no written rules on how to behave on the east side, just as there are no written rules stating that basically "anything goes" on the west. It's just a given in Manhattan. Once you've lived here for any length of time, you get it. You feel the difference and you know where you belong. Personally, I belong on the west side of the Park, no doubt about it. I'm a west side girl.

As I exited the 7 train and climbed the stairs, I was hit again with the phenomenon of cleanliness and order. There were people walking in their business suits, evenly spaced, along walkways—no shouting, no riding bikes, no bouncing balls. Honestly, I wasn't really sure I'd like it over here. This may be way too "east side" for me. I looked around for some sign of this passageway.

I noticed to my right a brightly lit walkway. It was three in the afternoon, so there were very few people in it, but it looked as if it might be where I was supposed to be, according to Alex's instructions. Yes, this is it, this is the passageway. I looked around to take in the possible acoustic contributions that the tunnel might provide me with this Valentine's Day. The Bryant Park tunnel was different than both the 34th and 42nd Street tunnels. It didn't have plain white tiles, or shadow boxes, but these tan-coloured tiles inlaid with matte-finished earth-tone tiles making scrolls of sorts along each wall. Chiseled into the scroll tiles were quotes ranging from Shakespeare to Aesop, from Emerson to Woodrow Wilson. Some of the oversized philosophical quotes were accompanied by pictures, some were plain, but the tunnel was certainly educational, to say the least. I took in the ambiance of the new tunnel and decided the best place to set up.

Now, by February 14th I was beginning to feel I was getting the hang of things underground. I felt as if I was beginning to acquire some kind of a rhythm. I felt so comfortable that last night I actually made a quirky little sign all in red to place in my guitar case, wishing everyone a HAPPY VALENTINE'S DAY. Being new in this tunnel, though, I wasn't really sure where the optimal spot might be, so I chose one end of the passageway where it had a feeling of a stage. I laid my case down and even before I unpacked my guitar, people were throwing money into my case. Yeah, I knew this was going to be a good day to sing. I tuned up and began in on my first song of the day.

I was just a verse or two into the tune when I heard a squeal, which I supposed, might have been an announcer over a loud speaker or something. (This, I've learned, happens all the time underground.) But the sound was getting so annoying that I stopped to try to decipher what was interrupting my day. Once I stopped playing I realized it was neither a train nor a loudspeaker but a saxophone blaring away right over my singing. I have to say something about the saxophone. It is a wonderful instrument, but one that, even more so than some other musical instruments, has to be played well when heard within an enclosed space. It's loud. The sounds coming out of his instrument were neither chromatic nor melodic in nature. He sounded as if he were playing scales he had not yet mastered, yet somehow you knew he had been playing forever, very loudly. Oh my God, that sound hurt.

The sax guy was stationed on the opposite wall, smack in the middle of the tunnel. He was a relatively large, older, black man with grey hair and a grey beard, wearing an overstuffed black down coat. He seemed to have a permanent scowl, perhaps, I thought, from listening to that torturous sound coming out of his horn. Heck, I'd have a permanent scowl too if I was subjected to that sound for much more than I'd already endured. Anyway, for the first time underground, I got pissed. Since I couldn't logically leave my gear and go over and talk to him about the situation, I was forced to pack up all my things and close up my, up until now, very lucrative shop. *Damn.* I shoved my guitar into its case, gathered the collection of bills that had already been donated, folded up the crazy Happy Valentine's Day sign, and swung my equipment onto my back once again. The Sax Man was very rough in appearance, but I decided to approach him nonetheless and see if we could work something out.

I stood a little in front of him so he could see me whenever he opened his eyes (which he seemed to do infrequently once I arrived) and waited for a break in the, well...in the "music." I resisted covering my ears during the wait, which seemed like an eternity.... finally a break. "Excuse me," I said. There was no response. "Excuse me." I leaned in a bit closer to the man, half wondering if I might be seriously risking my life with this move. He slowly turned around, mouthpiece poised at his lips as if he either didn't have time to chat or was threatening me with more of his playing if I didn't go away. "Excuse me, but I was playing over there." I pointed to the other end of the tunnel, "I was already playing when you started."

"I didn't hear anything," the man said in a monotone, as if to say "case closed."

"But I had already set up and was playing, and then you came and played over me!" I was now more than frustrated at this exchange, as he was appearing to be as stubborn and unreasonable as his "music."

"Well, I didn't hear a thing," he replied, poised and obviously ready to resume his horn sounds.

I gave one last shot at resolving this issue before the mouthpiece disappeared once again entirely into his mouth, leaving me without any recourse whatsoever. "I was wondering, since it seems as if we both got here at the same time, if...maybe...you could go to that end of the tunnel..." and I pointed to the far left end, opposite to where I had been set up, "and I'll stay over there." I pointed to my right, where my former stage lay empty. After a relatively lengthy silence through his mouthpiece, he replied.

"I'll move a bit."

I thanked him, feeling hopeful, but as soon as I turned around, the Sax Man stuck the mouthpiece right back into his mouth with the confidence of a sword eater swallowing his sword on stage, and began wailing some more.

This time I was fuming. I was so upset at having had and then lost such a great spot on such a great day, but decided to try my best at finding a replacement spot quickly. So I reluctantly swung my guitar over my shoulder and left the tunnel.

Back on the 7 train, I rode to Grand Central Station, a Mecca for musical acts. But, not surprisingly, it was booked. I kept searching: Times Square—booked, 34th Street—booked, even all the way down at 14th Street/Union Square, where there are lots of spots—booked, booked, booked. I felt my energy to search for a holiday spot wane and decided to go home, completely unfulfilled, and feeling somewhat wronged. I just hoped the rest of my evening would consist of something other than confrontation. As I hopped on the last train back home, I stared out at the platform wishing I could have played for just even half an hour. I daydreamed until that odd, kind of creepy, female "Star Trek" voice announced, "Door closing," accompanied by the two chimes with that trademark just-too-long-of-a-pause pause between the two notes. Just then, as the musical door show was happening I noticed, outside the car window, a woman. She was very tall and had a definite regal carriage about her. She was walking fast, taking long strides with her unusually long legs along the platform past the subway car, her long robe flowing out behind her like a superhero's cape. Her robe was a solid dark colour and she wore a multi-coloured headdress of sorts. But what really caught my eye about this "African Queen" was the roll of toilet paper perched on top of her head, the end of it unraveling with every giant step she took so that the farther she walked, the longer her "Procter & Gamble Train" became. I torqued my neck, plastering my face right up against the window to watch more of her and also to see when and if the TP train would finally break. Just then, the train lurched and pulled out of the station. So, I have no idea how it ended up. Had I been on the platform, I most certainly would have followed her to see if: a) she actually knew there was a roll of white toilet paper perched on her head, and b) to see how long it would continue to unravel before someone would step on it and break her train. I wonder if she even really knew it was there. I wondered if some kids played a joke on her as she napped in the subway car and placed it on top of her headdress, figuring she'd never notice (which I guess she didn't). Or maybe this was some new fashion statement she was making. Did she consider TP a sign of royalty? She was certainly well dressed otherwise, so I wondered, did she go to work daily with fresh roll of toilet paper on her head? Gosh, it's either the former and she'll end up on You Tube, I mused, or the latter and she's got one super curious job. Well, even though I didn't actually get to sing, at least I'd gotten my requisite dose of "crazy watching" for the night. And oddly, that entertainment in and of itself almost satisfied me for the night.

Tuesday, February 21st, 2006

Sleight of Hand, Flowerpots & Saxophones

I now have a first choice as far as tunnels to play in goes, thanks to Alex and her creative input, and the 42nd Street/Bryant Park passageway is it.

I have returned half a dozen times or so to play and each time, I'm learning more and more about the underground and how it works. I have learned that rush hour underground doesn't start at five, but around four, sometimes even three-thirty. I've also learned that if I'm to get a spot, I definitely need to arrive before the rush starts. Today, I made a point of arriving at the passageway at four on the nose. This way I'd be sure to get a good spot and be able to really play the tunnel.

As I meandered through the station and arrived at my favorite passageway, I saw an old man, white, thinning hair, perched in a beat up old wheelchair, wearing multiple layers of pants and leggings, socks and sweaters, gloves and scarves. Hanging from either side of his chair were two large, long, cone-shaped flower holders, the type you might see outside a flower stand displaying bouquets of cut flowers for sale. Inside each of the long containers were bunches of dingy plastic flowers of all varieties, with only one or two brightly coloured stems poking out here and there amongst the heavily faded variety. I wondered if they were there for decoration only or if he intended to sell the almost ghost white synthetic garden ornaments. Personally, I didn't want to get near any of them. They just struck me as creepy and somewhat "death-like." The man, not dead, however, seemed to be humming, interspersed with a few mumbled words in Spanish, followed by a few blows into his harmonica that he had steadied on the top of his chest. He did the hum, mumble, harmonica thing once and then the cycle would start all over again; hum, mumble, blow, hum, mumble, blow. This went on for a while and every so often, a passerby would throw a coin or a dollar into the tin he had resting on his lap.

I observed the scene for a bit and felt, morally, I couldn't play close to a man in a wheelchair as he was handicapped and had enough to deal with, tending to his plastic garden and all. So I continued down the tunnel and began to unpack in a spot farthest from him. Then suddenly on the opposite end of the disabled guy, I heard The Sax Man. *Ugh*. I grunted to myself but continued to unpack, determined to have a good day today performing underground. But a few moments into my set it became painfully clear that there was no way I was going to compete with The Sax Man, and I wasn't about to waste my breath reasoning with that dude today. I packed up once again and wandered back toward the wheelchair guy, just to see if he was still there, hoping he was finished for the day. Oddly, I noticed that his chair was there, but the man, formerly wheelchair-bound with his mini arboretum, was actually taking a little break. He was leisurely walking around stretching his legs, as his apparent "prop" wheelchair remained empty for the time being…so much for his handicap. The beauty of illusion.

At this point, I went ahead and unpacked out of his way, and out of The Sax Man's range. Without hesitation, I set up, and began to play. The two days I had taken off were definitely showing in my voice for the first half-hour but after that, I was warmed up, finding my space in the tunnel and within myself. After about forty-five minutes, as I was finishing my water, my nemesis, The Sax Man, was suddenly standing in front of me. Oh God, he's come back for retribution from our "encounter" on Valentine's Day, and he's going to either kill me or play his horn until I die a torturous death.

"Hi," he said matter-of-factly, seeming to want to start a conversation. *I don't know about this. He better not ask for my spot.* I ignored him just as he did to me on our first encounter and began to re-tune my guitar. "You know—" The Sax Man began again, "You have a really great sound. You're good. Your sound reminds me of Bonnie Raitt…the way you phrase your music and all…yeah, kind of Bonnie Raitt meets Eva Cassidy."

"Thanks," although I was genuinely wary of his true intentions.

"So…have you been playing in the subways a long time?"

"No, not long at all. I kind of just started a few weeks ago. But I like it," and I paused, remembering that my one and only negative experience had involved the guy standing right in front of me. And I added, "Mostly, yeah, I like it."

"I've been here, on and off, for thirteen years," he informed me. "I've seen a lot of things go on down here. You see a lot when you play underground."

"I'm gathering that," I rebuked. Then he got to the point of his approach.

"So, how long do you think you'll be playing today?"

"I don't know. I've run out of water." I turned my empty water bottle upside down to demonstrate how empty it was. Then, catching me off-guard, The Sax Man—the biggest annoyance I've had underground to date—said: "I'll go get you water if you want."

Up to this point, I hadn't looked him in the eye because I wasn't sure of him, was still angry from our first encounter, and honestly he kind of scared me. But now I looked at him, straight in the eye.

"Really? But that'll allow me to stay even longer, and I figure you want this spot. Don't you?"

"It's okay. Just give me one dollar twenty-five, and I'll ask the station manager if he'll let me out and back in again, and I'll go out and get you some water. My name's Sam," he said as I handed him the cash, thinking, *You're insane, Heidi. You're never gonna see that dollar twenty-five again.* But either way, it was worth the risk for me to play a little while longer.

Sam left and I began to play once again. Money was being thrown in at a pretty steady clip when I noticed this really old, witchy-looking woman, with pasty white skin resembling unleavened bread dough, standing to my left. She was bent over and dressed in layers

Slight of Hand, Flowerpots & Saxophones

of skirts, sweaters, shawls, and head dressings. Every garment she wore had one common theme: they all had pockets, many pockets. She looked exactly like something out of a Charles Dickens novel. For the right beggar scene, any casting director would have snagged her up in a heartbeat. She was the real deal. I didn't pay her much mind because she was far enough away from me to not interfere with my work. But with every verse I sang, she shuffled closer and closer towards me. Then I noticed that every two to three women, and sometimes men, who passed her, stopped and gave her money. I hadn't noticed this exchange when she was standing farther away. I hadn't noticed because this woman was crazy fast like a magician and a card trick: within milliseconds the dollars hitting the palm of her hand would disappear into one of the numerous pockets that her top layer of wardrobe cleverly provided, and immediately following the snatch-and-grab, her hand would be back out, empty, waiting for the next donation as if she had just begun her routine for the day. As hard as I tried to ignore my new neighbor, I was a bit dumbfounded by the whole display. No matter how I tried, I was never able to see the bills once they left the donor's hand. They were simply gone, out of sight. Despite her elderly and decrepit appearance, this woman was fast and nimble. She was nimble, at least where it counted: for her survival. In fact, throughout the entire time she stood there I didn't make one dollar, whereas she must have pulled in at least thirty to forty dollars. Maybe I should switch gigs. It seemed I was playing for her benefit, not mine. I wondered if she and the wheelchair guy were a team. Although, if they're a couple, I'd say she is definitely the main breadwinner. I also wondered if those two panhandlers were really "closet" rich folk who just do this...well, just because they can. I've heard stories of beggars in New York City who are actually millionaires. Crazy, eccentric millionaires, but millionaires nonetheless. In my mind, these two fit the bill, so to speak.

Just then, Sam the Sax Man showed up, as promised, water in hand. I smiled, thanking him, and pointed to the major "slight-of-hand" act going on to my left. "I haven't made a dime since she showed up." I wanted someone else to witness what was going on.

"Yeah, they do that. They plant themselves right next to you on purpose and they make money off you. They do that by lookin' all frail and needy. It's a psychological thing, because even though you and I, we're workin', these folks," pointing to the crowd rushing by, "the people, when faced with a choice whether to give to her or you...they'll always choose her kind, outta guilt. It ain't fair—you know that an' I know that—but these guys," he pointed to the old woman, "they feed off that."

"Wow. That's crazy, but I sure do wish she'd..." Just as I was about to say the word "leave," the woman seemed to sense our conversation and mysteriously shuffled off into the crowd, disappearing as if she'd never been standing there at all.

"I'm gonna hang around for a while 'til you're done, okay?" Sam said as he wandered off to the other end of the tunnel.

"That's cool." Grateful, finally, for a clear space to perform in, I got back to my singing and earning money.

I played, made most of my bill money for the day, posed for some random photos, and finally felt back in the groove. That is, until my bladder got the best of me and I had to pack up. It's always one thing or another down there: no water, no bathroom, the cold, the heat. But it's okay. I started out and found Sam. "The spot's yours, I'm going home."

"Thanks." He hoisted his saxophone in its case over his right shoulder.

"Hey, thanks again for the water."

"No problem. You have a good night, ya hear?" As I turned to walk to the train, he added, "Hey! Good sound, you!"

Friday, February 24th, 2006

Clean Sweep

    Yesterday, I realized how dependant I've become on the work in the trains. While doing my bills, I came up short. I have a few days until they're due to make it up by singing. Each day I'm grateful for the fact that I can sling my guitar over my shoulder, swipe my card at a turnstile of choice, pick a spot, open my case, and begin to play. My body, neck, and head are slowly, but steadily, feeling better. And because I can now be more consistent in my performing, I'm beginning to see how I might actually earn enough to live on. This is heaven. Not only am I doing what I love, but I'm getting paid for it.

    So today, I took my trusty "axe" and entered the Times Square station. I was sure every good spot would already be taken, as it was much later than my normal four o'clock/hit-the-rush-hour start time, but I was really surprised to see no musicians in the longest of the tunnels leading from the ACE trains to the NRW and 123 in Times Square. This particular tunnel is the largest in Times Square and is normally lined on both walls with the most eclectic group of musicians and entertainers, and the array of religious preachers. The musicians range from steel drummers to fiddle players, from keyboardists to conga players. The list goes on and on. Often it feels like a museum of music as one either strolls or rushes through. Each time I walk through this tunnel I think, "This tunnel really should have a name of its own, given the diverse conglomerate of sounds that competes daily with the "Jews for Jesus" and Dianetics prostheletizers." But today, as I passed through this normally sound-filled tunnel, it was empty. That's odd...I wonder why there's no music? I mean, it doesn't smell particularly poor today (the odors in any given tunnel or platform sometimes being a deterrent to musical expression). Today the air was fresh—well, as fresh as a subway tunnel brimming twenty-four-seven can be.

I kept walking along the tunnel, looking and listening...but still there wasn't one musician. It made no sense that they were all gone. It was rush hour. In fact, the tunnel was almost completely void of any sound, except for the shuffle of the many commuters' rushing feet along the tunnel in both directions, accompanied by their breathing, a little talking, and every now and again the bleed-through from someone's iPod turned up super loud. The tunnel had an almost eerie feel to it today. As compared to the normally pulsating and alive vibe that the tunnel usually sports, today it was desolate and vacant. The only people left were the bootleggers, who consist of immigrant families, primarily women and children, who sell bootlegged DVDs laid out on bed sheets on top of the cement ground as their husbands and fathers work as day laborers, soliciting above ground for various types of construction work. The kids usually work one sheet, the mom the other. It's an entire operation that attracts many buyers. In addition, these portable storefronts can be rolled up and made to disappear in a matter of seconds if the authorities show up. There have been times when I've walked through the tunnels and at the far end are bootleggers all set up doing business. Then somehow, through some silent means of communication, by the time I get up close to them, they're gone, completely packed up and the space vacant. I always wonder where they scoot off to. It's like a magician with his doves—poof and they're gone, without a trace.

While walking, the vibe just didn't feel right. As I passed the bootleggers and came to the end of the long 42nd Street tunnel, I heard that now too familiar muffled sound of a cop's walkie-talkie. Coming right at me were two cops escorting a pretty, light-skinned, black woman wearing a large curly-haired strawberry blonde wig. "We've told you, you can't set up down here!" one cop said to the woman.

"But I'm not doing anything different than anyone else down here....I'm just tryin' to make a living, just like anybody else, and I'm not doin' nothin' wrong, only keepin' the peace..."

As they passed me by and out of sight I heard the second cop cut her off with, "Yeah, yeah, yeah, but you know the drill by now. We've pulled you in enough before." I heard the click of handcuffs as he pushed her along. "Let's go." Having never seen anyone being arrested underground like that, I thought about what she might have done to warrant being hauled in. She was pretty enough and seemed well-spoken, so I couldn't imagine what the big deal was. I kept walking to the end of the music-less tunnel and jumped on the N train to Union Square, mulling over that last somewhat eventful scene along the way.

Once off the train, I picked my place of choice in the 14th Street tunnel since it was completely musician-free. Within the first musical measure, money was being thrown in my guitar case. I felt finally at home for the first time that day. I was just heading into song number two when a cop approached me. *Oh no, not another cop. Wonder if it's candy or being cut again today.* He had that same sheepish look on his face that the other two had that day in Times Square when they evicted me. It's the look that says, "I really don't want to be doing this...but so and so told me to..." Then he blurted it out: "You have to leave." This time I'd done my homework online about the subways and music, read all the rules, and knew I wasn't breaking any laws. The rules clearly say, according to our First Amendment/Freedom of Speech, that a person can set up and sing anywhere in the train tunnels as long as it's without amplification. "But—" I started to protest. "But, I—"

"You have to leave," the cop repeated, interrupting me. Okay. Okay, I get the picture, I have to leave, geez. I just don't get it. I'm just singing with a guitar. I really don't see what the big deal is, I mean, besides the fact that this guy has a gun, and I don't. Even though I was fuming inside, as I was packing up, I went ahead and blandly asked him, "Hey, how come I've not seen one musician today from here to 42nd Street? What's going on?" At first, he evaded my question with some politically correct answer that filled me in on absolutely nothing, zilch. And then, getting that I wasn't going to settle for a non-answer, he finally clued me in.

"Ok, so here's the deal, and I'm not even supposed to be telling you this, but we've been instructed to make a clean sweep of all the musicians in the subways today."

"What? Why?"

"Well...it has just gotten kinda out of control. That's what they say, at least."

"I don't understand?" I persisted, "What do you mean it's gotten out of control?"

Finally, he leaned into me and lowered his voice, "Okay, between, you and me...there's this new chief of police...and it's ridiculous and all, but all of us have been instructed to move all of the musicians out of the subways in the event he decides to come down and take a tour. You know, so we look good and all." He looked at me with a look that almost pleaded for my understanding. Then he added, "Listen, we don't like this any more than you guys. Between you and me, I don't see no difference today from yesterday in the number of musicians. Always looks the same to me. But hey, I gotta do my job." I still wasn't buying it, so he continued on the defensive at this point, "Hey, we don't like comin' out here in the cold and havin' to walk around tellin' you guys to pack it up. Listen, I'd much rather be inside, where it's warm, and drinkin' a cup-a coffee or something." He motioned to the police command station at the end of the tunnel. "But, yeah, we've pretty much cleaned you all out of all the stations today. And to be honest, what I'm really supposed to do is haul you in. If the chief was looking or anyone was videotaping right now, I'd be reprimanded for not cuffing you right here and now and takin' you in. But we hate goin' through all that, so most often we just move you guys along."

"But you left the bootleggers!" I suddenly blurted out.

"Yeah, we do that on purpose," he confided. "We leave 'em alone. If we pull 'em in, we have to separate the mothers from the children and we don't like to have to do that."

"But, I'm not breaking one rule!" Now the cop changed his tone a bit, perhaps sick of playing "good cop" and "confidant."

"Yeah, you know that, and I know that, but what you don't know is that there are a million other, random things that I could get you on, so if I were you, I'd take that guitar and move along before I confiscate it!"

With that, I slung my guitar over my shoulder and started to walk. Then, hating to lose such a battle, I turned around and bragged, "You know, the other cops I met last week at 42nd Street gave me candy," as I threw him a small, almost defeated, smile.

"Gosh, now I feel like the Grinch." He mumbled as he looked at his shoes.

"Well, you should," I shot back.

"Hey, watch it!" he playfully teased. Then he walked over to me, leaned in and whispered, "You know, you can go to the platforms." He pointed to the staircase that lead back down to the NRW lines. "We won't bother you there."

"Really? Thanks." I was feeling better. "I'm Heidi."

As the officer walked away, "Rodriguez's the name."

"Bye, Rodriguez!" I shouted back to my newfound partner in crime. Gosh, what a crappy job to have, doing stupid, unreasonable things to reasonable people that aren't hurting anyone. I don't know the guy, but Rodriguez seemed too nice to be a cop. I mean he seemed to like the sitting and drinking coffee part enough. But the rest didn't seem to really grab him all that much. I kind of wished inside he'd find another profession. One that let him do better things than stopping musicians from playing music. He could probably even find something that still let him sit in a warm office and drink coffee now and again.

Saturday, March 4th, 2006

A Bit More Music, One Less Saxophonist

I woke up depressed about this whole "clean sweep" nonsense and change in the underground vibe, but regardless, I went back today. When traveling through the 42nd Street walkway, I noticed an oddly familiar figure hunched over, playing a set of three white plastic paint buckets, singing old R&B covers to the beat. Paint can drummers are guys who have a collection of large, plastic paint buckets, each one propped slightly different to allow for variation in tone, and with the buckets and a pair of drum sticks, they make music. It was the same curious figure, dressed all in black, from my first day in the trains. He was a small guy, not sure how old or young because he was covered up with the hood of his sweatshirt, oversized dark glasses, and layer upon layer of dark clothing. Even beneath his layers, however, I could tell somehow that he was thin and wiry. He had a spooky, almost mysterious air to him but I approached anyway, as I wanted to get the "daily buzz" on the cop situation and he looked like a credible source. "Um, um, excuse me," I meekly inquired as the Unabomber-sized sunglasses turned my way. There was no response, just a reflective "lenses stare." "Um, well...I just wondered. Have you had any problems with the police lately? You know, today at all?"

"Nope," he replied with cool words. "Well, I haven't yet, but they just hauled in this saxophone player right there." He pointed to the other side of the tunnel, opposite to where he was playing. "But they haven't bothered me none." I looked down at my feet, suddenly feeling a knot in my stomach. "What's wrong? You okay?"

"Yeah, why?"

"Well," and he suddenly sounded oddly concerned, "you just turned white as a sheet when I told you about the sax player getting hauled off. Thought you were goin' to hurl all over me right then and there. You know him or somethin'?"

"Oh no, just met him few times in the Bryant Park tunnel. But, yeah, it threw me that someone I've met has been hauled in for music"

"Well, girl, I dunno if I'd call that music, but yeah, they hauled his ass in so quick he barely had time to pack up his stuff. I even got a stray dollar outta it that he left on the ground. But, man if that makes you wanna hurl, just wait till you get to the Uptown NRW. Better get your stomach in order for that. Now that's somethin' they actually *should* haul in, in my opinion."

"Who? Who should they haul in?" I was still lost in the saxophonist being arrested, wondering if it might be Sam.

Then the dark and shadowy guy suddenly cracked a smile, making him not so intimidating. "Ha-ha...so, you're new down here, are you? Can always tell the new ones. You looking for a spot, huh?" I guess my guitar strapped to my back gave it away.

"Yeah, I am." I thought for a moment about what he had shared with me. "So, this saxophone player...what did he look like?" I had to know if it actually was my nemesis-turned-ally, Sam, from Bryant Park. "Was he wearing this large, oversized black, down winter coat?" I asked.

"Yeah, and I don't know *how* he played in that thing."

It *was* Sam, Sam the Sax Man. This was all getting a bit too close to home. "Anyways," the drummer continued, snatching me out of my own head, "he was just there counting his money and the cops came right on by and grabbed him right up. They didn't seem to notice me, I sort of blend in with my "camouflage" an' all." (He completely bastardized the word, but I knew totally what he meant.) "And so I just waited 'til they'd taken him away and kept playing. Been okay so far." He looked around to his left and right to make sure he was still sitting in a safe zone. "I dunno. They didn't look too happy 'bout him playin' there, that's for sure."

"Wow, this messin' with musicians stuff is confusing me. I'm Heidi. So, you sing and back up your singing with those buckets? I like the sound."

"Whoa, girl! I mean, what, Heidi, is it? Yeah that's what I do but first of all, these here ain't buckets, these here are called cans. Not buckets, *cans*." He paused, then continued with a grin, "Well, I guess I'll forgive you this time. I'm lookin' to get myself a drum set, you know. I like my cans 'cause they make me mobile and all, but every now and again I wanna play a set of real drums, you know, to mix it up a bit. I'm One," he said, briefly peering over his glasses.

"Well, nice to meet you, Juan."

"Ummmm, Miss Heidi, it's *One*, not Juan. One, like the number? Not *dos*, not *tres*, but *uno*. *One*. Yeah, those cops, they've been acting really strangely for the past few weeks. Don't know really what's goin' on, but it's been kinda stressin' on me. Hard to keep my groove goin' with all this distraction, ya know?"

"Yeah, I know, and thanks, One. Got it. One. Maybe I'll see you playing your buc…cans again?"

"Sure will!" he shouted as he started his rhythm. "I'm in the trains every day except Sundays. That's my day for God. I'm sure I'll see ya around." I walked away to continue my search for a spot.

I headed back over to Bryant Park, thinking, how can they haul someone in for playing an instrument? Now I had to sing, if for no other reason than to try and erase this nonsensical tug of war between authority and art, and this random hauling away of musicians, ones I actually *knew*. Determined, I jumped off the 7 train to find my voice.

"Rain On Me"

Standing at the crossroads of
Do I let you in
Or do I trade this moment for
What might have been

Not sure I can weather
More pleasure and pain

A Bit More Music, One Less Saxophonist

'Cause every time I love
I taste the rain

I wonder what you're thinkin'
And how to let you know
My heart is feelin' scared now
But, I don't want to go

Where will I find shelter
If you don't feel the same
'Cause every time I love
I taste the rain

Yeah, every time I love
I taste the rain

Saturday, March 11th, 2006

That Touch

It's Saturday. I'd only played one other Saturday until today, having now made a routine out of the weekday evening rush in the tunnels. But I needed to play this Saturday for two reasons. One was financial, brought on by the fact that my very lucrative Friday rush hour was denied me by the city's random ridding themselves of all of its unsightly musicians. And the second reason was to prove to myself that I wasn't going to be scared off by cops. I'm feisty like that. I've tried to 'lay low' in life about stuff I believe in, but I've found it's just not in my nature.

I not only decided to play despite the sweeping nonsense, but to try the platforms for the very first time since my first day at 59th Street. I picked the 123 line. I unzipped my case, feeling both a bit nostalgic about being back on the cement again, and intimidated at that same fact. I arranged my belongings and lifted up my guitar. Before I had even gotten the guitar strap over my shoulders, a guy passed by and threw me a dollar. Surprised, I looked up, smiled, and said, "Thank you." He smiled back. Hey, maybe the platforms are where you make all the money, just like that beret-woman had told me.

A different rhythm exists on the platforms as compared to the tunnels. I also noticed that, as a musician performing next to the trains, I actually have an audience for sometimes up to fifteen minutes at a stretch, versus a few seconds in the tunnels. The tunnels are quick, like a snack on the run. People are rushing by. They may only hear a few notes, one bar, at the most, one verse or a chorus of a song, and then they're gone. The platforms, on the other hand, are different. Aside from all the noise of the trains, wheels, brakes screeching, announcements, it's more akin to a regular performance in that there's a captive audience for a pretty predictable period of time. Granted, it's not an eternity (with the exception of major delays on the tracks), but it's long enough to sometimes get an entire song in, and that's for the same audience. That, to me, was luxury. So it also quickly sunk in that I'd have to change my rhythm to make the most of the now comparatively lengthy "show time."

As I set up, I recalled my first day on the cement and compared it to how I felt now. Some of the same uncertainties remained, like fleeting thoughts of "I wonder what people are thinking as I'm setting up my gear here. I wonder if they are thinking with curiosity or with pity or a little bit of both?" But as compared to my first day at 59th Street, where everything was going so fast and became a blur, now things moved slower as I watched those initial jitters quickly transform into a sense of "ownership" of my space on that platform. That's what I'd gotten good at doing over these past months, finding a spot and quickly "owning" that spot with my energy and my intention to make music. I thought, what an interesting skill I'd now acquired.

I saw only one other performer around, a relatively young, black guy with an acoustic guitar set up on the opposite side of the tracks. Once the trains passed, I could hear him engaging the crowd with an air of an emcee. An emcee, in fact, with a slight, yet quite endearing, Southern stutter. "Com' on ya'll. It's Saturday. It's party day! Ya just gotta sing cuz you sure ain't going to work...well most y'all ain't. But I'm workin', workin' on making you smile, just you watch." And he began to play a Motown cover tune.

Stuck amidst the crowded platform, I began in on my own playing, now and then looking up to take in my surroundings. Sometimes a certain person would stick out and catch my attention and I would observe them as I played. New York is funny that way. People *love* to people watch. So, undoubtedly, while you're busy watching someone, there's bound to be someone watching you as well. Any

New Yorker will tell you it's one of the most entertaining benefits of living in this city. So, as I'm sure people were watching me (I mean, that's the point while performing, right?), I'd now and again pick someone out of the crowd to watch also.

About a quarter of the way into a set, a man dressed in a business suit, trench coat, with briefcase in hand, flew down the stairs. He was scowling to scare the toughest on Wall Street as he repeatedly looked at his watch and headed straight to the edge of the platform. He parked himself near a column, standing next to it like an obedient soldier, as if doing so would guarantee him to be the first on and off the train. I played on. And there he militantly stood, frowning, tapping his foot, and repeatedly flipping his wrist to check the time. I wondered if he thought by continuously flipping his wrist he was speeding up time and the arrival of the 1 train. I closed my eyes and sang with complete commitment and emotion, without any doubt, fear, or hesitation, forgetting everything around me but only the truth in the song.

"Sometimes It's Easy"

Sometimes it's easy
To just walk away
Sometimes it's easy
When they don't stay
Sometimes it's easy
But it ain't right
Sometimes it's easy
Babe ~
Just not tonight

When I opened my eyes at the end of the song, I saw that the rigid man had changed. He was no longer standing erect but leaning against the column, his briefcase now parked between his feet. And he wasn't doing that twitchy, stressed wristwatch thing. Instead, he was resting his hands comfortably in his coat pockets, just staring at me, listening. *I'd got him!* I grinned inside as the softened man pulled money out of his pocket, walked over, and placed it in my case. We smiled at each other as he disappeared on the train.

That guy, probably a high level CEO, CFO, heck, he may even have been CIA, for all I know. Maybe he was headed to some high-end or top-secret board meeting uptown. Whatever it was, however high or lowbrow, I'm sure there was money and power at stake. I'd like to think, though he'd be a bit more chill, once he arrived wherever he was going, or at least, some innocent secretary was, perhaps spared from being yelled at just because the 1 train was running late.

I kept on playing.

> *Sometimes it's simple*
> *To just let them go*
> *Sometimes it's simple*
> *To watch 'em walk out your door*
> *Sometimes it's simple*
> *But it ain't fair*
> *Sometimes it's simple*
> *Whoa Whoa, babe*
> *Except when you care*

Then a mother carrying a cumbersome stroller, holding a screaming baby and an overstuffed shoulder bag, struggled down the cement stairs. I noticed them as I was playing because you could hear the baby screaming at the top of her lungs from way up on the landing, and it only got louder as they approached. The child was so unhappy, I almost considered ceasing to sing while they were on the platform, not wanting to compete and not wishing to make things worse for the mother who was doing everything she could think of to quiet her child. After the mother had turned the stroller around so the child faced me, she suddenly stopped crying and just sat there, completely silent, transfixed. One remaining tear lingering on her puffy left cheek was wiped away with her hands as she began to clap in time with me. The little girl looked up to her relieved mother as if to say, "Clap, Mom. Clap, Mom!" The mother joined in for a few rounds of rhythmic clapping as the captivated baby joyfully kicked her legs. When the 3 train pulled up, the now relaxed young mother gathered her child and belongings. "Thank you so much." She smiled in complete gratitude as she threw a bunch of mangled dollars from her overflowing cluttered diaper bag into my case. "You have no idea how long she'd been crying." After entering the train with her load, she placed her hand to her heart and mouthed another "Thank you." With that interaction, I thought...*That's it. This is why I do this.* I sincerely hoped, for the sake of that poor mother, that her baby would be happy and quiet for the remainder of their ride home, however long that was. Maybe the train's rumble and sway would take over where I left off and be just the ticket to get them home in peace.

So many people descend the concrete staircase a) in their own world, and b) determined to stay in that private world until their train arrives. I've noticed that when an artist is "on" with their voice, sound, instrument, and mainly their emotions, that's when you get them: you pull them from deep inside their intentionally closed-off world, out to your world. And that world may be whatever you create at any moment according to the song. It's fascinating. You can see it in their eyes. They lose track for an instant. They lose thought of that train. They lose consciousness of, "I don't want to be here." They forget, "When is my train coming?" "I don't want to see, hear, touch or acknowledge anyone around me." They don't remember these things and really start to listen. They are moved in some way; moved enough to forget their normal platform defenses. It's interesting to watch it happen right in front of your eyes. I can say with complete certainty that it's truly a gift to receive as an artist. It's something an artist doesn't necessarily get performing on a stage, in a club, on a cruise ship...or anywhere else really...except while busking. And the subways are probably the most extreme forms of busking, because no one wants to be there to begin with. It's not a lovely outdoor plaza, it's not a park, or a field, or a beautiful, warm summer day...it's the New York City subways and no one wants to be there. In that environment, touching another human being becomes all the more powerful.

So take a look at me
Now that you're leavin'
Now that you're gone
Now that you're leavin'
I thought I'd be strong

That Touch

Where is my courage
Where is my pride
Thought it'd be easy
To let this one slide

So much for simple
Not part of this ride
Guess this is just how you
Know you're alive

Know that you'll see
One of these times
'Cause I've got my eye on the easier side
The easier side

Sunday, March 12th, 2006

"I'm a Producer"

From the first day underground I found myself being bombarded by everyone and their brother, each one of whom swore they were a "producer." I've since learned that, especially as a female, this is a common occurrence. But the frequency of these guys, along with the numerous random notes and "offers" written on the back of everything imaginable, never ceases to amuse me. The most common reason that random strangers are "producers" underground seems to be to secure my phone number. The second most common reason someone's a "producer" underground seems much more complex, involving much more planning and preparation, and actually borders right there, teetering on the edge of being flat-out creepy.

One day, I was on the platforms and I saw a guy standing right in front of my case, chewing gum, wearing jeans, some name brand, pretty expensive looking sneakers, and a leather jacket. He was wearing headphones attached to an iPod, one earpiece of which was left to dangle, resting on his shoulder. He gave me five bucks.

I'm a Producer

"Hey, so, listen, I wanna know somethin'?" The guy continued in his intensely thick Brooklyn accent, "Are you signed?" he asked, putting great emphasis on the word "you," as if he had just stepped out of a *Sopranos* episode.

"Ah, no. No, I'm not signed yet." Having already been through this drill on a few other platforms already, I was not giving any serious weight to his words about signing. Apparently, he was oblivious to my indifference, because he continued intensely on.

"Well, listen, I know this guy. He's a pro*du*cer, and I'm pretty sure he'd like ta meet you. So, if you got a numbah or somethin'?"

Having gotten good at cutting to the chase with these guys, and half wishing I could just hand them a Xeroxed copy of my now well-honed monologue, I blurted out, "Listen, I appreciate your kind words and all, but I really don't give out my phone number to folks I don't know on subway platforms. But if you have a card, or the number of this producer guy," (trying to hide my sarcasm), "I'd be happy to get in touch with one of you later. Either that or I can give you my email address."

"Ah, yeah. Yeah, you know, I had cards, but, yeah, I ran out, and this dude, yeah, he don't like the internet much. So why don't you just gimme your number and I'll pass it on to this buddy of mine. It's no problem."

"Umm, yeah, well, yeah…No, I don't think so." I was now getting slightly annoyed that this gum-chewing bozo was eating into my work time. "I really need to get back to singing, I have bills and stuff to pay, you know?" I said, hoping that the sheer checks and balances of it all would somehow bypass the gum chewing and sink in. Amazingly, it worked.

"Well, your loss, 'cause this dude could really help you, you know, make it and all. I'm tellin' you."

Always the diplomat, I tried not to be rude. "I'm here a lot, so next time, bring a card. I'll be happy to take it and call."

"Yeah." His cover now blown, and completely rejected, he immediately got busy securing the lone dangling earphone back into his ear. That was a lot of trouble to go through for a number.

~~~~~~~~~~

Another time, there was this guy in his late twenties, covered head to toe in "bling-bling" who kept pulling out his cell, flipping it open and closed, open and closed, as if he were feigning making a call. I thought for sure the hinge would break and the pieces go flying, given the rate that thing was being flipped around. Every now and again, he'd hold it up to his ear and pretend to talk, nodding, gesturing, and looking "oh-so-serious." Given that there's absolutely no cell phone service underground in New York City, the effort was impressive. When I finished the song, his focus moved from his cell and the ground to me. He said oddly, yet kindly enough, "Sing something else, that's why I stopped. Sing something else. Sing something pretty and smooth, but with rhythm." Honestly, it really didn't matter to me which tune I continued with, so I decided on a song that seemed to fit his request, all along really wishing to ask him what the heck all the phone flipping was about.

"I really love your voice," the bejeweled guy said to me when my chosen smooth-but-with-rhythm song was over. Then he pulled out one of the thickest wad of bills I'd seen on the platforms to date, threw a bunch in my case and asked, "Hey, do you have a card?" Thank goodness I'd had special "subway cards" made up just for this type of encounter. The cards have on them, my name (first only), an email address, and my music website.

"Here you go." I handed out the first of my subway specific cards to the guy.

He looked at my card and then back at me, "I'd like to work with you. I am a producer."

"I'm a producer." There it is again. Same line, different guy. I thought, as I commended myself for the lack of phone number on the card, in anticipation for just such bozos.

"Really?" I said, this time making no attempt to hide my skepticism.

"Yeah. I am a producer, really." He proceeded to back up his claim with "hard evidence": "I was with Paul Schaeffer last night. Look." He whipped out that handy-dandy cell phone and explained, frame by frame, the contents of each picture. "Yeah, so, here's me..." The phone flips and gets shoved in my face. "And here's me and Paul Schaeffer..." Phone in my face again. "And here's the Tonight Show, and there's David Letterman, and there's me again, and there's

Paul..." The photos continued, one after another, until the guy was suddenly hit with an even better idea, "Oh! Hey, wait. I've got this video...."

Great, I need to see a cell phone video like a hole in the head. What I really needed to do is to get back to my singing. But the guy was intent on making his point by showing me his teeny tiny phone video of he and Paul Schaeffer (a la *The Late Show with David Letterman*). "Okay, that's cool." I was trying to sound interested and encouraging, all the while hinting that I really had to get back to work by simultaneously tuning my guitar.

While I was tuning, the guy pulled out the card I had given him and inspected it. "Hey, there's no number here? How am I supposed to reach you?"

"Well, my email is there, you can reach me through that. Or if you have a number, I'll call you" Now we were getting down to brass tacks. A producer, right.

Then, somehow, oddly, I suppose thinking that this would change my mind on the number issue, he added, "I'd like to take you to lunch and work with you."

Yeah, right! *Work with me*...yeah buddy, I don't think so...come on, you gotta have better game than that! "Well, hey, if you have a card I'll be happy to give you a call this week. Otherwise, the email's cool," I replied, covering what I was really thinking as best I could with sheer politeness that seemed oddly out of place, given how hard this guy was trying in all the wrong ways.

"No, I don't carry cards." Obviously, he was just "too cool" to carry business cards.

"Well. I look forward to hearing from you," I said again, bullshitting, but trying to stay polite and politically correct while inching my way back to performing.

"Yeah, all right," the guy mumbled as he moved away from my case, obviously upset that he had not succeeded in securing a phone number. Ah well... But cell phone videos of *Late Night with David Letterman* and no business cards? Come on, that's just not enough to get a girl to give out her phone number to a stranger on a subway platform in New York City. You've just got to do better than that.

I don't get it though. I mean, why don't they all stop being "producers" and just say what's on their mind? Why don't they just say,

"Hey, I want your number so I can take you out." Why the whole producer nonsense, I don't get it. But, trust me: it's a daily revolving door of insanity with these guys.

~~~~~~~~~~

But not just with guys, because a few days later, a woman approached me. She was about five foot six, light-skinned with short, black hair, holding a video camera and wearing the smile containing the joy of a twelve-year-old. She stood there for the entirety of two of my songs and afterwards came up and said, "Very, very beautiful." She gave me a dollar, and her card. "My name is Minor, Poet Minor. This is my card." She placed it in my case. "I have a television show called *Different Voices* that highlights performers in New York. Have you heard of it?"

"Ah, don't have cable. And I don't really watch TV that much, as I'm usually making music."

"Well, I just heard you sing. You're very talented and I would like you to perform on my show."

Thinking, "what's to lose?" I responded with, "Sure."

"I left my card. Email me or give me a call," she said as she got on the train.

I don't know, but this Minor person seemed to stand out a bit. I mean, at least she had a business card.

~~~~~~~~~~

Then, one time I got approached by another "producer." This time it was a "producer" with a "studio." His name was Michael. He had given me a number which, it turned out, didn't work, and a "studio" address which, when I walked down there, turned out to be an empty lot next to a church. Go figure. It's odd; he seemed nice enough; unassuming and kind. Not pretentious like some. But, still a dead end. It's so odd.

So, that was the end of that "producer" episode. Really, the trouble these folks go to blows me away. Their motives seem as varied as the subway lines themselves, most congregated on wanting to get my number and take me out, but many seem to possess some other odd element of insanity. There's something bizarrely self-gratifying it seems to these guys. I have no idea what thrill they get out of their games of make-believe, but some seem to go to some pretty extreme lengths to "play house," as it were.

~~~~~~~~~~

Finally, one of the most exaggerated and I must say, most impressive preparation-wise, in the "I am a producer" category, occurred one night in February. This one's definitely in the "creepy" category. It was about six p.m., and a well-dressed man carrying a briefcase and wearing a designer overcoat stood and listened to me for almost twenty minutes. Once I took a break, he approached me. "You're very good, are you signed?" I looked down at my feet, my first internal reaction being *Oh, no, not again.*

"Thank you. No, not signed."

"Well you should be. Here, take my card." And the smartly dressed, corporate gentleman handed me a professional-looking business card with what I supposed was his name and Columbia Records and a phone number printed on it. "I work with the producers at Columbia. Call tomorrow and ask for my assistant, Cathy, and she'll set up a time for you to come in. I have to catch my train, but I'll talk with you soon." And the man boarded the approaching A train.

I looked down at the card in my hand, the most concrete evidence any "producer" had handed me to date, it seemed. I played a few more tunes, packed up, and rushed home to do some googling. All night I searched and searched for the guy's name, the number on the card, and any other information so I could brief myself prior to calling the next morning, but found nothing that matched. I was baffled. Although it was almost midnight by the time I'd finished googling, I dialed the number on the card, just to see what was at the other end. Nothing. Nothing was there. I went to sleep, baffled and confused. The next morning at nine a.m., I called again.

"Hello, H and S Realty," a woman's voice answered.

"Ummm...is this...?" and I repeated the number on the card to the voice on the other end of the phone.

"Yes, may I help you?"

I proceeded to give the Cliffs Notes version of how I got the number, to see if she could shed any light on the situation.

"I'm sorry, dear; we've gotten some odd calls as of late, but I have no idea who this guy is. Seems like a nasty game to play on anyone though."

I hung up the phone and just sat wondering, who on earth goes to all that trouble? I mean, he had cards made up, a fake number put on there, stood there all dressed up listening for over twenty minutes, and had all these props to back up his story: clothing, numbers, briefcase… Who does this? Who goes to all that trouble to mess with a musician's head? This guy didn't have sex on his mind. That was pretty clear. It was far more convoluted than just picking up a girl. That's what made it so kind of creepy and icky. I wondered if he was some kind of wannabe musician. Maybe his family never let him do what he really wanted to do, and maybe that was playing/producing music. Maybe he never made it into therapy. Maybe this *was* his therapy. Maybe…gosh, my mind just wandered at the creepiness of it all, but was actually grateful the guy had found a relatively harmless avocation into which he could channel his make-believe "powerful-me" alter ego. Needless to say, that "I am a Producer" episode took the cake.

~~~~~~~~~~

This "I am a producer" stuff happens so often underground I can barely keep up with it. It's like spam in your inbox: you innocently log into your email account, and there's a new message; you open it, only to discover it's nothing, nothing at all…just "hot air." That's what happens underground. And just like spam, they never stop coming. Every other guy it seems is either a "Producer" with a capital P or "knows someone, who knows someone, who knows someone." It's a maze of nonsense, but I'm learning to wade through it. And believe me, I've got my high-waders on.

Monday, March 13th, 2006

A Still Silent City

This week I learned the ban on all musicians had spread to both uptown and downtown stations further and further away from the main hub at Times Square. I guess I was just lucky to get that day in on the 123 a few days ago. There were quite a few musicians wandering around underground with their instruments. I'm sure they had been kicked out of their original spots and were now looking for a more ironclad replacement. Ultimately they'll probably be forced further underground to the platforms, like me. Seeking more information, I approached the station manager in her booth at the 59th Street station. "Excuse me, but do you have any idea why all the musicians are still being kicked out of the subway stations?"

"Girl," she shook her head side-to-side, "I have no idea." All the while, she was counting money behind her glass partition.

"When do you think it'll end?" I persisted.

"I have no idea." Then she did the ever popular lean-in thing that the station workers were doing these days, when they've chosen to express to me their true, heartfelt feelings about this crackdown situation. Only, this time she did the lean-in from behind her Plexiglas window, simultaneously covering her microphone with the palm of hand. "I'll tell you…" She lowered her voice to a half-whisper, "I know there's all this security now after 9/11 and everything, and that's why all these constant bag checks, twenty-four-seven, around me and all, but I just think it gets over the top sometimes, and kinda ridiculous to kick out the musicians. I have no idea what's goin' on half the time, why they do what they do, who decides on all this stuff, but it disrupts everythin'…that's for darn sure. And to be perfectly honest with you, you know, between you an' me, when they kick out all you musicians…I miss the music!" She uncovered the microphone, sat back in her chair, and continued counting the money.

I was about to enter the turnstile as subtly as possible (these days I'm feeling as if I stick out like a sore thumb simply because I'm carrying a guitar) when I noticed a congregation of cops around a long collapsible table right next to the turnstile. I watched as they seemed to be stopping almost everyone. They were creating quite a backlog of angry commuters while asking them to place their bags, purses, and brief cases on the table. The policemen rummaged through everyone's belongings one by one. "What's all that searching stuff about?" I asked a suited man standing next to me, leaning up against the cement wall, also watching the procedure.

"Oh, they're checkpoints," the man with a briefcase answered. "It's new. Something to do with homeland security, and a new chief of police. They were here and there last week. They're all over the city this week. It's a real pain in the ass." (Words you least expect come out of the best-dressed people in New York City and it never fails to crack me up.)

"Thanks," I mumbled, now to an empty space, since the man had relinquished his place on the wall and had quickly disappeared into the crowd. I guess this new chief is really trying to make an impression on someone. Maybe the mayor? Regardless, it's putting a lot of musicians out of work, and causing even the "regular Joes" to jump through numerous random and annoying hoops.

I stood for some time, leaning on the wall, just observing, while kind of hiding my guitar, resting it on the ground behind me. Then I decided the whole scene today is just way too over the top in homeland security and cops for me to feel relaxed and comfortable playing, even on the platforms. After the three encounters in two or so weeks that I'd already had, albeit one warranting sweets, I decided I knew my limit in that "art against authority" department, and took the train home. There are way too many authorities all focused on preventing things that haven't even happened, and way too much silence for this normally musical city.

Tuesday, March 14th, 2006

Settin' Up on Me & Tag Teamin' the Sweet Spot

My friend Dimitri is an underground veteran of two years. I'd met Dimitri about three years ago at an audition, years prior to my braving the underground. Dimitri is originally from Estonia and is a phenomenal guitarist/musician. He is somewhere in his thirties, over six feet tall, strong Russian features—round face, wide set large brown eyes, fit—with a very "put together" look. He regularly pulls in fifty bucks an hour underground. Music is his entire life. In his world, neglecting music is neglecting the very essence of existence. When we first met, I didn't really understand his gig playing the trains. He explained at the audition how he plays the subways for a living. In fact, the director we were both auditioning for actually found him performing in the subways at Union Square and asked him to show up. I remember when we first met he came right up to me and said, with his thick Russian accent, "Why do you not notice me? Everyone notices me. Why do you not notice me?" He's a big flirt, that I learned right off the bat. I explained that I'd been concentrating on the audition and had simply missed "noticing" him.

"So sorry," I answered with a sarcastic smile. He still seemed baffled that I didn't notice or fall all over him. Okay, so checking his ego was *not* one of his strong suits. I always wonder where one acquires an ego like that. I've always thought it'd be interesting for just one day to walk around with an ego of that size, just to see what happens, you know? Just to see how people react. I mean, would people have the urge to swat you as I do with Dimitri at times? Or would you actually get more accomplished, have more results with an ego that size? I know it's definitely not for me, but it'd be a curious one-day experiment nonetheless.

I'd forgotten Dimitri was a player underground because we had lost touch for so long, perhaps because I had not "noticed him," who knows. But now that his subterranean world was mine as well, I gave him a call and we reconnected. When he first learned of my playing the trains, he immediately expressed the following, clothed, of course, in his thick Russian accent, "I am glad to hear you are finally taking care of your music."

These last few months I've called Dimitri on several occasions for his extensive knowledge and experienced insight of the underground. Recently, I've kept lists of his first picks in the categories he gave me. And I refer to them often: Rush Hour Weekdays, Non-Rush Weekdays, Weekends, Holidays...the list is both extensive and intricate. I was more than grateful to Dimitri for sharing his accumulated knowledge of the underground with me. Though I hadn't seen him since my existence beneath the city, he responded to my inquiry regarding good spots with the following, "Listen..." (Dimitri always begins his sentences with "Listen.") "If I can help make someone else's journey a little bit easier than my own, then I'd like to do so. It has taken me two years to learn the underground. And, finally, now, after two years of playing the subways every day, I finally know them. Now I know exactly what I'll make in every spot at any time of day, any day of the week, and any week of the year." Dimitri has been yet another angel, although a somewhat cantankerous one, along my journey. "The Uptown 123," Dimitri filled me in, "it is the best spot in the city. If you can get that spot, you are very lucky; everyone wants that spot."

"I've played before at the Uptown 123...and you're right, it's a brilliant spot. Maybe I'll try for it tomorrow."

"Listen. If you get that spot, you must let me know, I will meet you there when you are done and play after you."

So, we agreed and made a plan. I'd show up first and get the spot around seven, which is when, he informed me, the cops leave. I'd

Settin' Up on Me & Tag Teamin' the Sweet Spot

play for a few hours and he'd come on by two hours later to take over the dollar-a-minute "sweet spot."

Dimitri gave me strict instructions, making sure I understood that I would have to get to the 123 around the time the cops leave He explained that they still have that station pinned down until seven p.m., banning all music. But, there's the Asian guy who plays this one-stringed instrument of some kind, and who typically arrives at least half an hour prior to the cops disbanding, just to secure the spot.

"Listen...that Asian guy," Dimitri explained, "he never misses a day. So if you want that spot, you have to get there before him. And he plays forever." I had time to kill before I hit the 123, so I decided to play the L line. Since I saw no one there, I set up and began to play.

Suddenly, a guy appeared from nowhere and tapped me on the shoulder, nearly knocking me over. "You set up on me!" He was one angry dude. I looked at him completely confused, as I had never in my life heard this phrase and was absolutely bamboozled as to what he was talking about.

"What?"

He repeated, more adamantly, "You set up on me; I'm playin' my vibraphone over there and you have to move. You can go behind the elevator over there." He pointed to an empty spot behind a tall elevator column where there were, by the way, no commuters. "I won't hear you there." Yeah, right, I thought, and neither will anyone else. Thinking it was no big deal since I could seriously not hear his vibraphone at all, I kept on singing. "Listen, not every other musician would be as nice as me; most would just pick up your stuff and throw it onto the tracks." He was back again and more adamant than before.

Okay, I got it; I now understood the definition of "to set up on." When one musician is playing in a space and another comes within audio range of that space and begins to play, that's "setting up on someone" and it's now more than obvious, it's not a cool thing to do. Kind of like Sam did to me way back when. Had I known the "lingo," perhaps I'd have been more successful at driving my point home with him on day one. But a learning curve is a learning curve and I'm obviously smack in the middle of one heck of a one.

Although this scenario seemed light years different than me and

Sam over at Bryant Park—I mean, I couldn't even hear this dude and I have zero idea how he could have heard me on the L—I decided that whole incident was my cue to pack up.

So I did, and went to check out the sweet spot on the 123, especially because Dimitri and I had an agreement. To my amazement, once I did arrive, no one was there: no Asian guy with his one-stringed instrument and no cops. Excellent. I chose an inviting pillar to act as my backdrop, put my case out, and began to play.

"On My Good Foot"

I'm on my good foot, baby
Now that you're gone
You had me wrapped around your finger
Now I'm on my own
Oh, you're cryin' now
But I'm a-smilin' now
'Cause babe I'm on my good foot now

The songs flowed, the smiles and money were given in exchange, and a lucrative hour and a half passed on the Uptown 123. Then, out of the crowd of people, I spotted Dimitri standing across from me, listening. Wow, he showed up. He's almost always late. "So, listen," as he stepped closer to me after my tune ended, "I am here. Listen, how much longer do you think you will be?"

"About half an hour more. I'm tired. I had this incident on the L before coming here," I started to tell him but he seemed uninterested in anything but the 123 and had no time for stories.

"Yeah, okay. Then I will see you in thirty minutes, at nine o'clock, alright?"

"Okay, Dimitri, but don't be late, okay? I'm already freezing and I know I won't last more than thirty more minutes. You've got to be here at nine, okay?" I sang on and Dimitri went cruising the stations.

Nine o'clock rolled around pretty quickly. However, there was no sign of Dimitri. I was spent. During this time, two other musicians, an upright bassist followed by a flutist, had the same inquiry: "How long you going to be?" I explained to them that I had just finished and was holding the spot for my friend who was going to "be here in just a minute." The mere fact that I was there was disappointing in and of itself, and then to hear that another musician was "tagging in" directly behind me, well, that almost sent them over the edge. But I stood my ground. I was getting very aggravated waiting for late Dimitri. So finally, I decided to go. I just could not stand there any longer. I was freezing.

As soon as I had phone service outside of the station, I called him on his to let him know the Uptown 123 was now free. "You left the platform already?" He sounded disappointed. "Oh, can you go back? Please? You must. I beg you; go back to the spot I will be there in five minutes, please!" His voice was so desperate that I reluctantly agreed and ran back to the infamous "spot." Alas, as I raced up the stairs, a trumpet player had already set up on the platform. Just then, Dimitri arrived, appearing just as out of breath as I had been. When he saw me his face immediately lit up, but then quickly dropped when he noticed the trumpet player.

"You were late, Dimitri!" I said adamantly.

"Yeah, I know, whatever." "Whatever" was one of the very first words Dimitri learned when he first arrived in New York City, as he was trying to fit into his new American culture. It stuck like glue and he uses it way too often. He explained to me that he picked up from his best friend, Patrick, another subway busker who he seems to spend much of his free time with doing multiple music projects.

We turned together and started to walk off the platform, back into the station. I told him that he really needs to work on this being on time thing if we're going to make this tag team thing work.

We wandered over toward Port Authority, going through the Times Square tunnel, passing a steel drummer along the way. Dimitri and I continued on through the tunnels, now exchanging "set up on" stories, and bringing ourselves to belly laughs in the process.

"Listen, most guys are cool, they'll just ask you nicely, but that guy with his vibraphone, yeah, he can be rough sometimes. Don't let it bother you, but now you know a new word, eh?"

"Yeah, yeah, I know a new phrase, Dimitri. Almost got my guitar thrown on the tracks, but I know a new phrase. Yeah!" I said half sarcastically.

As we walked I contemplated this learning curve, and I realized that there really is a rhyme and a reason to the workings of the

New York City underground as a community. It is an unspoken and unwritten code of sorts. The only way to learn it is to inadvertently step on someone's toes, at which point it is explained in no uncertain terms. In thinking about this system, I'm amazed that a) there is one, and b) there is, per se, no one in charge. Yet, despite these facts, it all actually seems to work. The longer I'm down there, the clearer it's becoming that there is a method to what may appear random madness. Amazingly, the underground works on a system of internal, unwritten checks and balances that function, in some ways, more efficiently than many of our heavily managed systems above ground. I mulled on these thoughts for a minute, then was snapped out of my own thoughts by Dimitri's voice.

"Listen, I'm going uptown now to see Patrick and do some recording. Sometime you should come, too. He is a very good musician. You'd like him."

"I'd like that Dimitri, thanks. Maybe next week sometime. What time do you usually get together?" Then I jumped in to answer my own question. "Let me guess, sometime after midnight, right?"

"Whatever, yes, we meet at night, always at night. I'll let you know. You call me. Whatever."

"Will do." And we went in our separate directions: he way uptown to Patrick's apartment in the Bronx, me back to mine in Hell's Kitchen.

Thursday, March 16th, 2006

Heartbeat of New York

    Before taking the descent, I peeked down the stairs of the Uptown NRW to see who, if anyone, inhabited the platform. All I could see was a huge overstuffed shopping cart, filled to the brim with everything, it seemed, in Manhattan. As I lugged my gear to the bottom of the steps to see if in fact the platform was free, I stood looking at the cart, overflowing and chained to the platform post, covered with an enormous cardboard sign that said something about "Jesus" and "God" and "Salvation," and wondered who it belonged to, friend or foe. Suddenly startled, I jumped when I heard someone say, "Hey! It's you! You came back." There was the same spritely older woman I had seen some time ago, scarlet red lipstick, beret, and all. She was wearing a long skirt, bright blue top, her guitar slung over her high shoulder, with that same metal holder dangling from her neck, this time housing an actual harmonica. Today she was sporting a red beret; I supposed to match the lipstick.

    "Yes. Hey," I responded, happy to see a friendly face. The cart with all its entrails hanging out was still marginally freaking me out. I swore I saw something move in that overstuffed haunted house on wheels, so I inched away from it a bit more as we began to talk.

    "So," the woman began in with her now clearly Caribbean accent, "you're likin' it down here, are ya?"

"Yeah, yeah I guess I am." Then I corrected myself, "No, I mean, I really am, I'm likin' it down here, I am. I don't know your name. I'm Heidi," and I held out my hand to her.

"I'm Izzy. So, where are you from? Here in New York?" Again her accent really shining through in the most soothing of ways now that I was listening more closely.

"Yeah, I live right near here, Hell's Kitchen. How 'bout you?"

"Oh, I live in Queens," she said. "But I like to play the city, better tips here. I've learned that in all the years I've been here"

"Yeah, I could see that. I like your beret; you had a different coloured one the other time didn't you?"

"Oh, yeah, these..." she said a bit bashfully, touching the red beret perched on top of her head. "You know, I wear these silly things 'cause I got sick a while back."

"What?"

"Yeah, I got sick and they sent me to the hospital and gave me some drugs..." and she pointed to the inside of her arm to where an IV would go. "But when I came out, I didn't have any hair, up here," and she motioned a circle at the top of her head. "Can you believe? I mean, man, I went in and just like that," she snapped her fingers loudly, "they gave me these crazy drugs I cannot even remember the name of and now I have no hair. So I wear these hats, you know, to cover up the spot on my head," she said as she pointed once again to the top of her head.

"But you're okay now, right?" I asked, having already warmed up to her and concerned of my newfound friend's health.

"Oh, yeah. They say I'm okay now. You know, I have to go back twice a year to make sure, but I'm okay. Just wish they hadn't screwed up my hair." Izzy paused and scrunched up her face. "Makes me *so* mad," her face quickly changing back to her cheery demeanor, "but guess this is my "new look" now."

"Well, I like it."

"What, you like it?"

"Yeah, I like your look. It's like a trademark. And you know, all the great people have a trademark of some sort."

"Well thank you." she smiled.

"So, you play acoustic too, Izzy? Without an amplifier?"

"Yeah, done so for years. I mean, I had an amp, but it was too heavy for me to carry and it hurt my shoulder. You know, my shoulder, it can't carry a lot of weight," and she massaged her left, slightly lower shoulder gently with her right hand.

"Oh, yeah, I could see that. But you could get a cart and that'd make it easier on your shoulder and all. I've just been thinking about getting an amp myself. I see lots of musicians with them and it seems like it might be nice to sing softly sometimes. Just now and then, you know? Not always having to sing loud would be kind of nice, I think."

"Yeah, I know. I'd like that too sometime. Well, for now I'm good though. And that amp I had, it don't work no more anyhow, too heavy and it don't work. So, for now I'm good. Anyhow, so you lookin' for a spot?"

"Yeah, I was, I was thinking here or the downtown side?"

"The downtown's better than the uptown at this station."

"Really?"

"Yeah, on the NRW it's the downtown that's better. You know, different at every stop, but here it's the downtown."

"Oh, okay, thanks Izzy, I'll check it out." Then I thought to myself, "Oh, unless you want that spot?"

"Oh no, sweetheart, I've already played for today. Just finished and am goin' home. I'm tired now. You go get the spot."

"Thanks, Izzy. Glad to bump into you again," I said as I gave her a hug, feeling somehow like I'd known her forever.

"Good luck, sweetie. Just watch out for that…" And she pointed to the shadowy shopping cart in back of me that I'd gratefully forgotten about by this time.

"Oh, yeah, what is that?"

"Don't wanna scare you, sweetie. Just steer clear, that's all." Izzy said as she made a crazy signal with her finger next to her ear, hoisted her guitar back onto her back, and walked towards the approaching train.

As I got to the bottom of the stairs on the Downtown NRW, I saw the now familiar shape of One, my bucket/can friend from the 42nd Street tunnel and the first day from a distance at 59th. He's easy to spot, as he's the only musician underground who seems to be both performing and sort of "hiding out" at the same time. Quite a feat, if I do say so. I'm not at all sure of One's past (or present, for that matter), but I get the distinct feeling he's seen a lot of life in his time. Probably enough life to fill more than a few Quentin Tarantino or Coen brothers movies. As my dolly hit the platform with a thud, One looked up from his playing. "Heyyyyyy! He–He–He…" he fumbled for my name.

"Heidi. It's Heidi, One," I said, feeling that we were now even in the name department.

"Yeah, yeah, Heidi. So how you been?"

"Good, One. I've been good. Kinda cop-dodging. But I'm good as long as I get to sing."

"I hear ya. So, you played already or you lookin'?"

"No I haven't played yet, I'm looking. Did you just start?"

"Ah, well, I been here a while; why, you want this spot?" One gave me the second rare glimpse of his eyes since knowing him as he peered briefly out from behind his dark glasses and grinned.

"Oh, no, no, not if you're still playing, I was just asking.'

"Well, I tell you what, Miss Hei-di," he started in, putting much emphasis on the first half of my name, continuing our now ongoing name game. "I tell you what, just because I think you're cool, I'm gonna hand over this spot to you."

"Oh, thanks, One, but really, I don't want to take it if you're playing. I can find another one, honestly."

"No, no, girl, that's okay, the spot's yours. These people are kinda buggin' me today anyways for some reason," he said, as his small frame rose and he started to stack the remaining buckets one inside the other, magically making them into one unit in a matter of seconds.

"Wow, alright, thanks, One. Thanks a lot. I've heard this is a good place."

"It's a great spot. It's a lot of people's favorite, girl," One said, now sitting on all four buckets, stacked one inside another, making a single seat at the edge of the platform.

"Yeah, I know. I'm lucky I live so close to such a great spot, I guess," I said, as I unpacked my gear, clearly not yet as organized or compact as One. Then I started tuning my guitar.

"So, Heidi, you know I do coaching, right?"

"Ummmm, no, One, I didn't know you coached," I responded, not really knowing and a little wary of what this Unabomber-looking guy who played paint cans really meant by "coaching."

"Yeah, I've coached some of the best. Used to have a studio on the Upper West. But ya gotta be committed for me to coach you. Are you committed?" I had stood up at this point and was trying to digest One's questions while at the same time getting ready to sing.

"Well, yeah. I mean, I'm committed to what I do, my music and all, of course. It's what I do. So, yeah, I'm committed, sure. But what do you mean exactly by committed? To what?"

"You know, are you really committed to do what it takes? What it really takes to be great?"

"Ummm. Yeah, One I...I guess so..." Although, now after daily encounters with "producers" and the like I was trying to stay as vague and nebulous as possible with my answers, as I was not really sure I wanted to know where One was leading me. I mean, if he was going anywhere near where the "producer" bozos had attempted unsuccessfully to lead me before, I wanted nothing to do with it. But One was so steadfastly determined to tell me what he had in mind, that I had no choice but to listen

"No, no, no, you can't be "I guess so," girl! See that's what I mean! You gotta be committed! I mean, lots of folks say "they wanna be this and they wanna be that," but I wanna know if you're really committed to work as hard as you have to work to be great. 'Cause I've had a lot of students I've coached, and it turns out they just fall off and most often turns out they don't got what it takes. So I'm now very particular 'bout who I offer my services to. You know?"

Still unsure and very wary about these so-called "services," or of any "service" offered to me underground for that matter, I stood momentarily speechless. I mean, I got that there was some sort of offer going on, and I got the whole drill about being committed (I've heard that my entire life as an artist), but wasn't at all clear as to what was really being discussed here. And it just felt confusing and relatively out of place hearing this offer of services/coaching talk from a guy covered head to toe in black, looking more like he's about to hold up the corner deli instead of giving musical advice. But who's to judge? Since I really wanted to sing, I just nodded and said, "Yeah, I understand, One. Makes sense." And I played my first chord, kind of hoping the "offer" might be at least temporarily withdrawn.

Little did I know I had just made a verbal contract to be "coached" by One, because I wasn't two verses into my first tune when I heard his voice in a half-whisper saying, "Breathe, breathe, focus, breathe…" This mantra went on pretty much non-stop with what seemed like microscopically small breaks at undisclosed intervals throughout my set. So, hit man or high-end coach, I have no idea, but one thing I do know is that as I started to incorporate bits of his running mantra into my performance, the sound was actually getting stronger with the tips coming faster. I kept singing and doing my best to focus on the music while simultaneously ignoring and incorporating the non-stop banter coming from my right.

"Long Walk Home"

It was a lazy day in summer
Mid-afternoon
You and I were walkin'
Nothin' much to do
Talkin' 'bout the weather
Politics and such
Sittin' by the water
Not doin' much

A few times, in between tunes, when I'd stop, One would talk to me. "You see? You see how the audience responds when you listen to me?"

"Ah, yeah. Yeah, One. I get the breathing thing. It helps, thanks," I responded, still not one hundred percent sure if I was better off solo or taking breathing lessons from this dark angel on an underground platform. The coaching banter back and forth continued throughout wave after wave of commuters. In between, I'd chat with him as I re-tuned my guitar. "Hey, One, you ever heard of MUNY?"

"The what? The MUNY? What's the MUNY, Heidi?"

"Oh, you know, that Music Under New York thing. It's that program they have for up there, on the mezzanines; you know, the musicians with the banners and all."

"Oh, yeah, the "banner people." Yeah, I ain't had much interest in all that. I like comin' and goin' as I please, you know, no one tellin' me where to be and all. Why? You thinkin' of goin' out for that?"

"Yeah, I see the banners all the time one level up, so I looked it up, how to apply and all. I'm thinking of it. I mean, it's not until May, but I had to send in my application in February. I like to audition in general, and I figure it'd give me another option to perform."

"Yeah, well, if that's your thing, then I say go for it. Well, Miss Heidi," One said, content, I suppose, that he had in fact secured a new student...me. "I gotta fly. I got stuff to do."

"Okay," I said half relieved that I'd have some vocal time to myself and half surprised that his dark mantra mumbling to me during the past hour had actually made some sense, and at times had made a difference. "What do you have to do?" I asked, not intending to be nosy, but merely polite in showing interest.

"Aw, girl, I got stuff to do you that you don't even want to know about."

"What?" I asked and then quickly retracted, "Oh, okay, it's okay. You're right, I don't think I want to know, One." Figuring it probably had more to do with his clandestine "hit man/hold up" look than his musical career. "Thanks for the coaching," and I smiled.

"You stay focused, girl, and don't forget to breathe!"

"I promise, One," I shouted, as his slim, black figure slipped sideways into the closing train doors, his stack of white buckets almost catching the doors as they closed after him.

You were just a pal
Nothin' on my mind
Just two friendly people
Sittin' 'round killin' time
Until we started walkin'
And you gently took my hand
And something in me moved
You gotta understand

It was a long, a long walk home
Whoa Whoa, babe, it was a long walk home
All I could think about was you and me alone

Not fifteen minutes later, a very tall black guy with long dreads, carrying a large conga drum, passed by and stopped. "Hey," he said to me between tunes, "I really like your sound."

Seeing his drum slung over his shoulder, wrapped in its bag of brightly coloured African cloth, I asked, "So, where have you been playing?"

"Union Square Park. I was out there with a bunch of drummers.

It was cool, we had a groove goin'. Made some cash," he said in a calm, laidback manner. "Sometimes we play Washington Square Park but today it was Union Square."

"I've heard that Washington Square Park is a great place to play, but I haven't gone yet. I hear it's got a ton of history, too."

"Yeah, it's like this kind of outdoor jam session for musicians and artists. Been like that forever. But, yeah, it does have a history: a history between musicians and the authority. Way back, they used to arrest people big time there. I think it was in the sixties they had this big to-do, where all these musicians were beaten and arrested, just for playing their music. I hear now that they're *cleanin' it up,* they want to *clean it out,* too. Of the *art,* that is." He paused and shook his head. "This stuff's been goin' on as long as time, it seems. Seems somehow our music is some kinda threat or somethin'. I don't get it, but it's been that way for as long as I can remember, as long as that Park's been around. It's too bad, 'cause it's what determines our culture, you know?" The man paused for a minute, contemplating his last statement, I suppose, as I was also. That was pretty profound, and true. Then he continued, "Still worth it, though. It's mostly on Sundays that we all get together and jam, right there by the fountain. You should come on down sometime. You come and you'll feel the history in the music."

"I'd like that. Yeah, I have to do that."

"You know we've actually met before. I asked you if you were signed, remember?"

Embarrassed, I apologized, "Sorry, I think I didn't recognize you with your drum and all. You didn't have it last time, right?" My "producer" armor snapping immediately into place as it seems to do these days.

"That's okay. I spoke with my producer, and told him about your sound. He said he'd be interested in hearing some of your tunes. So if you have a demo or whatever, I'll hand it to him."

"Okay." I was trying to keep back that internal laugh that rises up every time the word "producer" is mentioned to me underground. "Sure, I can get you a few tunes."

"Here's my number," the guy said as he wrote down a phone number on the back of a Union Square's Farmer's Market flyer, suddenly flipping the situation completely, adding refreshing credibility to his words. "Give me a call when you have a demo with you and I'll swing by and pick it up when you're down here playin'. Anyhow…" He slung his colourful, oversized conga onto his back, "You have a really good sound, keep it going. You have soul in your voice, I can hear it."

"I appreciate it." Then, for some odd reason, I decided to spill to this drummer guy a sentiment that had been on my mind since I'd landed on the platforms today. I'd been searching for my center in my sound. That place where a singer feels grounded and at one with the music. And all day it had eluded me, despite, or perhaps because of, One's "coaching." So, suddenly I blurted out, "You know, sometimes, it's tough…it's tough, to find that 'place' where you're completely relaxed and at one with the music. That 'place' where the music just flows, you know?"

"Yeah, I know. But, it's always there. Just remember, it's always there, regardless of how you're feeling. Some days it's just a bit harder to hook into than others, but it's still there. Same thing happens with my drum here." He gave the drum bag a pat with his palm. Then he held out his fist for mine to meet his. We bumped fist to fist and as he was leaving he turned to me and said, "Remember, just remember, when you're playing down here, you're the heartbeat of New York. You're the heartbeat."

Friday, March 17th, 2006

East Side Them–West Side Me

Today is St. Patrick's Day, and I decided to be extra bold today and try a platform I hadn't yet tried. I decided on the NRW, on the east side, at the Lexington Avenue stop. The east side is new territory for me, as I have only played the west side on the platforms thus far (with the exception of the tunnel at Bryant Park, which splits the border between east and west, so it's not truly the east side, just nudging that way). I was therefore not sure how my sound would be received by the east-siders of Manhattan.

Luckily, I found this superb spot. Both the uptown and the downtown trains run on either side of the platform at the Lexington Avenue stop, unlike the ACE, 123, or even the NRW, where the uptown and downtown platforms are separated by multiple rows of rail tracks. On this east side Lexington Avenue platform, there was a constant flow of people coming through the station. Some were coming from work, others obviously from the parade, and some appeared to just be on their normal everyday route to do errands and the like. The Lexington Avenue station is also unique in that the ceiling over the platform is arched, lower and lovely in both shape and design: making it feel much like a performance space. I figured when the trains weren't running or screeching to a halt, the acoustics bouncing off the arch couldn't help but be brilliant. This was the best of both worlds: the acoustics of a tunnel with the traffic of the platforms.

Even though those moments were few and far between, given that it was rush hour on a Friday, the sound was superb and alive during those brief quiet breaks in the trains. I will say, that even though I still felt a "West Side Me" on an "East Side Them" platform, it didn't take long for me to achieve that "this is my home" feeling. And the fact that folks were dropping money quicker than I could stash it away from the subway back draft didn't hurt any.

As it was St. Patrick's Day, the outfits on the platform and in the city were a hoot. Green everything and anything, reigned absolutely everywhere. New Yorkers tend to go all out on any holiday that involves dressing up. There were green hats, green glasses, green pants, green mini skirts, green hula skirts, green gloves, green boas, green thigh-high boots—all of this being worn by both men and women alike. The visual was more than entertaining. On St. Patrick's Day, the bars are open and filled, overflowing from dawn 'til dusk, so, many times in the middle of a tune, I would inhale deeply with the intention of taking a big breath for the next phrase and felt as if I had just inhaled an open bottle of vodka. The folks passing were...well, pretty much smashed and all unusually happy for a weekday on the east side of Manhattan, leaving a very clear trail of "Eau d' St. Patrick" in their wake. Honestly, it felt more like National Lampoon's *Animal House* than Fifth Avenue today.

New York is truly a "work hard, play hard" kind of town. And once that "play hard" mentality sets in and folks get into an enclosed space, such as the New York City subway system, the energy can rise to levels bordering on insanity. I can tell you with complete sincerity that, given the high level of craziness in the city in general, it was hard to keep focused on my music today.

It was also interesting to me to see that on the east side, for many of the travelers, drunk or sober, it seemed almost routine to drop money in a musician's case. Many pulled out dollars appearing to have barely heard a note. Some wearing headphones pulled out their wad of ones and threw me a piece of green as they walked by. It almost seemed as if that compact wad many of them possessed was just for buskers.

Then there were the few folks, mostly men, who, as they sprinted out of the train door and were flying down the platform at breakneck speed, would spray my case with whatever change they had in their pockets. Funny, that doesn't happen on the west side. I think the platforms are too crowded, or the transfers are too far away to make a sprint really worthwhile there. But, on the east side, it seemed to be quite a normal fare. Seeing as this was the first time I'd experienced this act of generous multi-tasking on a subway platform, with trains whizzing by, I was literally watching, in anticipation, each time a handful of shiny coins were thrown my way by a commuter at a clip, and actually landed in my guitar case. That's quite a skill, to be running full out, put your hand in your pocket, grab all your change, and throw it into a relatively small target (my guitar case), all without dropping a dime. It looked like a frat house relay event, given the amount of alcohol involved today. I half expected Kevin Bacon, the late John Belushi and the rest of Delta House to be next to pass by, beer in hands, decked out in their togas, and sporting full insanity. Honestly, it would have fit in perfectly.

The whole scene was so very "New York." I don't know if it was peer pressure, politeness, or just the east siders appreciating a little west side "urban street art" coming their way that made them seem so instinctively generous, but it was definitely swaying me. Although I'm still a west side girl at heart, the generosity, dexterity and ready wad of bills shared by the current crowd was quickly softening my mini east side prejudice.

I continued to play, doing my best to dodge the distraction of costumes, alcohol, and flying coins. The only drawback to the day was that I was finding myself beginning to get cold quite quickly. I was bummed at the cold, because the energy was so much fun and I so wanted to stay for another hour and have a shot at making some decent change. But that goal I would unfortunately have to leave for another, far warmer, day.

Saturday, March 18th, 2006

Danny Boy

Like a bee drawn to honey, I went straight back to revisit the east side. Even though everyone except the "liquid lunchers" would be sober today and it would still be cold, I wanted to get another glimpse of this curious world of great wads of bills and handfuls of coins flying. As I stepped off the train and back under my new favorite acoustic arch, I heard the most tremendous voice. It was a male voice, just dripping with soul. It had a strong, high tenor timbre to it that must have been amplified, as it cut through every other sound in the underground. And every other sound is a boatload of noise, let me tell you. It was obvious even before I looked that whomever this voice belonged to had been singing for a very long time. It was clear from the sound, they *were* music. I peeked down the platform and saw, attached to the voice, of all people, the guy with a limp who I'd seen passing by in the 34th Street tunnels, the one who'd had that air of composure and centeredness about him. But this time he was sitting on one of his speakers, his shopping cart beside him, eyes closed, just singing. Singing, in fact, with zero amplification on that voice. I had wondered about his cart that he pushed full of speakers and amplifiers, but seeing him and mostly hearing him now there on the east side NRW, it all made sense. He was a subway musician as well. He must have been mid-fifties, maybe sixty, black, with a medium build. His shopping cart that stood by his side was now empty except for a few empty plastic bags and a newspaper. I was a little intimidated about inquiring about his spot, mostly because he looked so established and seasoned, which made me feel very new and a bit "unworthy" of a good spot in his presence. But I gathered my courage, I think encouraged slightly by the fact that he kept sighing and leaning back for small breaks to just look around. So, in my mind, I thought perhaps he was nearing the end of his set. I walked up as he was adjusting his cassette player for the next song. "Excuse me," I said politely as somehow his air seemed to render extra politeness. The man turned toward me and as he grinned, friendly creases formed around his twinkly and surprisingly blue-grey eyes. "Hi, I'm Heidi, and I just wondered if you knew how long you're going to play for?"

"About half an hour more," he replied.

"Can I wait? Is that okay?" He smiled again, a smile that looked oddly familiar. At first I couldn't place it, then it hit me— *Santa Claus!* When he smiled, he had the exact same twinkle in his eye as St. Nick. He grinned, his body slowly nodding, at this point, to the rhythm of the intro to his next song, which had begun to play on the trusty cassette player. I jumped in quickly with one more question before his vocals started. "What's your name?" I asked.

"Danny." The first long "Ooooooo-oooo-oooo-oooo" of his next tune following his name without a breath as if talking and singing were one in the same to him.

I moved my guitar out of his stage area so I wouldn't distract his audience. I've learned now, that that's what you do when you're waiting for a spot. If your gear is visible, and it's obvious you're a musician, you become invisible while you're waiting so as not to pull focus from whoever is making their money.

So, there he was, sitting and singing, happy and regal on his amplifier, which seemed to serve as a seat as well as a power source. At his side lay two wooden amplifiers, very distinct with an older, classic look, almost like homemade tube amps. Ingenious setup, I thought. Using one amplifier with two inputs as power and connecting two other amplifiers with superior sound to the battery-powered one is pretty smart. Plus, he's got a seat. I'm always so curious about musician's various and individual setups. From the look of this guy's setup, he'd obviously been underground for a while. "Nice amps," I said during one of his cassette re-set moments.

"Thanks, yeah, I built 'em myself. They're tube amps ya, know," Danny explained with a scoop of his head accompanied by a thick Southern drawl on the word "tube."

"Really? They're beautiful. I've been looking at amps, thinking of getting one, probably smaller than those though. I'm not sure I'd be able to lug something that big all over the trains; they look heavy, and I'm a little afraid of the cops if I use one. But the sound *is* amazing"

"Oh, I don't mind that none. I'm down here anyways might as well have 'em with me. And those cops, they'll git you with or without an amp, so you might as well git one and sing like you like ta sing. You play the gui-tar?"

"Yeah, I sing and play, and write music"

"You write music. What kind of music you write?"

"Oh, some blues, soul, folk-rock; it's a mixture. But I really love your sound, Danny. You've got some kind of voice there. I mean, you're not even using a mic, right?"

"Nope, I used to but then my voice, it just seemed ta grow, ya know? It got bigger an' now I don't need no mic. An' ya know, I ain't neveah had no trainin'. Folks think I have. But I ain't."

"How long have you been singin' for?"

"Ah, I been singin' forever. I been singin' from before you were born most likely. I sung with the Blind Boys of Alabama, Clouds of Joy, my band The Young Professionals, and Caprice. But that wuz years ago, ya know. Prolly you don't know those guys."

"No, I do know of them. And you've sung with all those groups? You've sung with The Blind Boys of Alabama?"

"Yup, me 'n' my band, we sang at Roseland, the Apollo, Copacabana, the Red Parrot, Latin Quarters... we sung all them places. You know once we, my band and I, we...we were at the Apollo...You know, the Apollo Theater up on 125th?" My ears perked up even more, as I love the Apollo Theater. "Oh, yeah, I know the Apollo. I got to see James Brown there once. I love that place."

Danny continued, "Well, yeah, we was at the Apollo, 'bout nineteen sixty-eight...we was there performin', you know, warmin' up an' all, and the Jackson Five were there too."

"*The* Jackson Five?"

"Yeah, you know, the Jackson Five. And don't you know that little Michael wouldn't get up on stage with us?"

"What do you mean?"

"I mean, we invited them to sit in with us and he wouldn't." Then Danny leaned in and spoke in a half-whisper, even though his speaking voice was oddly quiet on its own, especially in comparison to his enormous singing instrument, "I think he was intimidated, that's what I think. I think that Michael Jackson was scared 'cause I was a better tenor, that's what I think. Anyway, he wouldn't get up on that stage with us for nothin'. Well, we all know ultimately he did get up on that stage, intimidation or not, and the rest is history."

"So you scared off Michael Jackson did you? The King of Pop? Well, you *go*, Danny."

"Yup, he wouldn't get up on that stage, not for nothin'. Too scared," he repeated. "Sure would like to play one of them big venues just once again though, but most have closed now. Not like it used ta be. Sure love playin' them halls with all them people. I love it here, but just once more, ya know? If one of them halls was still around, and me too, if ya know what I mean." He grinned again. His cassette player now re-set, Danny started to play for his last set.

"Well, you sure have got some pipes on you, Danny." At which he smiled and started in on his last half dozen tunes.

After his last set, most of which kept the entire platform in motion as they either danced, sang along, clapped, or some combination of the three, Danny started to pack up and I moved over to set up in the space, this time with a sense of honour to follow such a voice.

"Where you from?" Danny asked as he packed the last of his belongings.

"I live here now. I moved from D.C., but was born in South Carolina."

"Well, how 'bout that! *I'm* from South Carolina!" Danny exclaimed as he hoisted the last amplifier onto his shopping cart. "So, you're a Southern girl, are ya. That means you got the blues in ya, that's what comes when you're from the South. We're probably related."

"Oh, I don't know if we're related but..."

"You got any Irish in you?"

"Well, yes, I'm part Irish."

"Well, I'm half Irish. Why you think they named me Danny? So ya know, then we're definitely related, bein' that we're both from South Carolina and both Irish and all." At which point I grinned, trying to picture how this sixty-something old black man with a thick southern accent and me with my oh-so-white New England upbringing were related. Heck, we both had the same blue-grey eyes goin' on, so one never knows.

"You know how to play 'Danny Boy'?" And he started right in on it.

"Oh Danny boy, the pipes, the pipes are callin'..." A beautiful a cappella version, since his gear was already packed.

"I know the song, just not on the guitar."

"You should learn it, it's your roots. You know your Irish roots, since you're Irish and from the South. I know you'd sing it good. Well..." He leaned on his cart once again full of amplifiers, just as it had been when I first saw him months before. "I'm gonna go get me some home fries 'n chicken. You like home fries 'n chicken?"

"Of course, I like most any food you put in front of me." I responded from the heart, as I'm an avid food fan.

"Yeah, I been havin' them home fries on mah mind all day long, so I'm gonna go git me some now. I'll see ya, darlin'...Alrighty then." And Danny dropped a dollar in my case as he took his time rhythmically shuffling his way toward the approaching train, leaning on his cart for balance.

"Bye, Danny," I shouted, sincerely hoping I'd see this wonderful soul again.

Sunday, March 19th, 2006

Projectile Pennies

Okay, so I'm, at least temporarily, diggin' this east side vibe. Who'd have guessed that I, of all people, would become a convert? I went back to the exact same spot I had played St. Patrick's Day and the same one where I'd met Danny the day after. I guess it's true: we humans are, in fact, creatures of habit when you get right down to it. Or perhaps Pavlov had it right: when someone's rewarded enough for a certain behavior, they will, in fact, repeat that behavior. For me the repetition came in the form of yet another visit to the first east side stop on the N train. I put myself in the middle of the platform, with a trashcan as my backdrop. Lots of us do that; it creates a small sense of enclosure for us when we play underground to use a pillar, trashcan, or stairwell as a backdrop. Plus I, personally, feel better when I'm sure no one's standing back there, staring at my butt. That always weirds me out. So, today it was a trashcan as my backdrop/bodyguard making me feel safe to sing. The energy on the platform was, of course, not quite as inebriated and nuts as that of St. Patrick's Day, but it was still a weekend night to some New Yorkers and surprisingly sometimes Sunday nights can be just about as drunk and nuts as two days ago. Nonetheless, I was doing okay. But, darn it, once again, the cold quickly got the best of me before reaching my self-imposed financial goal. Sometimes I get so pissed when I want to keep on singing and my fingers just freeze up, especially in winter.

Having stayed even longer than my body would have wished, and shaking ridiculously, I was finishing my last tune when I noticed down the platform a pair of feet wearing nothing but socks. I quickly scanned upwards to check out what was standing in those socks: an oversized homeless guy, completely disheveled, wild hair standing mostly straight up in the air and wearing, I'd say, half of the Salvation Army men's section. He was standing at the other end of the platform, just staring at me. He was just staring, his gaze not moving from me, all the while rummaging through his pockets. He'd every now and again take a quick glimpse into his pocket and quickly look back up at me to make sure I was still there. And each time he looked up, unfortunately I was. *Oh, no…Please don't give me anything from…from…those pockets…please!* Then suddenly, a penny came flying at me from across the platform, and then another. Just as I was trying to pack up, Sock Guy was shooting hoops with pennies, my guitar case being the net! Damn. What on earth am I going to do now? I sure wish someone would intercept the enormous homeless linebacker. You know, now would be a superb time for a cop to show up, not to ticket or arrest me, but to actually help. But no, I can only surmise they were all in their cozy offices drinking coffee or whatever they do when not arresting musicians.

Then Sock Guy wandered over, picked up the pennies he'd already shot and matter-of-factly wandered straight back to where he had been standing, directly across from me, leaving a very unfortunate odor in his wake. I brought my winter coat up to my nose, as did everyone within spitting distance, as the smell was just "blow-you-over" bad. At this point, I was cold and shivering and not inhaling very much, and my body and hands weren't really cooperating with the task of packing up and getting the heck out of there. Finally, lowering my coat away from my face and shaking, I managed to do what I always do first: lay my guitar down carefully in its case, and begin the process of removing my capo and finger picks, one by one. I was in the middle of all that disassembling, having momentarily blocked out Sock Guy, when suddenly… Wham! Projectile penny, round number two, came flying across the platform. This time, however, it landed *in* the sound hole of my guitar. Do you know how tough it is to do that? Really, what are the odds? I looked around, just to see who had actually noticed the event, and it appeared almost everyone had. The incident just happened to have occurred during one of those rare silent times on the platform when you can hear a pin drop. And a penny ricocheting off the inside of the body of a guitar was more than audible. Thus, it appeared almost everyone within spitting distance had witnessed the one-cent missile.

Now, as with so many times before in this sub terrestrial three-ringed circus I perform in, I was having a very difficult time maintaining a straight face. Somehow the shivers were now being replaced with giggles; giggles with very little air inhaled, as I was still quite afraid of the smell. I managed somehow to put two fingers into the body of my guitar and searched around- relatively aimlessly, of course, since I have very small fingers and the inside of a guitar is…well…just as large as the outside, so you can do the math. Plus, with frozen fingers, I wasn't sure my fingers would even recognize a penny if it ran smack into them. I looked up to see folks still staring at me, mesmerized at the whole scenario. I lost sight of Sock Guy as I was busy poking around, my entire body doing this alternating, I'm sure somewhat convulsive-looking, dance of shivering-giggling-shivering-giggling. So who knows who they thought crazier at this point, Sock Guy or me. For all I know, they might have thought of us as a team. *Oh, God!*

Then, suddenly, that smell was back, but Sock Guy was nowhere to be seen. Then I heard a rustling sound right behind me. Then it was quiet. I covered my nose, and listened again and still heard no more noise, so I turned my head around to sneak a peek. As I turned around my coat slipped from away from my face and that now way too familiar pungent odor hit me like a brick. It was so horrible it nearly knocked me down. I won't go into all that was contained in that one whiff, but trust me it was one serious smell. I was too scared to take my next breath and replaced oxygen with my down jacket. I hid my nose in my sleeve and breathed that way. Well, at least the shivering had stopped. So, it's true, when one part of your body is in pain, a surefire way to forget about that one painful area is to torture another part of your body. Then, like magic, first pain gone! As I performed this careful breathing routine, I looked around and saw everyone in the now increasingly widening circle covering their nose as well. We were all suffering. We all knew who was creating this horrible smell but were pretending it wasn't happening. It baffles me in this city when this happens. It floors me when someone walks around so obviously pungent and yet so completely unaware of it. I'm not sure exactly how the smell switch gets turned off in a human being, but I'd probably have given my right arm right about then to learn that secret. I don't know, but the olfactory senses must somehow get numbed or something after a time of continuous assault, leaving the perpetrator safe and the rest of us to suffer mercilessly. It's a curious occurrence, and one I wouldn't wish on anyone with a functioning nose. I have persevered through a lot of stuff down here. But this silent and seemingly inconspicuous guy…I wasn't sure I was gonna survive him. So, the disheveled lunatic that was once pitching pennies from "over there" was now, most unfortunately, "over here." He was now leaning against the industrial-sized trashcan and, oddly, casually reading a salvaged edition of *The New York Times*. Here's me: a calm and collected girl with a guitar, just trying to get the heck out of there, framed by this huge, smelly, trashcan-rummaging Sock Guy who strangely began to resemble Bigfoot as he stood so close behind me, hair flying every which way. But this oversized creature was, in fact, standing there, stinkin' up the subways, and reading *The New York Times* with an air of what strangely bordered on sophistication. I mean, what was he looking at? The real estate section for a multi-million dollar Manhattan home? Checking his investments on Wall Street? Reading the sports page and/or the leisure section to figure out his next vacation destination? Or is he another one of those billionaire beggar people I keep hearing about? If so, he definitely needs to start using his gold-plated bathtub more often. What on earth interested or distracted this poor deranged soul in *The New York Times* was beyond me.

Finally I managed to remove the dastardly penny, at which point I heard a voice say, "Hey, if you shake it, it'll come out." I looked up to see Sock Guy now standing right in front of me, sans *New York Times*, as intrigued as anyone at the show he'd instigated.

"Thanks, that's okay." I kept my nose covered and head bowed.

I had absolutely no desire to get any more involved with Sock Guy. In fact, I feared that if I did, I'd actually pass out.

"I wish I could've given you more." He was now almost standing in my guitar case. I reached into my case and made a trade with him, his penny donation for a handful of my earnings for the day, hoping that would entice him to be on his merry, smelly, sock-happy way.

Sock Guy, however, just stood there, looking at the money in his hand. *Damn he's not leaving!* "Hey, what's your name?" he asked.

"Uh, Mary" I blurted out a fake name while packing, trying to breathe and wishing to un-involve myself from the whole situation stat.

"Mary...hum...Mary...." He repeated over a few times. "Hey! What's your sign?"

My sign? My sign? What on earth did he need to know my sign for? Ah, he must have been reading the horoscope section of *The New York Times*, if, in fact, there is one. Or maybe he just imagines he sees one in his own private crazy, smelly world. I just kept on making up responses to the "What's your name," "What's your sign," and finally, the ever popular "Where do you live" questions being rapidly flung at me. Consequently, as a result of all of my made up answers fabricated in my half frozen, shivering state, Sock Guy now thinks my full name is Mary, I have no last name, I live in the country, far away from New York City, and, for some odd reason, I don't know my sign nor do I know my own birth date. Oddly, all the answers satisfied him. In fact, from my responses I probably appeared more like him than most folks he meets. Yeah, that's what I was going for, resonating a stinky, oversized homeless dude in socks. I finally escaped the inquisition by explaining to the penny shooter, still through my coat, that I really had a long trip back to the country and I had to go before it got much later. And so I left, leaving stinky Sock Guy there all by himself, shuffling back to the trash can to resume, I assume, his search for hot real estate deals in the *Times*.

I scooted around to the front of the escalator and practically ran up the moving stairs and out onto the street, finally feeling safe enough to let my coat fall from my face and breathe again. I needed a bath.

Saturday, April 8th, 2006

What Ya Can't Buy

    Having had the magical yet fleeting "East Side Spell" at least temporarily broken by my last trip over last month, I've been sticking to the west as of late. I'd been scurrying around all day searching for a wheelie-cart, or dolly, to help me transport what was feeling like an increasingly enormous guitar, around Manhattan. I finally purchased one, and by eight p.m., I entered the subways. I wasn't quite sure what spots would be left at that point since I was late getting started.

    I began to set up, excited to land my now most favorite spot on the first go: the Uptown ACE at Times Square. *Excellent, it's empty!* I thought to myself as I unpacked. There seemed to be lots of people on the platform, and almost as much garbage surrounding them. The platform looked like the aftermath of a Manhattan street fair, but indoors. I kicked away some trash, cleared the spot, and began to sing. People were clapping and smiling, and the money was coming in left and right. To my astonishment, one group after another kept filing onto the platform and not really going anywhere, providing me with the most upbeat, party-happy, and joyful audience to date. The trains had long breaks between them and that left me a decent amount of time to get some serious singing in. It became an impromptu celebration of sorts, with people clapping, hooting, hollering, and dancing.

Soon after, a maintenance worker for the ACE came by. I chatted with her about the crowds and unusually large amount of trash. She finally clued me, "Yeah, girl, it's the A train. The A train is runnin' on the E track and the E is runnin' on the A track. Been this way all evening. It's a mess! Yeah, there've been folks waitin' on this platform for over an hour. They'll be standin' there on the A track and have no idea their train was running right in back of them on the E track the whole time! That's why all this trash." She went back to her tiny broom and dustpan, trying to make at least a small dent in the piles upon piles of stray paper and other products littering the platform. I felt for her, one of those mini bulldozers would've been far more effective at this point.

I decided to help where I could with the confusion by, every now and again, making an announcement regarding the night's mixed-up train patterns. I started to feel a bit like that Southern showman I'd seen after a while.

Then, speak of the devil, I noticed, across the tracks on the downtown side, the friendly face of the southern emcee, guitar in hand. He too was "directing traffic" amidst his "routine." When there was a lull in the trains, I suppose due to some odd acoustic fluke, I could hear his banter clear as day, as if I were standing right next to him.

"Hey, ya'll, what's up today? Now, I'm here to do two things for ya'll. My name is Ron. Yup it's Ron, not Don, not John, but Ron with an "R-uh" and I'm hear to entertaiiiiin you. Yes, you, you and you, pretty lady, aaaaaand to explain these messed up trains today. Well, as best I can. See, these trains. These trains, well they ain't runnin' like they should." And then he strummed a chord on his guitar.

Man, I thought to myself, *my lowly train banter can never compare to that show*, and I continued to listen from across the tracks, as enthralled as anyone sitting two feet away.

"Yup," Ron continued, "these trains..." And then the next line he sung his entertainment, his slight stutter disappearing completely,

"The-heeeze tr-a-hey-hey-hey-hey hey-hey-hey-hey-nzzz, no, they sure ain't runnin' like they should, but if ya keep on list-en-in' to me, yeah, I'm gonna tell ya'll wha-ah-ah-t they could, yes I am." Then the hum of an approaching express train drowned out the rest of the show; well, the long distance version at least. So I went back to my (now seemingly pedantic) singing and train directing, feeling completely overshadowed in the emcee category, but soon settled into my own musical rhythm.

"Just Another Monday"

Oh if was just another Monday
Runnin' from the Sunday
Tryin' just to do
What I should

Then the unexpected
Found me in the hustle bustle
And I turned the corner
And there you stood

I don't know what happened
And I can't explain
How you turned my life
Around and around

But ever since that one day
I'm diggin' Mondays
'Cause you're beside me
And you take me down

As I sang, a group of teenage girls gathered around two columns to my left and started chatting: comparing hair, nails, clothes, purchases; going through each of their numerous bags one by one as they stood there at the edge of the platform. It was more than obvious they had been shopping, as they each had their respective purses hanging off one arm and a load of shopping bags dangling off the other. Each bag sported a different trendy label: Bloomingdales,

Macys, Forever 21. Once I started to sing though, the girls stopped their chatting and primping. Their shopping bags slipped to their new home, at their feet, and they simply stood there. Their focus was now completely on the music. The girls stood there moving, tapping their feet, and clapping their hands on the sides of their legs. Once I was done, they clapped loudly and reached into their respective glittered purses to pull out tips.

Teenagers inspire me. I think their interest in live, acoustic music moves me more than any other age or sociological group. Today's teenagers have an unreasonable number of very adult choices to make. They are bombarded by so much material and crazy unattainable visuals that for them to acknowledge something not spoon-fed to them by the conglomerates and corporations all after their dollars, makes me feel as if what I do serves a purpose. Even if it's just for a minute that they listen, for that brief minute, they are not focusing on what they've purchased, or need to purchase, or want to purchase to be "in," or feel accepted. For an instant, they are enjoying something relatively intangible, something non-material. For just one minute, the music takes over. I love that. I love that everything that was important to them a mere second ago, and will be important again once they are on their train with their friends, disappears. It melts away. Even if this switch lasts for only a few seconds, the priorities for that moment change, and art, music, and the conveying of pure human emotion take precedence over materialism.

Even as they reach in to their pinky-purple, glittery, "all-that-and-then-some" handbags to give me money—I know they have been touched by something they can't buy.

Wednesday, April 12th, 2006

Duck 'n' Run

    The money came in at a steady clip, one to two dollars a minute, on the Uptown 123, the platform I'd done so well with during my tag teaming attempt with Dimitri a while back. Directly across from me was a homeless guy surrounded by everything he owned in two shopping carts poised at either side of him. I reasoned I'd be "safe" from cops since they'd have to remove him as well as me. And they never touch the homeless.
    I started in on my music, and just like clockwork, the money came in at a steady one to two dollars a minute. Folks were smiling, clapping, laughing. Then, just about fifteen or so minutes into my lucrative and upbeat set, entertaining the crowd, they appeared: those men in blue. Two of them sauntered over to me and one said, "You gotta get your stuff and move along. You can't play your music here."
    The other added a reason d'jour, "The platform's too crowded, it's a hazard, it's too dangerous, you gotta go." I looked up at the three cops standing in front of me.

Then one added, "Come on now, pack it up or we'll take you in."

My heart sank. Take me in? Take me in? Because I'm "too dangerous?" Too dangerous for what? Music? It's not too dangerous for the homeless guy to sit there with a ton of loot, and who knows what inside of those carts, but it is too dangerous for me to stand with a guitar and sing? For some reason, this time, being evicted almost broke me: it made a slight crack in my soul. All of this and more I wanted to say to the cops, but was afraid I'd cry in the process, out of pure emotion. So, I bent low over my guitar case as I put my guitar away so I could safely hide everything I was feeling.

I'm really getting tired as an artist of being singled out, and what felt, honestly like being harassed. As an artist, I felt picked on; as an American, I felt cheated out of a basic American freedom. All of it saddened me to the core. I'm just singing for God's sake. I'm not trashing a platform, I'm not hurting anyone, not that I know of at least, and I feel as if I might be doing some good in moving some souls, by the looks of what had already come into my case.

I understand the increased security following 9/11, but these underground "musician sweeps" started long before 9/11; they've been going on for decades, in fact. There have been court battles over this particular tug-of-war. As long as there have been artists on the planet, it seems, there has existed, a kind of "push and pull" between art and the status quo. It just gets heightened in times of national crisis, and the spinoff from a crisis, artists often becoming scapegoats and targets of government crackdowns. These random sweeps underground are run by fear. I also believe *fear begets fear* and at this point, it seems as if the country is being run more by fear than freedom. It feels out of whack. That's what breaks me. And on a personal note, this particular cop scenario was giving me an oddly familiar twinge, a twinge dating way back to my childhood. I was being stopped again. And man do I hate being stopped, especially if I'm stopped for doing what I do. That kind of familiarity I could do without.

I quickly went back to thinking about my current world. If, in fact, this community of musicians that I have embraced, and that has embraced me in turn over these past few years, was run by fear, it would simply not exist. It exists, only *because* of what it is based on: trust. If we as musicians and artists went underground every day afraid—afraid of what people would think, afraid that people would steal the money in our cases that publicly sits there exposed for hours, or afraid that someone might come and fight us for a spot—we would not exist. We would fall apart the minute we'd begun. But, in fact, we don't fall apart. We do exist, thrive, and grow stronger...individually, artistically, and as a whole.

I know it's a stretch, but, having been underground for a while now, I often wonder how this "trust not fear" part of the musicians' social template might translate above ground. Perhaps someday I'll get to witness that.

As I put my guitar case strap across my shoulder and started toward the stairs, I kept my head bowed. I just couldn't look those guys in the face. I just kept walking, fearing any minute I would burst out in tears, part from sadness that this is where we are... still... and part from being just pissed off. The one and only thing I did notice, as I exited the now banned sweet spot, was the homeless guy, across from whom who I had purposely parked myself, cleverly, I thought, choosing him as my buffer. Clever, except he was still there as I was being escorted out. They'd left him alone, sitting directly across from where I had been not a minute earlier, surrounded by all his belongings, taking up three times as much space as I had. They didn't touch him. So much for my plan.

I traveled for about an hour looking for another spot. I noticed a number of other homeless folks on the other platforms, some with instruments, some without, but all of them free to be there, surrounded by all their possessions, without issue. But I saw no musicians. Finally, I found a spot on my favorite Uptown ACE, right there at Times Square, where there were no homeless and amazingly, I got to sing, and no one stopped me.

"Walk On Through The Rain"

There are things I don't want to see and
There are days I don't want to be
Alone, with myself

There are things I don't want to know
Like how they run that show and

THE SUBWAY DIARIES

Just why those cards are dealt

But I see it, I seen it all
And I'll take the fall
Yes I see it, see it all

I've had the days the deck feels stacked
Things I believed in have cracked then
Then night begins

Though it seems a losin' hand
I don't fold my cards
I take a stand

Strength has a way of
Finding truth within

And I feel it, I feel it all
And I'll take the fall
Yes I feel it I feel it all

I walk on through the rain
Don't stop me
I won't be afraid
Gotchya
I can play your game
Won't you watch me
Walk on, walk on, walk on
Through the rain

Thursday, April 13th, 2006

Mad Man of the NRW

Today was rough. The police presence is ever widening again. They aren't only in the walkways and tunnels but they are now paired up on the platforms. The initial act of going down underground and opening my guitar case in the middle of Times Square all alone was challenging in and of itself. But when there are cops everywhere, and they've been stationed there solely to kick you out, it becomes much more challenging to open that guitar case and start to sing. Believe me.

I went to four stations today looking for a cop-free stop: 42nd, 34th, 14th, and finally ended up on the NRW at the Times Square station. There I set up shop far enough away from a guy with a violin so we wouldn't clash. The guy didn't actually play the violin, but simply ran the bow across it, causing an incessant bit of sound to emanate from that part of the platform. I chose a pretty good backdrop of the stairwell at one end of the platform. With the exception of the enormous exhaust fan humming over the tracks, which gets truly loud at times, the acoustics were good in my new spot. I settled in, sang, and began to make some cash. Suddenly, I heard this never-ending noise. I poked my head around the corner to see what all the commotion was about. There he was (and I swear he wasn't there when I started): the craziest person underground, the creature everyone, Izzy, One, Rodriguez, all of them had warned me about.

I gathered from the others that this being seems to be a permanent fixture on the NRW at Times Square. His height is average, but I can guarantee you that's the only thing about him that fits into the "average" category. He has long, thin, straggly, dirty blond hair that begins two-thirds of the way on the back on his scalp and falls in thin strings down to the middle of his back. He's dressed in pants that stop mid calf, exposing his ankles and his chronically bare feet throughout both the summer and winter months. He seems to always park and chain his upright shopping cart, the large kind, filled to the brim, at the same pillar on the uptown platform. Attached by string to the cart, which is spilling over with anything and everything he has collected along his journey, is a huge sign made of aging, white poster board. The sign is filled, corner to corner, top to bottom, with writing which focuses on the subjects of God, Salvation, and Hell. Hell being the most popular subject on the sign. There are no complete sentences, but somehow any reader still gets the gist...*the end is most definitely near.* This "Mad Man" verbally augments the sign now and again by mumbling without a break something about "Damnation" and "Christ." Perhaps that's why the nonsense on the sign seems to actually "make sense": his audio version of the poster board consists of a non-stop barrage of non sequiturs, all spoken at a very low volume while he stomps his bare feet left, right, left, right onto the cement platform. The Mad Man has one more item that is a staple to his signature "look"—his guitar. It was originally a twelve-stringed acoustic guitar, you can tell by the number of now barren tuning pegs poking out string-less and lonely at the end, but it's now more like a random seven-stringed instrument, most of the strings long since left his highness. He wears this around his neck, secured with a strap, whether playing it or not. He moves, as he preaches and strums, in a slight hopping fashion from side to side—left, right, left, right—lifting one bare foot and then the other off the ground, all the while strumming madly on what's left of that guitar. He wails away without any particular melody and very few discernable words, except, of course, "Hell," "God" and "Damnation," those seem to be some of his favorite. Mad Man only plays one thing— madness. I mean, really, it's "madness"... no chords, no rhythm, no melody, just madness, for hours and hours on end. Finally, I'll add that this creature has apparently been stationed on the Uptown NRW line *forever*. You can ask almost anyone in the city who rides that line, and they'll most likely know of whom I am speaking.

Reluctantly, I decided not to compete with the maestro and I began to pack up. But as I was placing my guitar into my case, Mad Man decided to waltz over to me, hopping and strumming along the way. He seemed to be on a mission, which actually concerned me. I began to pack faster. *Oh, no, please go away.* But apparently my silent pleas didn't transmit because he hopped right up to me, within smelling distance. Whoa! What an odor. Not as bad as Sock Guy, but ripe enough. I was now multi-tasking madly; rushing, praying, packing, and holding my breath. Thank God it was warmer so my hands worked faster this time. Then he spoke.

"Listen, I just had to leave for a bit to call and report something to the police," Mad Man declared to me so very matter-of-factly that it was as if this entire scenario was no different than someone leaving a seat in a movie theater to get a box of popcorn. "Otherwise, I wouldn't have left." And he stared down at me with a mad, fixated glare. Then he insanely mumbled, getting louder and more passionate with every grunt, "Awe na na, ya gotta, know, God comes down, and yes, yes, don't you know, na na na, the citeeeeeee, um um, the, yeah, um, don't ya know, um um um, saaaaave yourself damnation. Yeah, well, I been sent here from him, you know, so this platform, this platform is *my* territory, it ain't no one else's but mine. So, if you're smart you'll leave an' go somewhere else to play. Got it?"

Oh, *now* I get it. This is his office, this is his job, and God is his boss. It was all becoming crystal clear now so, yeah, this was definitely my cue to exit. I scurried away, holding my breath, deciding to add to my list of below street level policies. I'd been making a private mental list for myself over these months in an attempt to make my life a tad easier underground. Rule #1- Don't haggle for space with anyone carrying a gun, baton and/or handcuffs; and now, Rule #2- Don't haggle for space with anyone not wearing shoes.

I'm sure the list will grow as I continue on my journey, but for now, these two will serve me well, of that I'm sure.

I decided to try the 123 line again since it had served me so well last week. I started down the stairs, excited about the possibility of an option. But my hopes were flattened again. Cops. Cops everywhere: standing in pairs, lining the platforms, all obviously bored and wishing for that coffee break, I'm sure. I swear, when these men and women are put on ban-the-music duty, they honestly look as if they'd almost prefer falling onto those train tracks than standing there doing nothing until a note is played. It's a ridiculous waste of manpower, in my humble opinion. (Not to mention that whole, you know, First Amendment thing.)

I hoisted my guitar up the stairs one last time. I thought about where I'd try next...Aha—the 7 train. I had tried that line before and it was a good one to play. I walked down the stairs and was pleasantly surprised. There were tons of commuters on the platforms and as far as I could see, no musicians and, most importantly, no cops. Maybe I'll actually get to sing.

The platform of the 7 line was a bit awkward due to construction going on smack in the middle of it. Blocked by floor-to-ceiling construction barriers, no matter where I stood, I wasn't visible to my most immediate audience. Nonetheless, I unpacked and began to sing. The acoustics were surprisingly good on the 7 line. No loud fan, no crazy guy without shoes, no cops with guns. *Heaven.* I played, finally feeling the slightest hint of peace. Out of the corner of my left eye, I saw a uniform. My heart skipped a beat as I tried to hold my voice steady. *Thank God.* It was an MTA (Metropolitan Transportation Authority) worker. I played on. My fear was replaced with endorsements as the transit workers all lined up, each one putting a dollar in my case, accompanied by a nod or a thumbs up.

It still bugged me as I walked home that someone like Mad Man gets to stay—in fact, he lives on the subway platform—but I and others who make music get booted. I don't know, maybe I should consider a different "look."

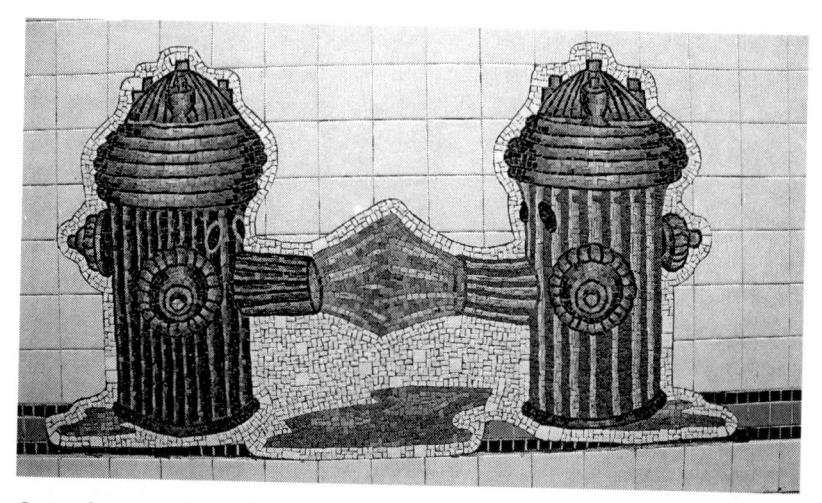

Saturday, April 22nd, 2006

"Ampaphobia" & Acts of Kindness

It's been a week now since I've been underground, the cause being a combination of too much daily "stuff" (appointments, meetings, etc.) eating up much of my time and the cop stuff temporarily knocking the wind out of me. Sometimes I need a break to regroup after a string of cop events. But now I miss the underground. I feel somehow incomplete when I don't perform underground. But that "incomplete" feeling especially hits when I ride the trains to just travel for appointments and the like, because I feel out of place when I'm in the trains but not really "in the trains," you know? So that's when it gets to me even more. I find myself, when traveling just to get somewhere, listening for the sound of a musician playing something, somewhere, just so I can feel connected. I seek out the sound, whether it is congas, violin, saxophone, paint bucket drums, or break dancers dancing to Michael Jackson (Michael's music being a steadfast and pretty permanent fixture as accompaniment for the dancers in the system). Tonight, though, as I entered the trains, I was surprised, not by the King of Pop, but by an entire Amish choir, in full Amish attire—long skirts, hats, and full beards—singing proudly at the top of their lungs. I never really know what the trains will yield, but its randomness is much of what I like about it.

So, tonight, thankfully, I was there to sing again. The good spots like my now most favorite, the Uptown ACE, were taken by other musicians, so I had to wander. Wandering is now an event since I have recently acquired an amplifier. Danny was right, amplification or not, the cops will still harass you and haul you in. And since I was getting tired of constantly belting out just to be heard *and* being harassed at the same time, I purchased one and was just getting used to it. There are always pros and cons to getting more gear, and the tradeoff here was the lugging of a guitar, dolly, and an amplifier with all accompanying gear up and down flights of stairs within the vast subway system. It now makes a local spot very appealing. Since my load became heavier, I've noticed that almost every elevator in New York City seems to be "Out Of Service." The MTA is always, "Sorry for the inconvenience," and promise it will be repaired as soon as possible, but now, with a guitar, amp, and dolly, I'm not buying it. The most intimidating part of climbing long flights of stairs is at rush hour, when all of the city is literally stampeding toward me. Somehow, I always feel I'm going in the wrong direction when that happens. When all of Manhattan comes towards me on a stairwell, it leaves no room on either side of the herd to attempt the stairs without the fear of being knocked over. Even for a regular, non-musician commuter with a tiny handbag in tow, this task of going against the grain is difficult and takes guts. So what I'm lifting with my petite five-foot frame becomes a feat, sort of an Olympic event. Each time I face such a sea of people coming toward me, I really have to prep both my mind and body for the ascent.

On the Times Square Uptown 123, I only lasted about forty-five minutes because the trains were on wrong tracks and a woman on the loudspeaker was continually announcing the mix-up. The thing with the loudspeakers on the trains in New York is that they sound exactly like the "wa-wa-wa" in Charlie Brown. You can't understand a thing, ever. So people were just not getting it. They were standing around, not understanding her, literally, for hours. New Yorkers are so used to not being able to hear the messages on the loudspeakers, they don't even do the normal, "turn-to-the-person-next-to-you and ask did you understand what she just said" thing, because they know full well that no one understands a word that's been announced. It's amusing. God forbid that anything more important than a convoluted train schedule ever occurs underground

"Ampaphobia" & Acts of Kindness

in Manhattan. Theoretically, this would've been a superb platform for busking, but the volume of the unintelligible speaker lady was so loud that I gave up and moved on.

The Uptown NRW was occupied by the permanent fixture of Mad Man. And that was definitely out as an option since he had made it unwaveringly clear to me that this was *his* rail line. Well, his and God's, I suppose. But the gist was, find another spot. End of story.

I scouted out to see if the Uptown ACE at Times Square was occupied, as I've really grown quite fond of that line. When I poked my head down the stairs, I was truly surprised to see the same woman with the blond wig I'd seen getting arrested. But this time she was cop-free and wearing a different, darker wig, and singing. Go figure, she's a singer. She was singing Karaoke-style, with her tracks and her microphone. Wow, so all that fuss with the two cops way back when was from her singing? Give me a break. I mean, she was *good*. She was digging into a Whitney Houston cover coming through an amplifier as I walked down the stairs to the platform. Her singing was interspersed here and there with, "Hey, you all, thanks for the donations, I'm Annette, thanks for the donations. You know this is helpin' to make my CD, so every penny is appreciated. Thanks for your donations and God bless." As I waited for a break in her music, I witnessed something wonderful. As she was singing, in the middle of her song, a homeless man came up to her. I hid behind a pillar and watched her as she saw him, and without giving a second thought, she bent down, picked some money from her bucket, and handed it to him, never skipping a beat.

If only Corporate America, heck, all of America for that matter, would just bend down now and again. If only those with more would, without a second thought, dare to share some with those who have less, just because, that action alone might change everything. No charitable deductions, no press about it, no one need witness it. Just make that happen.

It was obvious to me, from the rhythm of that particular routine, that it happens on a regular basis with Annette. Witnessing what I had just seen, in a matter of seconds, cleansed my sense of humanity. During a water break, I decided to ask her about her schedule. "Hi, I was just wondering how long you might be at this spot?"

"Oh, well, at least another hour. But you can have it then if you want."

"Okay, then maybe I'll come back. Thanks." I turned to explore more territory.

"Wait, girlfriend. I've never seen you before, you new? Nice to see another female in the system. What's your name?"

"Oh, I'm Heidi."

"I'm Annette. Come back then, if you want the spot. Gotta get back to work here."

"Okay, thanks. Good sound."

Her offer was nice, but I was so eager to sing that I continued searching for a more immediate spot and landed on the downtown side of the same line. I spent the evening making friends with my pesky little, yet surprisingly heavy, amplifier. I had been so used to singing without an amp that it felt strange to perform with one. I'm really a purist when it comes to singing, feeling more comfortable with acoustic and raw. At the beginning, I found myself turning it off after only one song. I felt odd, squirmy and out of my zone, as I adjusted to the amp's sound. But this evening I got it. I experienced a breakthrough with my new toy. I now know I can be so much more intricate with my voice. I can use subtle vocal changes within my music and vocal range because people can actually hear me now. I finally got to the point tonight where I actually enjoyed the new sound. Tonight, I was able to sing the quietest, most intimate songs I have ever written, and do it on a subway platform in the middle of Times Square. My repertoire virtually doubled in a day. How cool is that? So finally, after finding a spot, overcoming my "ampaphobia" issues, and making a good amount of cash (highlighted in the middle by some very random and powerful acts of kindness), I felt good. You can see why I miss all this when I'm away.

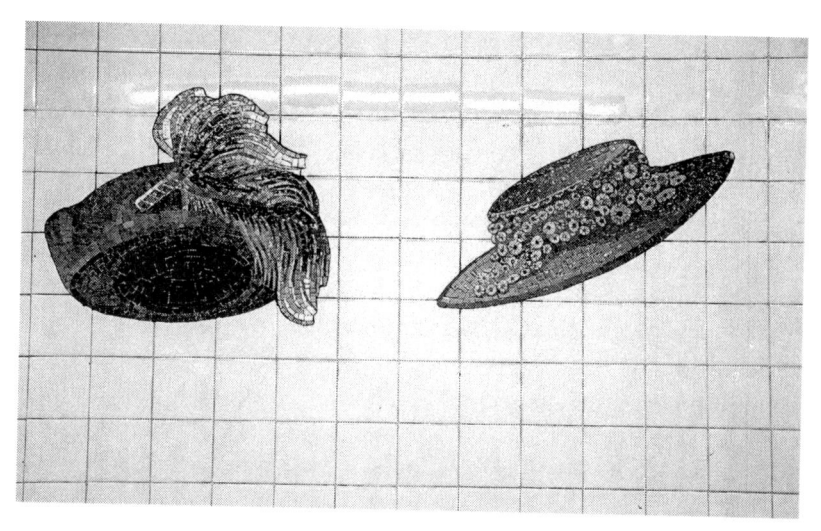

Tuesday, May 9th, 2006

Izzy

    My gear felt unusually heavy today as I pulled it to the trains today. Some days it just feels heavier than others. As I got to the bottom of the steps of our mutually favorite second home, the Uptown ACE, I saw the now familiar and friendly shape of Izzy. I've now exchanged spots with her many times in my travels. I asked her timeline since I could see she was taking a break and I thought she might be done. But I've often noticed some of the older performers take substantial breaks while on the platforms, just silently standing, sitting, or pacing back and forth, simply to regain their energy, I suppose. Whereas the younger lot, we just bust on through, singing, playing, sweating, freezing, until we can barely carry gear and ourselves out of the station. Don't get me wrong, we all work very hard; just all at our own pace. "Oh, I just started, dear," Izzy smiled at me through her brightly painted lips and over her harmonica holder.

    "Oh," I answered, privately hoping for a different answer today. I've missed a few days underground and, although somewhat distracted and disoriented from a crazy week above, I decided that the cure was the trains. I decided that I needed to remember how it feels to be there, if even for a minute, just to center myself and find my groove again. That usually fixes everything, I've found.

"I just began and that man," (she pointed across four rows of train tracks to the downtown side), "he is coming after me."

I strained my body, neck, and eyes, while hanging on to my guitar and amp, to see whom it was Izzy was referring to on the downtown side. Then I saw him, across those four train tracks, through the pillars, on the downtown side: an Asian man, sitting, wearing a white t-shirt, bowing his one-stringed instrument back and forth, back and forth. I asked Izzy what time this particular one-stringed instrument guy was making his appearance. "Around ten."

"Okay."

I unknowingly must have seemed a bit bummed, but I was just preoccupied when Izzy asked, "You okay?"

"Oh, yeah, I've just had a tough two days and have this audition for MUNY—you know the banner folks—and I just came down to play for, well, just even half an hour, just to…" and I didn't get to even finish my thought when she jumped in and finished my sentence.

"Just to know you've been here."

"Yes! Exactly!"

She knew. She knew exactly what I was talking about and responded with, "Half an hour? Well, I can give you half an hour. You offered me a spot before; I can give you half an hour now, that's okay with me."

"Really?" I was surprised that this offer was even being considered, not to mention actually extended to me. "But Izzy, you just began."

"No, it's okay. You only want to play for half an hour; go, play, you helped me, and so it's okay." She motioned that she was going to leave her tambourine and small instruments there, which she promptly put, right *in* my gig bag where the money goes. But I didn't say a thing, as I just felt lucky to have a chance to sing and get centered for thirty minutes, without traveling the length of Manhattan to do so. She could lay down in that guitar case while I sang for all I cared, and I'd still be happy to sing.

She broke down as I set up. I could see she was debating what she felt comfortable leaving with me. I stopped my song and said to her, "Just leave it, Izzy. I'm not going anywhere." She seemed to feel comfortable with that as she carefully tucked her harmonica and brace into my gig bag as well, right next to her tambourine. With both of our gear lying in the pathway, we were taking up twice the normal space, but it seemed natural for some reason. I just let it be and folks would have to simply walk around us.

A half hour or longer of singing went by, and Izzy showed up. I told her I was on my last song.

"You did well!" she said as she perused the contents of my case.

"Yeah, I did, Izzy. Thanks again for the time to play. It changed my day, you have no idea."

"You feelin' better?" she asked shyly, but in that unique, caring way she always has about her. I stopped for a second, amazed that this relative stranger had not only given me her job for thirty minutes, but also had remembered that I wasn't feeling too chipper to start with. She remembered enough to ask if the half hour donated to the cause had helped.

"Oh, yes. So much better Izzy, thank you. That half hour helped me so much. I think it's fixed everything. I feel one hundred percent better about auditioning now." I grinned with relief. She grinned back, I suppose glad she had done some good. And she actually had. Had it not been for her reminding me I had felt a bit "off-kilter" thirty minutes ago, I most likely wouldn't have thought about it again, my mood had changed one-eighty just from her giving me the opportunity to sing.

As I was getting ready to leave, I dropped a dollar in her tall, construction paper-covered donation can. "Thanks, Izzy."

"It's okay, you helped me the other day," she said for the third time. "We must look out for one another, you know?"

"You're right, Izzy." I leaned in to give this angel a hug.

"I'm all sweaty," she said.

"I know, me too." I gave her a hug regardless. "See you later, Izzy. Good luck."

"Good luck on that audition, dear." Izzy waved as she put her freshly painted lips to her harmonica and began in on the rest of her day's work.

As I exited the trains and got to the sidewalk, I heard a voice say, "You walk like you own New York City. Like you don't got a care in the world." I turned to see a vendor sitting on a stool selling cell phone accessories.

"Ha-ha, no, not New York City," I responded, "just my music with a little help from the subways." And with that, I knew that with Izzy's help, that thirty minutes in the trains had done the trick.

Tuesday, May 9th, 2006

Tell Me Off

"Excuse me." I pulled two dollars from my guitar case, as I stood in front of a large man who looked to be about fifty or so, but very weathered, sitting motionless. On his head was perched a small, round cap made from African tie-dyed fabric. And once again, as many of the poor in this city do, the man was wearing multiple layers of clothing, the top layer being a ski jacket, despite it being mid-spring in Manhattan. He was sitting against the tile wall on a milk crate. Beside him was a bright red shopping cart on its side; next to it laid an enormous big black box, honestly the size of a coffin. The coffin/box was covered with empty plastic bags and a large piece of cardboard lying on top of the bags. The cardboard looked quite like the side of a moving box used to transport wardrobe. In front of him was a cardboard sign, leaning up against a small, white bucket. The sign, painted in black magic marker read, *"TELL ME OFF FOR $2.00."* I swear, only in New York. "So, I don't want to yell at you or anything, I'm not really in the mood," (having just finished a blissful two hours of singing on the NRW on the opposite side of course to the Mad Man's abode, who was thankfully not at "home" today) "but do you mind if I take a photo of you instead?"

"Yeah, sure," the man answered in a deep slow voice. "Do you want me to move the sign or anything? Like to a different place?" He put both hands on either side of his creation.

"No, no, that's fine, where it is." I was amused at the man's concern with the composition aspects of the shot I was taking with my cell phone. "It's perfect, exactly where it is." I took the shot, wondering about the back-story to this intriguing setup. "Thanks." I put the dollar bills in his white bucket. "I like your sign. Hey, so how many people actually do that? Yell at you and all?"

"Some do. Mostly kids and tourists. Sometimes cops, when they take me away, but they don't give me no money for that," and the large man cracked a smile, revealing a perfect set of pearly whites that seemed as large as the black box looming behind him.

"Well, it's one unique sign. And I've never seen anyone else with a sign like yours, that's for sure. So, thanks for letting me take a

Tell Me Off

photo; hope you get lots of takers today," I said, feeling both a bit sorry for him and impressed at his ingenuity.

"Sure." He didn't move a muscle. As I put my camera away, I wondered what that other piece of cardboard said on it. Was it a duplicate, in the event that "TELL ME OFF FOR $2.00" got lost or sold for a king's ransom or something? Or was it a whole other angle that this guy pulls out when the first sign isn't doing the trick? Maybe even that coffin thing played a role in his gig and maybe he had a sign that said, "Try Out the Coffin—$1.00." Gosh, with that collection of items, the options are endless, I thought, as I strolled away to a low, muffled "Bye" coming from Mr. Photo Op.

Wednesday, May 17th, 2006

Bohemian Nights

    The 1 train stopped at 242nd Street in the Bronx. It was a warm night. I'd never been that far uptown before, so it was all unfamiliar. When I got out of the station at ten o'clock, it was completely dark. Dimitri had called yesterday to let me know he and Patrick were getting together for some music around ten, and that I was welcome to join them. Since they were both buskers as well as musicians, it seemed a likely fit, so I agreed, figuring we'd have at least those two things in common.

    "I'm sorry. The train stopped at 59th Street, Dimitri, and it didn't move…for ever. Hope you've not been waiting long?" I asked, immediately spotting Dimitri's face as I came up from the train. He was the only familiar thing anywhere in sight so I was more than glad he was there when I arrived.

    "Whatever," Dimitri responded, taking my guitar for me as we started walking. I skipped a few steps to catch up.

    "So, how far is Patrick's?"

    "Three blocks, but you don't want to walk them alone, trust me."

    "Thanks for meeting me then, Dimitri. Guess that means I get to live tonight," I joked, unsuccessfully, to the seemingly unflappable Estonian. Must be a Russian/Estonian thing, I thought to myself, of the chronic lack of any visible joy in this guy. We walked the three blocks to Patrick's address, chatting about music, busking, and our mutual desires to see the globe with our music, along the way. We were buzzed in and walked up the five flights to Patrick's apartment, a rent-controlled, large two-bedroom that he shared with his black cat, Bojangles. Dimitri made half introductions, moving straight to the percussion instruments and computer, guitar in hand. I finished off the intros. "Hi, Patrick, I'm Heidi. Dimitri's said a lot about you, all positive of course. Great to finally meet you, and thanks for having me over."

"Oh, no problem," Patrick responded. "Dimitri's told me a lot about you as well. All good, too." Patrick stood about five foot eight, Hispanic, and Dimitri had said mid-thirties, although he looked about ten years older than that due to the years of drugs and alcohol that he'd apparently traded in for a firm devotion to God. "He really turned his life around. He does a lot Christian Rock stuff now," Dimitri had previously explained.

We three settled in, the guys on two chairs and me on the lone couch with Bojangles, who chose to nap on the far end. We jammed all night, trading mostly original compositions with one another, each of us taking a turn with our guitars and songs, the other two joining in where we wanted, either vocally, on guitar, or percussion. In between making music, we talked music. Patrick filled us in that a label that heard his CD had called him in to audition in a few months. He and Dimitri both were really hopeful about it.

At about midnight we ordered Chinese food, took a short break to gather together enough bills to pay the delivery guy and eat, and went straight back to the music. We three jammed until almost three a.m., when I, reluctantly, began to fade.

"Hey you guys, I'm fading here." I filled in the two late night minstrels. "But you guys keep playing. I should get the train home though, I have a long ride back to Times Square."

"Okay," Dimitri said without inflection and not looking up from his guitar.

Patrick piped in, "Dimitri, you have to walk her to the train; it's late and this is not a safe neighborhood. In fact, if you were really polite, you'd take her all the way back to make sure she gets there safe and all." Dimitri stopped playing briefly and looked down at his feet, obviously not "jazzed" about the thought of taking a forty-five minute trip downtown to Times Square, only to turn right around and repeat it to his home on 148th Street. But finally, an "Okay, whatever," came out of his mouth, which Patrick took as a positive and stood up to help us gather our things.

"Thanks so much, Patrick. This was great; I'd do this again anytime. It was as much fun as the trains, and I rarely say that, honestly. Hey, how come I never see you underground?"

"He is lazy," Dimitri jumped in, as he put his guitar into its case. "He is lazy, he goes underground only once or twice a month with his CDs and plays for six or seven hours and comes home with enough money for the whole month."

"Are you kidding? You make that kind of money all at once?"

"Yeah, usually, as long as the cops don't get in my way." He then proceeded to fill in Dimitri about the prior week, when he'd gotten all the way to Times Square, set up, laid out his CDs, and not twenty minutes in, got a ticket. "I was so pissed. I was doing so well and this pissant cop just needed to ticket someone. I mean it was like one a.m. and...anyway, I lost money that night. Haven't been back since, I got so pissed off."

"Listen. You need to play more often," Dimitri replied. "Otherwise you get lazy," he reiterated in his typical "Dimitri" manner.

"Hey, Dimitri, I'm really okay getting home by myself if you just make sure I get to the train," I jumped in as I walked toward the door, giving him one more out, as chaperoning me all the way home seemed beyond the "call of duty" at that hour.

"Listen. Whatever, I take you. See you later, Patrick. You fill me in with the producer and label, okay?"

"Will do, bro. Have a safe trip home, Heidi. Really good meeting you. You've got some great material there and a big, soulful sound for such a little white chick," and we both gave Patrick a hug goodbye.

"Thanks again Patrick. Hope to see you again soon." I was dizzy-tired so the train ride back to Times Square was a bit of a blur. I had to catch myself a few times as my head kept ending up on Dimitri's shoulder as I'd nod off. With any other friend, I'd have just let it rest there, but I never really know with Dimitri. He's an odd dichotomy of ego and "untouchable," and I never really know how he'll digest stuff. So I worked overtime at trying not to nod off, so as not to create confusion.

As we exited the sparsely populated subway onto the street, I was shocked and slightly giddy to see a sight I'd never seen in New York City: 42nd Street was completely empty. Living in the midst of it all, it was a rare and crazy sight to see absolutely zero cars on the pavement, only a few pedestrians on the sidewalk, and one or two late night eaters in the still open restaurants and diners along 9th Avenue. Before we turned the corner toward my apartment, I said, "Hold this, Dimitri. Hold this, just for a second," and I handed him my guitar.

"Why? Why are you giving me your guitar? Come on, it's late, we must keep walking."

"No, just for a second, here hold it for a second." I got up on my tiptoes and manually put the guitar strap over his shoulder.

"Whatever," was of course his response, which I'd gotten really good at ignoring at this point, and I ran out into the still vacant 42nd Street. I looked up and down the street to make sure it was truly void of traffic and proceeded to lay down in the middle of the pavement, which was still warm from the days of spring sun. "What are you doing?" Dimitri shouted. "You're crazy, come on, you cannot do that you will get us into trouble or you will get run over!" I laid there on the ground for a few seconds more, absorbing the feeling of a warm, empty 42nd Street on my back, then stood up and went back to a now marginally uncomfortable Dimitri, still standing at the edge of the sidewalk. "Here, take your guitar, you crazy girl." And he started to walk again. "You are crazy, you know that? Crazy! It is too late for this stuff." And then he mumbled something in Russian, the meaning of which I could not imagine, but it sounded like some cursing or something, which I quickly ignored.

"I just wanted to see how it felt. You know, to say I had done it. That I'd laid down in the middle of 42nd Street, just once." This only spurred on more Russian out of Dimitri, so I reveled silently to myself, now completely awake.

"Okay, come on, you're home then. Good night." Dimitri said succinctly.

"Thanks so much for the escort home, Dimitri. Really, I could have managed the train ride myself, but thanks and it helped to have someone to hold my guitar for the 'detour.'"

"Yeah, whatever. Listen I go back home now. See you later," and as the sun began to peek out in the Eastern sky, he leaned over and gave me a gentle kiss on the cheek.

"Thanks again, Dimitri. I had fun, really. Tonight was as close to the trains as I've ever felt in this city and your friend Patrick is great. Thank him again for me, will you?"

"I will. Okay. Good night. See you." And Dimitri started his now hour-long trip back up to his apartment on 148th Street.

Gosh, if all the social events I went to were as musical and bohemian as tonight, I'd be staying up 'til four a.m. every night of the week. Heck, I might even surface from the trains a bit more often, I thought to myself as I took the elevator up to my apartment. That was one brilliant evening.

Friday, May 19th, 2006

MUNY

MUNY time was finally here. I felt centered and ready for the new adventure. The MUNY auditions are held in Vanderbilt Hall in Grand Central Station. Vanderbilt Hall was built by the Vanderbilts, who built and used to own the station itself. It used to be the main concourse before the current one was built, but now it's used for special events, and I guess MUNY auditions.

Just the mere fact that it was built by the Vanderbilts gives you an idea of the scope and grandeur of the space. It's an enormous hall with ceilings that go up at least four stories straight to the top. The grandness of the hall mirrors that of the train station itself in both its history and mystery.

I've always been intrigued by Grand Central Station. The station is an intricate and mysterious structure. It's grand in every way, from the seemingly endless astronomical ceilings, where the sky is backwards and the stars are oddly displaced, to the enormous four-faced clock and intricate carvings that adorn the atriums and passageways. Whenever I walk into Grand Central Station, I feel as if I'm going back in time. I'm not sure how I found this out, but there's actually a spot, in a certain vestibule, about twenty yards in diameter in Grand Central Terminal, where two people can stand on opposite sides of this vestibule, put their faces to the walls, and hear each other whisper as if they were standing right next to each other. I've always thought it would be a great spot for a proposal, so unexpected and magical. There's also this "secret" sub-basement with this very "James Bond" kind of name: the M42. Nothing else, just the M42.

The M42 lies under the Terminal. The exact location of M42 is this closely guarded secret and can't be found on any map, I've been told—although it's been shown here and there on a few TV shows. Isn't America wonderful? It's all "secret" and yet it's been shown on TV. Superb, still. It's all so fascinating. To me, these little "mysteries" are perfect encapsulations of the magic I feel when entering Grand Central.

As I walked into this huge, somewhat intimidating space, I found the people there completely opposite to the vibe of the hall itself. The Great Hall was filled with every kind of musician and musical act you could imagine, from all corners of the globe. There was everything from bluegrass groups to Indian vocalists to tap dancers to African drum groups. They were welcoming, organized, and friendly, and I'd say at least half, if not all, of the volunteers were subway musicians themselves, helping "herd the masses" for the day of the MUNY auditions.

Each year, hundreds apply for MUNY, and sixty or so are chosen to audition. Then they choose a handful from the final candidates to become part of the program.

As I checked in, I was welcomed by smile after smile from various monitors and volunteers. They were answering questions and herding us into our respective line-ups to warm up, line up, go on stage, et cetera.

The stage area itself was the interior of a large semi-circle of tables, behind which thirty-odd judges were seated. Behind them, a wall of press with cameras and notepads. The judges all looked like musicians themselves, men and women both of various ages and with distinctive looks. A few seemed to be MUNY players; the rest I'm not sure where they were recruited from, but they seemed to take it all quite seriously. In front of the tables was the stage area and at the back of that was the emcee podium. Behind the podium stood a flamboyant PT Barnum-like man wearing a brightly coloured shirt, a wide brimmed hat, and glasses, doing a fabulous job of not only keeping everyone moving but also keeping judges and talent alike fabulously entertained in between each hopeful musician that performed.

It seemed like forever that I waited to sing, although I know it was only ten or so minutes. But once I was called up there in front of the judges, the time flew. It always does.

The semi-circle was interesting to sing to, as it was a challenge to make contact with everyone since a good chunk of the judges were poised at my sides. But I did my best and sang my allotted two tunes happily, absolutely loving that space the Vanderbilts had built so many years ago.

Once done, I was escorted off by the guy allotted that duty, then quickly bombarded by press people. I'd seen that was the drill by watching those before me, but it caught me off guard nonetheless to do interview after interview right after an audition.

All in all, it was a fabulous experience: the people were fantastic, the space amazing to sing in. I did a solid performance and felt as if I could easily stick around and chat for the rest of the day. But I decided instead to follow the audition with trains and sing, especially since I had all my gear with me and I was right at the subway entrance there in Grand Central.

I hopped on the train, recounting the adventure in my mind and now wondering about the outcome.

Sunday, May 21st, 2006

Madness & Marley

I'd had the MUNY audition about two weeks ago, and although I felt good about it, I wanted to put it aside in my mind until the results came in a few weeks. I went back to the Uptown NRW at Times Square. This time, Mad Man was "at home" and, as usual, Mad Man was doing his non-stop manic strumming and sidestepping on the downtown side. Since I had played there last night, and it went well, I set up shop again, figuring there was a good chance of a repeat in the success department.

I wasn't even three songs into my set of tunes when I opened my eyes, and right in front of me were Mad Man's two bare feet, even though he had been on the complete opposite side of the tracks when I started. He was hopping left and right, strumming madly on that guitar of his, flailing his head and the small amount of hair on his head back and forth, and side to side. He had actually traveled all the way up and down the stairs from the uptown to the downtown side, solely to harass me. He suddenly stopped and addressed me: "Listen, I didn't say anything the other day, but this is my platform; go and find yourself another platform!"

I pointed out that I wasn't playing on his side of the tracks. But it didn't seem to matter to him in the least. He seemed to believe, with complete and utter conviction, that the entire NRW line, both the uptown and downtown sides, belonged to him, and him alone. "You have to go, you have to find yourself another platform!" I bent down to put my guitar away, and reminded myself of my new rule involving not arguing with folks wearing no shoes, as the two bare feet firmly planted in front of my case seemed to stare at me without flinching.

I scooted down the platform a bit to try to diminish the raucous noise coming from this threatening beast, and hoping that he wouldn't care as much if I stood far away from where he played. But he was on a mission to get me off that line no matter what it took. Consequently, he and his feet stayed right on me, on my side of the tracks, and madly strummed, screaming louder and louder, all without a break, until finally: mission accomplished. It was just too much, I had to go.

On my way to find another spot, I felt a bit freaked out by the whole face to face encounter with the Mad Man—his feet, his hair, his...well, everything. I decided to approach the station manager about it. I walked up to the booth. "Excuse me," I said through the glass. "Excuse me, but may I ask you a question?" The man in the booth took a few beats to acknowledge my presence. He looked up slowly, and gave a "What? Do I really look as if I care?" look and said nothing. "Anyway, I was just singing and that crazy guy on the downtown side, you know who I mean?" Again, not even a flinch from the station manager behind the glass. "Well, he came barging over and harassed me off the platform for playing my guitar. Is there anything that can be done? Is there anyway someone can just tell him not to mess with other musicians?"

The station manager looked at me and with a completely straight face, put some money in his drawer, as if intentionally making me wait. He finally said, "Well, if you want, I can call the cops and they'll take you both in. If I call them, they'll come and clean out all of you guys. And to tell you the truth, if they take him in, he'll come right back, just like you will."

Okay, not really the answer I was expecting. Anyhow, after the station manager inquired two or three times if I would like him to call the cops, which would result in me being "hauled in" (his words) to jail along with the Mad Man, I smiled and politely declined his offer.

Honestly, I'm still very fuzzy about this legal/illegal thing where it pertains to Freedom of Speech. I think I remember the

Constitution protecting us in that regard, but since performing in the subways of New York City, that subject has become blurry in my brain. I'll admit, pulling my mind off the now accumulating encounters, one with barefoot Mad Man and the other with the warm 'n' fuzzy station manager was tough. But I kept on walking, trying to shake the whole thing. And just before I was about to leave the station for the night, I looked down the stairs to the platform of the Uptown ACE at Times Square, just to see who was there.

This guy from Trinidad was there with his headphones, Walkman, CD player, and cart filled with stuff. He was singing what he sings all the time: Bob Marley. Most of the time he stands on the bottom stair, leans against the railing with a Walkman in hand, headphones on, and just rests all his belongings, taking up the actual "performance space." He takes breaks, I think, more than he stands and sings, which always seems so bold and quite interesting to me. Bold because he knows that the ACE is a coveted spot; and interesting because he seems to possess a very different life rhythm than everyone else down there, who is on a fast-track pulse. Once his break is over, he reaches the spot with his headphones still on and shuffles his feet side-to-side, relaxed and in, one would guess, perfect rhythm. Even though at this point there is no audible music to those of us not connected to his Walkman, somehow you do actually feel the beats. Then after what I suppose is a number of measures of musical intro (I only surmise this via his body movements), he begins to sing.

At the end of each of his performances, he—with his headphones still on—makes an announcement. "That was Bob Marley, ladies and gentleman. Bob Marley, the legend, Bob Marley. Thank you very much. Have a good evening." Now, there's no way for me to tell if he's simply continuing to follow what's being broadcast through his headphones, or whether that portion of his performance is off the cuff. Somehow, it really doesn't matter.

And like the rest of us down there, he is a prime example of a singing experience that is somewhat cathartic. He is most definitely in his own zone while singing— it's as if you're watching someone through a candid camera singing in their kitchen, completely oblivious to the world around them. He always seems completely and utterly blissful.

So even though at first glance you'd think this setup would have no chance, it actually works. The CD player, the headphones, the slight movements, the voice...it all works. People listen and are somehow magically calmed and transported for a few seconds. I suppose this happens simply by virtue of complete commitment for the few songs he sings.

A good friend of mine (not a subway performer) actually mentioned to me the other day how "The Bob Marley Guy" is her favorite subway performer. And until I informed her of his limited repertoire, she had for the past year thought that she had just been "super lucky" to catch him singing her favorite song, "No Woman, No Cry" every single time she got off the A, C or E at Times Square. *Ah, the beauty of illusion.*

He's an interesting one underground, the Bob Marley guy is. I waved silently to his headphone-laden self and continued on my mission, walking to the downtown side of the station. There I found a home and played.

Monday, May 22nd, 2006

Listen Closely

Tonight, right before my last set, I was in the middle of one last tuning on my guitar amidst the masses of people. People were coming and going, running, walking, and waiting, when I noticed a pair of legs standing right in front of my case. I looked up to see a well-dressed, thirty-something guy looking down at me, wearing dark glasses with a serious, contemplative look, hands behind his back. With a furrowed brow, he disclaimed, "Your high E string is off." Stunned, I looked at him.

"What? You mean…" I stammered in amazement. "You can hear that, even with all this noise and commotion?"

"Yeah. It's off, your high E, it's off. And your D is a bit sharp."

I was floored. This guy passes me amidst the noise and chaos of the Uptown ACE, smack in the middle of Times Square, and he seemed to have been listening so closely that he could hear that my high E and D strings were off? I was momentarily speechless. I regained myself enough to utter, "Uh, wow, okay, thanks."

"Sure, no problem." He continued to stand, feet firmly planted until the issue was resolved.

I looked back down at my electric tuner and went to work. He was right. There they were. The two notes were off, the high E and the D. Once I'd fixed them both, the guy's hands came from behind his back and he shook the right hand hard, quickly unfolding a collapsible cane used by the blind.

"Thanks," I said, looking up at the blind man, who obviously had the hearing of a feline, or better. He nodded and, tapping his cane, was able, it seemed, to board his train in peace.

The crowd down there was quite responsive and supportive tonight, including my tuning Sherpa. I played on, mulling over the complete randomness of these and other such acts that happen to me underground. They surprise me every time.

Tuesday, May 23rd, 2006

One

"You done, Heidi?" I heard as I looked up to see One standing on the ACE platform just as I was breaking down my gear. One has this stealth ability to silently appear. He often surprises but never scares me with his "covert" appearances. Perhaps he uses them in that "other" life of his and they've now just become second nature.

"The spot's all yours; good timing, One."

"So, how's your mom?"

"She's good. She just had her hip replaced, but it's all cool now. She's fine. Thanks."

"Tell her to take it easy, girl, okay? Will you tell her that, Heidi?"

"Yeah, One, I'll tell her."

I've never quite figured out One's consistent interest in my mom's welfare. As with the coaching, it surprises me that such an unlikely person would be asking after my mother. But nonetheless, he does. And on quite a regular basis, too.

One took over the spot and pulled out his paint cans. He began his lesson regardless of the fact that he was the one performing today, not me. "Back in the day, when I first started, I used to rest this can here. I'd rest it right on top of my foot here." He lifted the right paint can up off the platform and onto his foot. "You know, to lift it off the platform a bit, for acoustics 'n' all." Then he tapped on the empty white paint can: "Hear that?"

"Yes," although I wasn't really sure exactly what I was supposed to be hearing.

He removed his foot and tapped again, "Now, you hear that?"

"Yes?" Again, I wasn't sure where this lesson of "the infinite number of sounds made by plastic paint cans on a subway platform" was taking us. But the lesson continued, moving from the intricacies of musical plastic paint cans to the fine-tuning of an echo in the various underground subway stations. One definitely rides on his own plane in life.

Needless to say, One always seems to be singing for his supper, lunch, breakfast...or whatever meal of the day he has yet to consume. I often feel badly that I don't have a sandwich or hotdog ready to give him. Then I remembered, I did in fact have something for him. "Hey, One. I have some drum sticks and they're yours if you want them."

"Finally! I ask you to take me for lunch every day, so ya finally brought me some chicken?"

"Oh, no. One, I mean, drum sticks. Like your sticks there, to play your cans with."

"Aw, Heidi, that's cool. Yeah, that's cool. One can always use some new drum sticks. These here get pretty beat up." He paused for a minute. "But when you takin' me to lunch, Miss Heidi? I been askin' you for months it seems, and you never took me to lunch yet. What's up with that?"

"One, One, listen— I'll get the sticks to you, okay?" I said, trying to dodge the "lunch with One" question.

"Sure, Heidi, I can always use a pair of sticks."

"I'll put them in my case so next time we bump into one another I can hand them over."

"Well, Heidi. You know I want 'em autographed."

"Okay, okay, One. I'll autograph them. See you soon, One, and next time I'll have the sticks. I promise." I decided to change the subject. "Hey, I did the audition—the audition for MUNY."

"MUNY? Ah, yeah, the banner people. So....how'd it go, Miss Heidi? You remember what One coached you on? You remember to breathe?"

"Yeah, yeah, I breathed, One. It went well. Now, I'm just waiting."

"I'm sure you'll get it, Heidi. In fact, I'm sure you've got it. Ya gotta think positive. And breathe!"

"Yeah, I'm stayin' positive. Hey, so I gotta go; I'll get the sticks to you though, promise."

"Autographed, Heidi! Don't forget!"

"Autographed, One, I promise."

So I wouldn't forget, I got home and pulled the sticks from a bag in my closet. I grabbed an indelible pen and wrote on the wood, "To One ~ aka bucket-boy/can–man ~ Heidi." Now, the trick is to find him again so I can hand them to him. This world that's adopted me isn't like an office job—when you bring something in for someone, it's likely that they get it within a few days. I mean, at least there's a permanent, stationery desk you can leave it on. Sometimes I won't see One for months at a time. I'm pretty sure he has other gigs that don't involve cans, music, or subway platforms that keep him busy when I don't see him. I mean, one day he pulled out an oversized key ring with what looked like at least seventy-five keys packed on it, all appearing to be from automobiles. Honestly, unless he owns a car dealership, I have zero clue what that was all about. But I don't ask anymore. I just say he's a busy boy and leave it at that.

One. He's a unique spirit down there. Perhaps that's why the name seems to suit him so well. I do enjoy bumping into him: catching up, being reminded to breathe, and feeling invited into this wacky world of secret "Oneness" every so often.

Friday, July 14th, 2006

Ron's Way

    I got the response from MUNY last week and it was a "Thank you but due to the limited number of spaces...blah, blah, blah" letter. The disappointment was still a bit on my mind, especially because inside I felt like the perfect candidate, seeing as I've been underground for a while now, but I was back enjoying my world and determined more than ever to try again and get in next year. Maybe it's the Taurus thing in me, but I rarely, if ever, give up. Not at least until I've achieved my goal.

    It was overly hot today. One of those "mugg-ed" (a word I learned in Vermont meaning "muggy" and "humid," all wrapped in one) days that makes everyone move in slow motion. Once the city heats up in the summer, the underground just holds on to that heat like a sponge holds water. Even if the temperature above ground dips to seventy or eighty degrees, the tunnels and platforms hold the heat of the preceding weeks and months like an oven. It's so hot underground that I find myself moving right up next to the subway cars so when the doors open, I can absorb as much of the car's air conditioning blowing out as possible. Compared to the inferno on the platforms, the cold blast from the trains feels like a huge walk-in freezer door opening. If I'm not in the middle of a tune, I usually stand, turned, facing the train doors, motionless until the train departs. The blast does its job by reviving me for another round until the next air-conditioned car approaches.

I left around five p.m., entering my favorite line, the ACE. I think I've actually fallen in love with a subway platform. Go figure. On the platform I saw, of all people, Ron, that showman extraordinaire who I'd heard and admired from a distance for the past so many months. I knew his name as I did Annette's, from overhearing his banter. He was parked on the ACE with his acoustic guitar and that's it: no amp, no microphone, nothing. I'd noticed that between his witty quips, he sings mostly covers: sixties, seventies, eighties, Motown, Pop, and the like, and always in the most uplifting manner. I watched him for a bit, having only heard him from across the tracks thus far. As I watched and listened to his banter, "Hey, y'all, yeah, it's me, your friendly neighborhood subway performer, here to make-you-smiiiiile!" I noticed that this Ron guy actually involves and engages the audience of commuters like no one else I've seen underground. Many of the musicians down here have adopted a pretty thick fourth wall: not engaging the audiences all that much, as we never quite know what that audience will hold on any given day. But Ron breaks that fourth wall all the time, actually encouraging the commuters to get involved. He does this by interacting with them "off the cuff" as well as the best stand-up comic in Manhattan.

After a few minutes of up close observation, I wandered up to him in between tunes and tapped him on the shoulder, as I was too small for him to see me otherwise. "Hi, I'm Heidi. I've heard you play for a while now. You really have a way with the crowd."

"You have? Well, ain't that somethin'. I've been seein' you around here an' there as well. How come you've never said hello?"

I laughed. "You were always across like three lines of train tracks. But your banter, your act, it carries, so I've heard it a few times. It's so cool what you do. I wish I could be so interactive with the audience like that."

"Yeah, well...Heidi, right?"

"Right, Heidi."

"Well, babe..." (I was a bit surprised at how quickly the word "babe" was in play.) Ron explained, his southern accent interspersed with that slight stutter of his: "Yeah, when I sing, I-I-I talk to the folks, I talk to them 'bout just 'bout everything: train delays, weather, news, whatever. Ya know, then the folks feel involved, they feel part of the show. They like that." "Well, it rocks, what you do," I reiterated.

"Hey, so, so, you, you want this spot? I'm only gonna to be a half an hour, if you want it."

"Yeah, sure, sure I'll wait. Thanks."

I stood back for the remainder of the tunes and watched Ron as he touched person after person with that effortless and entertaining banter on that steamy and sticky subway platform. People not only dropped money, but made sure they told him how they loved his performing. Soon, Ron laid his guitar in his case and began to count his money. It's interesting how each musician counts their money. Most guys count their pull right there on the platform, at the end of their playing. Not me, I wait. It's odd. It's not that I feel scared or vulnerable, but I would feel awkward because it just seems kind of rude to me. It's not like my folks ever said to me while growing up, "Now, Heidi, when you're playing on the platforms in the subway, don't count your money in front of everyone, that's just rude. You must wait until you get home, do you understand?" So, honestly, I have no clue why I do it the way I do, it's just one of my things, I guess. So I choose, instead, to plop my guitar right on top of all of the cash and deal with the banker portion in private, once I'm home.

Now finished counting and packing, with a grand sweep of his arm, Ron indicated that the spot was mine. "Thanks, Ron." I started to unpack. "I've been away a while. Some bug, I guess. But even when I'm away for a minute it seems, I miss the subways."

"Yup, babe. This is about as close to the people as you can get."

Moving a bit closer (the label "babe" not making me feel the least bit uncomfortable anymore), I confided, "It's about as close to heaven as you can get, in my book. So often I'm down here in the subways, and I'm so happy that I actually feel I could die, right here in this moment, and be content."

"Ha-ha. I'll second that, babe."

"Hey, so do you know One? The small guy, all in black, who plays those paint buckets, or as he calls them, cans?"

"Yeah, yeah, sure I know the dude. Wiry. Always wears dark sunglasses, right?"

"Yeah, that's him."

"Why? What's up?"

"Well, I have these drum sticks I've been meaning to get to him, but I haven't seen him for a while now, so...well, I'm having a tough time finding him, that's all."

"We-we–well, I seen him just a few days ago, so I'm sure you'll run into him sooner or later."

I continued to set up. I plugged in my tuner, but for some reason nothing was registering. "Let me see." Ron fiddled with the cord. "You're right, it's not workin'. Where's your battery case?"

"It's on the side, here." I pointed. "I'll open it; it gets stuck all the time."

Ron removed the battery and touched it to his tongue, "It's got a bit of life left in it, but this might be the problem." I felt my face fall. Darn, I had been looking forward to singing today, more than any other time I could recall, since I'd had such a long absence. The thought of not performing due to an equipment mishap was bummin' me out. I've gotten pretty good at being prepared when I play this gig; it's a bit like a "musical camping trip." I have double everything: capo, strings, batteries for my microphone, wire clippers, nail clippers, and so on. But, the only things I didn't have in twos were a patch cord—the electrical cord encased in rubber that runs from my guitar to my amplifier—and a battery for my pickup. I guess because I've never had either one die before.

"Hey, Ron, do you want to play a bit longer while I go up to 48th Street and buy a new patch cord and battery? I need to sing but I don't think these are going to do the trick."

"I'll go. You stay and play acoustic."

"What? You don't want to play? I can go, Ron. I don't have any cash yet to give you to pay for it...only a dollar, so..."

"It's no problem, baby. I'll go. You stay and sing." He left his guitar with me to watch.

I played unamplified until he returned about an hour later.

"Here. They had a lot of cords, but this is the only one I could afford." He whipped out a brand new shiny patch cord.

"Thank you so much."

"And here's the battery."

"Thank you. Thank you!" I looked into my case. "Here, I've made almost enough here to pay you." But as I counted the money in my guitar case, Ron interrupted, "No, no...it's fine, really. Don't worry about it. It's fine. Don't worry, it's only ten dollars." Ten dollars is probably a good percentage of his take that day, though, and that's not counting the two dollar subway fare back to hand the things to me. He picked up his guitar and black plastic bag. "Oh, do you want me to take the sticks to One for ya? I probably see him more often than you. You know, the autographed ones."

"Oh, yeah, sure, thanks."

"Good luck, babe. And be safe."

I stood there for a second, dumbfounded. Once again, the contrast and the polarity hit me. The contrast between the way things function underground, and what, at present, represents a "functioning" society above ground. The contrast of the two worlds I live in floods my mind on a daily basis as I continue my journey through the New York City subway system. Whatever these guys run on down here, well, they should most definitely bottle it and share it with a few CEOs, landlords, world leaders, and anyone else in power who's in charge of the well-being of others. I'd like to see *that* transformation happen. Yes I would.

Wednesday, July 26th, 2006

I Travel

This is kind of a milestone for me. It's been just over a year and for the first time since the accident, I have accepted a stunt job on a film. Over this past year or so, I have been focusing on getting stronger and singing in the subway. This job is a personal challenge; I'm going back to stunts with great anticipation. Taking full advantage of my trip, I booked a gig in Southern France, opening for a great band from Africa called "Buru" at Le Volume, a club in Nice. So at least my "axe" will be traveling alongside me, making me feel a bit less removed from my newfound second home.

Just as I was about to head off for my reunion with high falls and the like, I bumped into a familiar soul. As I exited the trains, I spotted ahead of me, at the top of the steps, the familiar, nymph-like figure and contrasting bright, white hair of Alex. I hadn't seen her for months.

"Alex?" I shouted as I tried to pick up my speed with my dolly trailing behind me, slowing me down quite a bit. She headed towards me, also picking up speed.

"Hey, Chickee. How are you? I haven't seen you in a while. Wow, you're actually playing the trains? Look at you! You really hung in there. Good for you!"

"Yeah. I kinda got hooked after that first day. It's your fault," I joked.

"Well, I love to see you with your music and, as always, you're just one brave girl, Chickee."

"Thanks. Hey, Alex, guess what? More brave stuff on the horizon—you did such a good job on my body that I'm going to do my first stunt gig since the accident. I'm really excited. I know I've said this before, but you're amazing. I'm actually stronger now than before the accident. I'm now convinced you're a magician." I grinned. "So, guess where I'm off to?"

"Where?"

"I'm off to France, to do what I do: sing and stunts. Thanks to you, Alex."

Alex's eyes widened with a bit of disbelief. "Wow. Well, Chickee, now I think you're the amazing one. Don't you ever forget that, okay? And be safe. Let me know once you're back. I want to hear all about it and more about your music. I gotta go now, but really, congrats on all of this! I'm so proud of you. And you seem happy. Let's talk soon, Chickee. Keep in touch!"

And with that, she gave me a bear hug and blew me a kiss as she skipped down the block. *I'm so grateful to that woman,* I thought to myself as I exited the trains.

Seeing Alex coupled with the decision to do the film and leave the subways, even for a short time, was a bittersweet full circle for me. These "veins of life" have become such an integral part of my existence over these past months, offering more healing and growth as an artist and as a human being than I could express. So, it's difficult to leave at all. It's an odd sensation...I'm being asked to travel to one of the most beautiful places on the face of the earth, the French Riviera, to do what I love—stunt work. Yet as I pack to leave, somehow the subways still call to me. I never would have anticipated this love and connection that has developed between me and the underground when I first got my courage up to brave this world. But somehow, I feel as if I'm leaving my family behind while I travel abroad.

Don't get me wrong, I'm excited about traveling to Europe and being given the opportunity to get back on that "stunt horse," so to speak. But these dual feelings have just caught me off guard.

The subways have most definitely carved out a place in my heart. I didn't realize how embedded they were until I was asked to leave. But they aren't going anywhere, I am. And I will return. I promise.

Tuesday, August 1st, 2006

Le Volume

 Although my guitar wasn't an issue at the airport customs, the X-ray operator did pull me aside and whispered to me, "Excuse me, Miss, but are those wire cutters?" He pointed to the monitor displaying all the treasures my guitar case held, including, yes, a pair of wire cutters. "Oh no," I thought as I took a breath and answered back.

 "Yes. They're for my guitar strings."

 "Okay." He didn't skip a beat. "Next." So much for Homeland Security.

 I arrived and pulled off both stunts in the film without a hitch, nailing them both on the first take with no rehearsal: one twenty-foot high fall from a yacht backward, flipping into the Mediterranean; and one fall, backward down a set of stairs while tied to a chair. Yes, it's one crazy business. It always surprises me what the body can do when the mind decides it's going to do so. That's one lesson I almost always glean from my stunt work, and it's the one I try to apply daily to the rest of my life. But now it was time for music, time to perform.

 While taking the train, not a subway, from the suburbs of Nice to the city, I began to miss the subways. If there was a metro system in the south of France, I'd certainly had jumped right on that and busked that town, as well. But alas, no such system exists. They were tearing up the streets severely when I was there, so who knows, maybe next time.

 After being completely lost with all my gear in tow for almost forty minutes, I finally found the club. I was amazed that I actually found it at all, given that I speak little to no French and the club has no external markings whatsoever visible from the street. But after repeating "Le Volume?" as a question to every single person I passed, finally I was close enough that one man I asked walked a few steps with me and pointed down an alley.

 "There, there is Le Volume."

 The entrance was in the back of a building where there were neither numbers nor signs of any kind indicating its existence. I looked down the very thin European alley paved in cobblestones and saw a small triangular billboard on the ground reading "Le Volume." A red arrow pointed left. *This journey reminded me of the subways.*

"I'm Heidi," I said as I walked in with my equipment.

"Heidi! Bonjour!" one staff member at Le Volume welcomed me. The salutations kept flowing in, everyone welcoming me. The staff showed me the stage, introduced me to Buru, offered me a beverage, and showed me where to put my belongings. Since I was opening for Buru, I tuned up, ate an apple, and got ready to go onstage. With word from the front of the house, I started my set. Surprisingly, I wasn't nervous at all. I suppose as compared to the A train, Le Volume felt breezy. What a boot camp for the world that underground has turned out to be.

The audience at Le Volume was so enthusiastic and friendly that I felt one hundred percent at home in this foreign country. Performing on the same bill as Buru was an honour. Every single one of the four musicians in that group lived and breathed their music, much like the musicians who surround me back home. The four of them, two women and two men, used their rich, honest voices, an acoustic guitar, hollowed out gourds, drums, and the sound of water that one of the female members lifted with her fingers out of a large hand carved, wooden bowl. Through living their music, Buru created a unique, organic, and undeniably moving musical experience that one just could not ignore. I'd never experienced a sound quite like theirs before. Collectively, they produced an energy that was so full of life, vibrancy, and truth that it seeped from their voices and instruments into the cells of my being. Even though most of the songs were sung in an African language that I can only assume no French audience member spoke, every single person in that room was riveted on the musicians. I was honoured to have been able to sing with such accomplished and truthful artists in Nice.

Once the show was over and we were packing to leave, everyone welcomed me back whenever I return to France. What a great gig, and a fantastic slice of humanity. Nonetheless, I was still eager to get back to my roots underground.

Tuesday, September 5th, 2006

Harmony & Subcultures

    Today is my first day back from France and I decided to hit the Grand Central Terminal, which I've really never played, except for my one stint upstairs when I auditioned for MUNY. I guess I was still in "adventure mode" from my trip, so it seemed appropriate to experience a different location beneath the sidewalks. This is the world with all its intricate subcultures that I missed while away.

    I set up at the end of the shuttle stop, which is on the lower level of the train station, at the end of a subway platform. That spot is actually a MUNY spot, one usually reserved only for MUNY musicians. But today, there seemed to be no one playing there, so I grabbed it. I thought it would be a cool experience to play one level above the platforms and see how it felt. I figured it must be a great spot, as MUNY books musicians there on a regular basis and there is less train noise since it's located in Grand Central. Those trains arrive very infrequently compared to the constant rush when one is playing on the platforms themselves.

    I set up at the coveted empty spot and began to play. Somehow, since it was actually a MUNY spot, I expected the experience to be one notch higher, but instead the opposite occurred. The people who surrounded me were running to catch one of two awaiting shuttles to take them from the east to the west side of Manhattan. Half the time

I don't think they even saw me there. It was insane to play to such a large crowd of marathoners, whose only focus was the awaiting shuttle. What's all the fuss about this spot? Just then, about forty-five minutes into my gig, a man approached with his cello in tow.

"I have this spot now."

"Okay." I packed up, somewhat relieved, as I was already missing the platforms. "Is this spot good for you, usually?" I asked inquisitively.

"I don't like it so much," the cellist said with a thick Spanish accent. "All the people, they just run and run. It is too difficult to play. There are much better ones in the system. But now and then it can be okay."

"Yeah, I was wondering about all the running people, how they actually stop to hear anything. Well, good luck." I walked up the stairs as the sound of the musician's first draw of his bow ran across the cello's strings.

Needing some fresh air, I rounded the corner of the staircase and entered a small vestibule within a hallway from which emanated the most beautiful three-part harmony. The energy in that hallway was circular in nature; quite parallel, it seemed, to both the room and the symbiotic give and take between the minstrels and their audience. Three black men, in their forties to fifties, were standing there singing a cappella. In front of them was a stack of photocopied papers, the title of each one reading, "Made Over." I picked up one of the papers. Each photocopy told the story of the group's journey from drug addiction to where they are now, and how their music has been their way out. I listened for a bit, propping my gear up against the cool, marble terminal wall. I observed as person after person discovered this group just as I had and was moved enough to drop money in their bucket. Barely a commuter passed who did not donate something to the group. Their music seemed to move the human spirit universally, and it brought a smile to every face that entered that vestibule. At times, they'd chat during the songs with their audience, thanking them and interacting with them, saying "God bless you," yet never missing a beat in their tight performance. Then out of nowhere, they began in on a gospel tune and pointed to me to sing as well.

"You sing, I know you do," the tall guy said, as he pointed out my guitar and amp. "Next verse is yours."

Surprised, I asked, "What?"

He reassured me, "You can do it, just feel the music. We know you got soul, we've heard you." They'd heard me? They'd heard me? Where had they heard me? Okay, now I was in a corner. I stepped up and sang.

I had jammed before with other musicians on the platforms, mostly with random folks who come up now and again and ask if they can join in. But that's stuff I already know. This was completely unfamiliar. Even though it was a cappella, off the platforms, and I was feeling slightly put on the spot, I still joined in. I liked the challenge. In an instant, I was "with them," singing what was now four-part harmony in the surround sound vestibule. Once a few tunes had passed, the tallest Made Over member pulled me in and introduced himself.

"I'm Barry, I've seen you for a couple of years and always wanted to say hi."

"You have?"

"Yeah, I've seen you. You've just never seen me. I've wanted to say hello all this time and just never got the chance, because every time I see you, you're doin' your 'thang.'"

Then Barry introduced me to his buddies, who then nudged him to get back to work. "Okay, babe, we gotta get some more singin' in here, but stick around."

I went back to the marble wall that I'd been originally leaning against, where my gear still stood. I'm not sure why I didn't think to keep a better eye on it, or even one hand on it while I jammed. All I can say is that when I'm underground with the musicians, all fear and distrust seems to vanish.

As I was listening to some more tunes from Made Over, I noticed a small white man in khaki-coloured pants walking behind the three singers. He gave a silent nod to the three troubadours, who nodded back in turn. It was clear from that mutual nod alone that this was a regular routine. At first, I thought he was a subway maintenance worker just doing rounds. Then the man got right underneath the low-hanging steam pipes, reached up, felt around, and pulled out a walking cane. At this point, my attention was no longer on the songsters but this curious situation unfolding in front of me. The man hooked the cane over his right arm, then stepped slightly to his left and reached up again. He felt around the next section of pipe, this time pulling down a cardboard sign, which read, "Please Help Hungry." The thin man laid these items briefly on the ground while he rolled his pant legs up to just below his knees. He then removed his shoes and socks and promptly placed in his "locker," which doubled as a steam pipe for the subway system. He picked up his two props and waved goodbye to his buddies as he skipped into the subways.

Is there a grooming or trade school of some sort for professional beggars in this city? Almost every one I've seen seems to be doing double-time, leading some sort of "dual life." One life of a beggar, the other of, well, not so much of a beggar. Maybe it's like bartending school: you go, learn your trade, pick your shtick, and go for it. All I know is that these folks in this particular subculture definitely have their alter-egos/day jobs nailed to a "T."

I looked around to see if anyone else had seen what I'd just taken in. I just know my jaw was dangling wide open, as all of this happened so matter-of-factly. I'm not sure I'll ever really get used to the supreme creativity underground...I'm not sure I really want to.

My contemplative state was only broken when the three guys stopped singing. "Okay, that's it for us today," Barry announced.

"You're done already?" I asked.

"Yeah, babe, we made our money. We're goin' home now. You can come on downstairs to the food court while we divide up our money, if you want."

"Thanks, Barry, but I have to get home. I'll see you soon, though, okay? Thanks for the amazing music. You guys rock. And now that you know my name, say hi, alright?"

"No, no, I'm glad we finally got to meet, it's been at least a few years that I've been trying to meet you down there in the trains. Okay, take care, babe, and we'll see you. And keep that great sound goin'!"

Tuesday, October 10th, 2006

In The Studio

    I've decided to take the next few months, the cold ones, to work on—at least make a start on—an album, a lifelong dream. I now somehow feel closer than ever to realizing it. That, and move to new apartment...that's always a fun adventure. That means weeks of packing, tossing, sorting, moving, sleeping in chaos, unpacking, etcetera. Although I'm eager to actually be *in* the new place, the thought of all that just described makes me want to run far away. It seems like a logical time to do all of this since I have returned from the stunt gig in France with a bit of extra money to help tide me over during these processes.

    So, instead of writing in *The Subway Diaries*, I'll be packing, unpacking, writing, and recording new music for a while. But I'm excited. Both are moves forward, and however temporarily uprooting these changes tend to be, I've found they're almost always life strengtheners.

    I look forward to sharing the musical part of the adventure with the platforms and the world once I come up for air.

Friday, January 19th, 2007

The System

Right at the bottom of the Uptown ACE staircase was Annette. She wasn't singing, but was bending over her bag. I approached slowly, as I never want to be rude or interrupt. As I got closer, Annette looked up and said to me in her always to-the-point manner, "You want this spot?"

My eyes, I'm sure, got very big. "Uh, sure. But, why? Are you already done?"

"Well, girl, no, but this cop...you know, the tall one, Hispanic, with that little mustache..." and she ran her two fingers pinched together over her top lip indicating how thin the mustache was. "He just came by and told me to move on."

"What?" I exclaimed "But it's Friday...and..."

"I know, girl, I know. But he always does it, and when he does, you just have to go. But, you should set up. You might get lucky and get in an hour of playin' before he checks back, you never know."

"Okay. But that just sucks. I don't understand that."

"I know girl, but I'm okay. I made my money; God was lookin' out for me. I'm okay today."

Just then, Ron sauntered up and gave me and Annette each a big hug and kiss on the cheek. Ron always gives the greatest bear hugs. "What's goin' on?"

Annette filled him in on what just occurred and, unlike me, she relayed the story to him just as if she had just bought a tube of toothpaste at the drugstore, all the while calmly packing up her gear.

"I know," Ron said. "Last week I got a sum-sum-summons." This information rolled off his tongue in the same casual manner as Annette's story had hers.

Only I, it seemed, remained hopping up and down on the platform, enraged. "I don't understand…a summons? But you don't even play amplified!"

"Yeah, a ticket, baby. Fifty bucks."

"For what?" I asked this in complete sincerity, as Ron plays guitar and sings totally unamplified, a hundred percent acoustic. He doesn't even sell CDs, or anything for that matter. Ron is a poster child for exactly what the MTA has deemed "legal" and "acceptable" underground on the platforms. Yet, he was given a ticket. I was floored.

"Baby, it doesn't matter what it's for, they don't care… they just write them. And if you say anything they'll haul you in."

Then Annette matter-of-factly responded to that comment with, "Yeah, I'm still angry that they have my picture as a mug shot in the system, makes no sense."

"It's-it's-it's like beatin' my head against a brick wall to do anything or say anything when they do this," Ron added. "It's just paperwork; it's just quotas, like parking tickets. It ain't fair, it's just the way it is… The-the-they just have to write a certain number of tickets within a deadline. They don't care what you do with it after that: pay it, not pay it, contest it…whatever…as long as the paperwork is in, that the ticket has been written and the cops have met their quotas. That's all they care about." Annette nodded as he continued, "And these tuh-tuh- two cops were angry. They don't like their supervisor who had told them to do this ticket thing… you could tell as they were writing the ticket. They were mumbling something about it when they radioed back, informing her that the tic-tic-ticket had been completed, as they were writing me the summons." Ron sighed. "I'll be going down to con-contest it next week."

I thought for a moment about what that actually means for a person. To have to contest a ticket, that means one has to take a day off work or cancel whatever you had planned, travel downtown, sit in a courthouse, wait to be called, and maybe get your case heard and hopefully thrown out, thereby saving you the fifty dollar fine. But if it doesn't go smoothly, you've wasted a day and are still stuck with the ticket. "We should nominate one of us down here to be in charge of all the tickets that are given out in a week, and for five or ten dollars per ticket, one person could take all of them down at once."

"I was th-thinking of that," Ron said.

"It would be a good idea, really…this is really a ridiculous waste of time on everyone's part."

"I know, baby, but it's just the system."

"Man, we need to start a ticket fund or something. It's nuts."

"Would be nice. But they'd probably only come after us more 'cause they'd know there was money."

Annette, by this time, had packed up. "Bye, you guys, I'm callin' it for the day." She smiled as she boarded her train.

Ron and I chatted a bit more about the cops versus art issue as I set up. "And do you know what the wor-worst part is?" Ron continued.

"What?" I answered as I was plugging in patch cords and tuning my guitar.

"The worst part is that right after I was given that ticket and told to st-st-stop playin' and move on, I was walkin' through the train station and saw a guy bein' mugged at gunpoint. And don't you know, there were no cops, not one anywhere around. The priorities are just reh-reh-ridiculous; they make no sense at all." Then, Ron stopped for a minute and looked down before he continued, as he gained momentum on this subject. "But, yuh-yuh-you know what? You know what?" he repeated for emphasis. "You know what bothers me the most is when those cops, they come right up to me and they tell me I'm breakin' the law. And I ain't breakin' no law. They don't even know no law. If they did, they wouldn't be accostin' me like that. I ain't got no amplifier, I ain't sellin' no-no-no CDs, and until the law changes… I ain't breakin' no law. I'm playin' acoustically, that's freedom of speech, pure and simple. But when I see someone in uniform with a weapon and a badge, misquotin' the fuckin' law, well, that just pisses me off. There ain't enough professional musicians down here anymore 'cause of all this sheeeee-shit to even bother with us. But they do. And I have been temporarily detained too many times to be messin' with them, so you know what? Now I just say okay and I leave. But it still, still ain't right."

After some heavy thought, Ron added, "But ya know…you have such a friendly, open-like personality, it seems like yuh-you'll be fine, no matter *what* goes on. It seems no matter what happens to ya… you're still gonna be okay."

Ron paused, "But you know, I-I-I wasn't sure of you at first."

"What?" I said, a bit taken aback. "What do you mean you weren't sure of me? You thought I was mean or something?"

"No….not that, I…" Ron started in and then stopped.

"Ah…" I decided to take a risk and finish his train of thought: "You thought I wouldn't survive, right?" He nodded. "Ah, but I have, right?" I flashed him an "I told ya I would" grin.

"You s-s-suure did, baby. You sure did." I smiled down at my guitar case, loving my newfound home. Ron paused again and then continued, once again changing the subject completely, "You know I met some c-c-cool folks, this couple, last week, Heidi. I seen 'em before an' they know I sing and all of course. I mean, they hear me most every week. Anyhow, last week the-they said whenever I want; I can visit them when they go to France in the summer. They have this-this guest house or somethin' I can stay in and sing there in France."

"Oh, man, Ron, I'd do that in a heartbeat! I've always wanted to busk the Paris subways. You gonna do it?"

"Yeah, I'm thinkin' 'bout it. For a summer, at least. Yeah, I'm thinkin' 'bout it."

"Yeah, you should do it. I mean, I hear the Paris subways are great to sing in. Wow, if you had a place to stay and you could be in Paris and be close to the trains and parks, and *busk* that'd be awesome. They'd love you over there. You'd clean up! Gosh, if you don't go, I will!" I said, half seriously.

"I'm probably gonna do it, just gotta figure out when and save up for it. So, if you don't see me for a while, you'll know that's where I am: Paris, France."

I was finishing setting up when Ron said, "Well, I guess I'm gone to-gone to-going to hit the other side," nodding his head toward the other tracks.

"Come back in an hour or so. I have had a hard day and may not be long. Just need to be here for a bit, you know?"

"Really?" Ron's eyes brightened with the thought of getting the uptown side on a Friday evening. "Okay, baby. Be safe." Those words definitely held vivid meaning for me that day, after all that

"Spooky talk."

I played, I loved it, folks danced…it was a typical Friday underground, packed and joyful.

The ones with most
Keep getting more
Send another young boy to war
To keep what's theirs safe from harm
A soldier boy dies for "the cause"

The ones on top say
"Don't speak your mind
Take what you've got
Stay in that line
And you will be as rich as I"
For the grace of God go I

Give me somethin' I can walk with
That you and I can talk with
And we won't stop 'cause
There's a brighter day
There's a brighter day

I played for just about an hour, until my voice and body were nagging at me to call it a day. I packed up my gear, dragged it up the uptown steps, and rushed over to the downtown side. I looked for Ron, but I didn't see him. I wanted him to have the spot.

Finally, I heard his unamplified cheerful voice and guitar wafting through the subway tunnel. He saw me approaching and I waved my arm, pointing to the uptown side, motioning for him to hurry up and go. He shrugged his shoulders as if he didn't care to move. I went closer. "Ron, you should go to the uptown side. I'm done."

"I'm okay here." As I looked into his case, I could see he had done really well. But I still wanted him to know the reality over there on the uptown side so he would be sure and make a good call for himself.

"But, you don't understand…it's packed! There was barely room for my amp on that side of the platform, it was so crowded." He gave me a look that said "Really?" and then quicker than I could blink he gathered up his gear, and like a jackrabbit, was headed over there.

"Thank you, b-b-baby." As he whisked by me, he gave me his trademark kiss on the cheek.

"Sure. Have fun."

Seeing Ron there as I handed him my spot made me wonder briefly if the people watching and listening are even aware that we are constantly threatened by the cops. I wonder if they know this element even exists for us. Perhaps some know. But if some know, it's very few. What they do know is that we entertain. We entertain and move. We move souls. We move souls enough to dance, clap, sing along, move, feel uplifted, reflect, and show it with a donation and/or a smile. From what I have observed in my few years underground, we are, as a whole, probably one of the happiest and most contented group of workers and artists in New York City. I hope at some point the cops just leave us alone and choose to pick on a somewhat more serious threat to society.

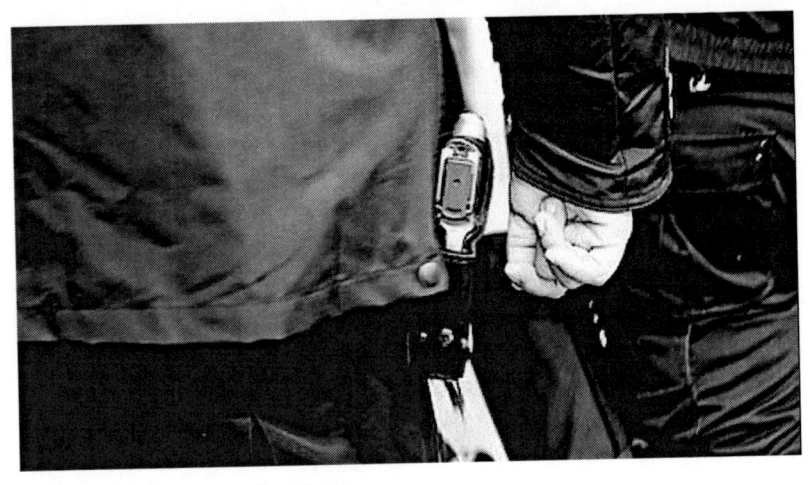

Wednesday, February 28th, 2007

Gimme A Break!

"Pack up your stuff." I looked up at the cop standing over me on the Uptown 123. He fiercely repeated himself: "Pack... up... your... stuff!"

Whoa! He's not messing around. I wondered what kind of person this guy must be off-duty if this was his personality day to day at work. He probably never wanted to be a cop. I mean, his dad was probably a cop, his grandfather a cop, his brother a cop, heck, his dog probably wears a badge. All I know is he hated his gig.

I put my guitar in its case and loaded my gear onto my dolly. I figured he was just going to escort me off the platform. How wrong I was. It seemed forever since I'd been back in my element. I'd finally gotten back down underground and now this cop was seriously "harshing on my rhythm." That I didn't like at all. But surprisingly, this time it wasn't breaking me as prior encounters had. I was pissed. This was an inconvenience, yes, but I wasn't feeling "violated" as I'd been feeling before. Just pissed. Maybe my skin was getting a little bit thicker down here.

The harsh cop told me to follow him to the top of the stairs. There he proceeded to take out a pad and a pen. He never once told me what he was doing. He never even allowed me to ask any questions, or allowed me to speak. I decided "meek and cooperative" was the way to go in this situation. He asked for my address, my ID, and my age. I decided to state the obvious, "But you have my ID."

Still never once looking at me, he stared at his pad with my ID lying on top and fumed, "I know. I don't feel like doing the math!"

I realized that meek and cooperative were getting me nowhere fast. So I decided, since my ID said Washington, D.C., I would play the whole "I just moved here" thing. Again, no response. *Shoot, I'm going to have to cry. I really don't want to cry, but it looks as if I'm going to have to. Damn.* I began to cry, just a bit though, not wishing to expend too much tearful energy on this guy. Again, not one hint of a response from the evil troll in blue.

Next he called up his sidekick, who was, I suppose, somewhat lower in rank. He appeared a far less infantile and power-hungry cop. The troll proceeded to describe the situation, I guessed, for the purpose of handing me over to the sidekick. The problem was the second officer couldn't even read what the troll had written.

Finally, the sidekick took over. Okay, it's now or never. I'll either need to cry full out now or I'll lose my chance. The tears ran down. I cried so hard, sounded so shaken up, confused, and scared that just as "Sidekick" was putting pen to paper to write the ticket, he looked up and saw my face. Then all he could muster was, "Uh, uh, uh...hold on, hold on...just stay there—hold on, I'll be right back," as he scurried back to his evil commander. I halted the tears while he consulted with his supervisor. After a bit of chitchatting, they both wandered back over (cue tears again.)

The original evil cop got right up in my face and said, "Listen Heidi, first of all: you can stop crying now. And second: my partner here is gonna give you a break. But..." He moved close to my face, his finger shaking waaaay too close to my right eyeball. "If I ever, ever, ever (yes, he repeated it three times for emphasis and I'm sure for the 'scare factor'.) "If I ever see you again, I won't give you a break!" The two cops turned to leave. Ah, goal accomplished.

Just then Ron walked past, saw me drying my eyes and asked, "Are y-y-you okay, babe?"

"Oh, yeah. I just had to cry to get out of a ticket. I'm fine. But really, give me a break, right?" I explained as I began to pull my dolly and gear.

"Oh, yeah, they're tough on the Uptown 123. You just cr-cr-crack me up though, cryin' to get outta a ticket. Only a girl can get a way with that. I just wish!"

We took the train uptown together to look for a spot, since now I was more determined than ever to play. There is no way this guy is going to win. I'm going back under tonight. I have to return and play. I have to play now to prove to myself I can. Otherwise…he wins.

So back to the trains I went, guitar and amp in hand. I entered the subways, found a different location, far away from the former "crime scene," set up, and started playing. I only had enough left in me after that earlier performance of non-tears and shenanigans for about half an hour of singing, but that really didn't matter. It only mattered that I sang.

I really think I may be getting stronger down here at letting rough experiences that temporarily stop my art roll off more quickly. A year ago, I'd have handled that encounter with the warlock far differently. I would have most likely been scared, intimidated; those tears would have been real, not manufactured, and I'd have probably walked away greatly shaken, holding a hefty ticket. But I didn't. I actually think the encounter with the tyrant cop and his sidekick, although it temporarily knocked the wind out of me, made me stronger. Even Dimitri, despite my protests to his reasoning, had said at my recounting of the event, "Good, you needed to go through that, it is good for you. Now you know, now you'll be stronger. This is good." And he's right. In his somewhat twisted and morose Russian way, he's right. I am getting stronger, I can feel it.

Saturday, March 10th, 2007

Lowdown from Annette & Saturday with Simon

I'm glad it's the weekend. I feel more comfortable on the weekends, as far less nonsense occurs involving cops than other days during the week. Of course the Uptown ACE at Times Square was stop number one for me to spy. *Ugh,* I mumbled to myself as I looked down the platform stairs and noticed a one-stringed instrument guy playing away. *Those guys play forever, Dimitri's right.* So, I moved on.

I ventured to 59th Street, the downtown side. It was Saturday so the platforms were busy and filled with music and dancers, like an underground carnival. I bumped into Annette, who was wearing that same funky, blonde wig she was wearing when I first spotted her almost a year ago. She had just arrived. As I watched her perform, I noticed that she emanates this energy about her: a drive and ambition that some of the performers don't display underground. You can tell she has a plan both in the way she performs and in the way she interacts with the audience. Many of the performers seem quite content where they are, doing what they're doing, which is great. But you can tell with Annette: she sees bigger, she sees farther than the trains. Annette is aggressive about promoting the CD she's working on, and makes it clear at every underground show that every dollar donated goes to that CD. I've found out via a few conversations that busking is her full-time gig and Annette, like Dimitri, knows these subways like the back of her hand. Whenever I see Annette singing, I know it's got to be an excellent spot and I take note. She's a great marker for me in the system.

Each time I see and hear Annette after a time of absence, she has grown a bit more, musically and artistically. When you see and hear her, you get the distinct feeling, as with so many of the underground performers, that she is giving it her all: body, mind and soul. She always has passion and joy in her performance. That joy is what brings in the rent.

I recounted the "Cliffs Notes" version of the nasty cop incident to Annette, as it was still burned in my mind. "Girl," she said, "you just wait until they arrest you."

"Arrested? What?" Suddenly, somehow, my "major" cop story had become quite a minor event. In one sentence, Annette had both freaked me out and silenced me.

"Girl. I've been thrown in jail so many times I've lost count. I've been doing this for twenty-five years. You know they even have a warrant on me?"

Okay, this was not making me feel any better about the goings-on the week before. And trying to feel better was the only reason I even brought this cop stuff up to her to begin with. "So, this jail thing, I mean, do they really keep you, like, overnight and all?"

"Yeah, girl, they put the cuffs on, take everything from you, and you're there, stuck in that tiny place overnight. You can't ask any questions, can't say a thing, and you really don't know much 'til they let you out, usually the next morning. It's not a pretty scene, believe you me. But that don't stop me from singing. They think it'll stop me from singing, but every time I come back. They do it 'cause they got their quotas. And then there are the new guys who wanna climb the ranks and make sergeant and they got their quotas, you know, they gotta get a certain amount of tickets in. It's all political. The homeless, they don't have the money to pay tickets. But they know us musicians do." Then Annette paused, and reset her CD player. She continued: "Girl, you think the platforms are dirty and cold, just wait 'til you see jail."

"Man, you're kinda freakin' me out, Annette. I mean, I figured tickets were as bad as it gets. But now I'm wondering if I have to "pack for the night" every time I sing. How ridiculous is that?"

"Ya gotta be prepared," Annette said. "But to be honest, girl, they don't let you have nothin' with you, so I wouldn't bother packin' too much," she educated me with a half smile. I have to say, none of her answers made me feel any more at ease. So rather than freak myself out any more, I decided to change the topic of conversation. This was stuff I had absolutely no desire of ever experiencing firsthand. I changed the subject.

"You recording an album?" I asked.

"Yeah, girl, been workin' on it for three years so far. It's comin' along. Just money, ya know. That's what slows it all down. Money."

"Yeah, always a challenge—doing an album without a ton of cash. Same deal here."

"But I haven't seen you for a while now. Wondered what had happened to you. Where you been?"

"Oh, I've been working some on my album, as well. Plus, I had to move. That's why I've been kind of MIA for the past few months. I bet yours will be fantastic, though. Can't wait to hear it."

"Yeah, I like it so far. It's makin' me proud."

"Hey, so, I'm auditioning again for MUNY this year. You know, the folks with the banners?"

"Yeah, I got one of those. Had it for years. But I like the platforms better, to be honest. And don't let the banner fool you; the cops will still mess with you, even with the banner. Not as much, but they'll mess with you just the same."

"Really? Well, I tried last year, didn't get in, so I'm givin' it another go."

"Yeah, I've heard of folks taking four, five, sometimes six years to get into MUNY, not sure what their criterion is. Not sure why they wouldn't accept you, I mean, really, you can sing and you're down here all the time anyway. I'm sure you'll get it, though. You'll be fine. I'm sure you'll nail it this year. When is it?"

"Sometime in May. It's always in May. It's in Grand Central Station, the Great Hall. I like auditioning there. It's a great space to sing in, so, regardless, singing there always makes my day."

The change in subject succeeded in getting my mind off jail and back to the subject of music. Once that goal was accomplished, Annette pointed me in the direction of a few good spots that might be open on a Saturday.

I scoped out the two spots she had mentioned. Both were busy with some of the best music I have heard in a long while. One filled with a jazz trio, as styled and polished as any performing in the most exclusive jazz clubs in the city. The other was occupied by a very accomplished conga player. Sometimes the underground feels like a World Music convention. Its diversity never ceases to surprise and intrigue me. I stood waiting for the C train to head back to the ACE, where I had left the one-stringed instrument guy, figuring there was a chance he'd have wrapped.

"My sister. Ah, how are you, my sister?" A cheery, upbeat voice with a Caribbean accent suddenly sounded from behind me. I whirled around and noticed this rather small, slightly hunched over figure, dressed in a pressed light grey suit, his right arm lovingly cradling his violin case, his left hand gently resting on top. Violin in tow, he was in a constant state of motion of some sort, seeming to me much like Alice's White Rabbit in her Wonderland.

"Hey! Simon," I shouted, now feeling very "Alice-like" myself. The darting man was named Simon. We go way back. Well, "way back" in subway terms basically means that we've bumped into each other, introduced ourselves, and have shared spots before. Simon is around fifty, I suppose, although it's tough to tell because he's always so "hoppy" and energetic. He's from Trinidad and Tobago and always addresses me as "his sister." The very first time I met Simon was on the Uptown ACE at rush hour. He addressed me as "my sister!" and has done so ever since. Between Danny and Simon, it seems, according to them at least, I'm somehow related to a number of subway musicians. I'd never have suspected so, but I don't argue with the two subterranean genealogists.

He's always been great to me, ever since I've known him. Today was no exception. He asked, "You looking for a spot?"

"Yeah, I've already checked the 1 train and the ACE here at 59th, and they're taken. Where are you going to look?"

"Come with me. I will show you. I will show you some very good spots." Simon held his finger up to his lips, "Ssssshhhhhhh." Off we went. We hopped back on the C train.

We rode trains, transferred here and there, hopped off now and again when Simon had something exciting "spot-wise" to share with me. I wish I had had a video camera. I felt as if I was in the middle of a "best busking spots in the city" documentary. Simon not only showed me the prime spots he had spent years researching in his travels, but he also explained why each spot was good and at exactly what times of day, and day of the week. I took copious notes on any stray pieces of paper I could wrangle from my guitar bag, not wanting for an instant to miss a shred of information.

We ended up at the E at 53rd Street, on the East side. "My sister. Here." Simon scurried off the train, still resembling Alice's rabbit, and pointed to a specific spot on the platform floor. "Here, my sister, this is where you perform on this platform. It's the best. The reason it's the best is because, you see, the travelers at Times Square are bombarded by music from the second they enter until the second they leave. But here..." And he waved his arm in a grand gesture, "Here at 53rd the people enter from the street above." He pointed up. "Then they travel down a long escalator and they have heard no music until they reach the bottom of the platform. You see, they get to the bottom of the platform and *wham*: there's music! So there you are. You see, my sister, in this way you are special; you stand out and they appreciate your music. And when you are special, when you stand out, you make money."

Just as I was mulling over his words and scribbling the location on my piece of paper, a cop passed, having ventured out of his little solo cop station at the end of the platform. As he walked by, he lingered, then stopped and looked at Simon and me. I turned to the cop. Having recouped my feisty spirit with underground cops, I said, "You don't even *want* to know what we're chatting about." Just as I said that, I got a whiff of the cop. He smelled like he'd been drinking. The cop moved closer. And as he moved closer, he smelled stronger.

"What?"

"My friend Simon here is sharing some very valuable information with me."

"Really?" The cop was now interested. Tipsy, but interested.

"Yeah. He's sharing spots with me." I leaned in and put my finger to my lips, just as Simon had done earlier and whispered, "He's sharing the best spots in the city to play music in." Then I put my finger to my lips and uttered a "Shhhhhhh…"

"Ah. Well, I can tell you some really good spots!" The inebriated officer winked and enthusiastically jumped in. He began to rattle nonstop about this spot and that one, where he's seen musicians and where he hasn't, honestly not making a whole lot of sense, but moving closer and closer to me with every spot contribution. To be quite honest, his intoxicated flirty manner combined with the strong smell of alcohol made me tune out everything he said and put my focus directly back on Simon.

As the intoxicated cop wandered, not very steadily, back to his station on the platform, I turned to Simon. "Simon," I whispered. Simon wasn't really paying attention so I poked him. "Simon, oh my God, that cop's been drinking! Could you smell it?" Simon turned to me, looked over to the cop, and nodded in confirmation. I continued, "Well, I guess there's an alcoholic in every business. At least he was friendly though. It's just too bad he's drunk with a gun."

"Well, my sister, at least he's walking away from us and not toward us, right?"

"Amen to that Simon. I suppose if I had to spend all day, every day, in that little, tiny cop house over there, I'd be drinkin', too. It's kind of sad though." Simon looked at the cop hut and nodded in agreement. "You know what? I think I'm going to go back to the ACE and see if the Asian guy is done."

"I will go with you, my sister."

We rode to 42nd Street, hopped off, and walked to the uptown side. The guy was gone. Simon smiled, "Ah, you see, this is your lucky day."

"Simon, you should come back in an hour or so. I probably won't be long, and then you can have the spot."

"Ah, my sister, this is your spot. Do not worry about me, I will be fine, just enjoy your singing." He skipped off, violin case tucked under his arm, most likely to peruse the rest of the underground system until he, too, found a place to perform.

Tuesday, May 15th, 2007

MUNY, Take Two

I surfaced today to go to my second MUNY audition at Grand Central. Since the first year I auditioned solo and got rejected, and since MUNY has solos, duos, and group acts and spaces open in these various categories each year, I decided to try the group thing this time around. I'd spent the last month rehearsing with five other musicians: a drummer, percussionist, fiddle player, bassist, and lead guitarist. It was a sharp deviation from last year's setup and took a ton of organizing to get it all together—all five people in the same place, at the same time, for numerous rehearsals and now for the audition. But I was determined to get in this year.

The audition day is always a party of sorts, a gathering of so many different musicians from all over the world, that it can't help but be a positive vibe. And I have to say, I've been impressed both times now at how smoothly MUNY runs the auditioning of fifty to sixty musicians and musical acts. All of the MUNY musicians who volunteer their time to help make the judging of others go smoothly, embrace you as you enter, like family. If it's your second year back, they all seem to know it somehow, and go out of their way to be extra encouraging.

The same cast of characters was there this year: the press, the PT Barnum emcee, and that panel of judges ala *American Idol*, just more of them, a lot more.

Our name was called (I'd made one up, Hudson Crossing, as the Hudson has been such a huge and positive influence in my life in New York). We set up in record time. Sound is always a challenge in the Great Hall—since it's so large and the ceilings are so high, the sound goes up and out and never comes back. It's an odd sensation to really not be able to hear your own music as you're making it, but I was used to it from the year before. We were announced by the jolly emcee, who remembered me from the proceeding year. He told a joke or two and we began in on our first of two tunes. It always goes by in a flash, it seems. You prepare, prepare, wait, wait, wait, then...*bam*, it's over. Both songs were well received however, applause and all that. People commented positively afterwards, various press folks came and asked us questions, then it was "wait and see" time. Although I kind of felt as I did last year, as if I could have stayed there all day, just hob-knobbing with the other subway musicians and subway hopefuls. But after I'd made sure the guys in the band were okay, I scooted back underground, where, if I landed a spot, I could be sure of the outcome.

Thursday, May 17th, 2007

Dimitri & Breath of Life

Today I finished my aboveground day later than usual. It was eight p.m. but I knew I needed to be underground to feel complete. Sometimes that feeling is so strong and so clear it doesn't matter the time of day or night, I just have to go. I have to sing.

So it was about eight fifteen by the time I ended up underground. After passing a phenomenal steel drum player on the Uptown ACE, I headed uptown and got off at 59th—seems to be my route these days, Uptown ACE to 59th Street (the option of the NRW having been adamantly eliminated from my list of choices by Mad Man). There, on my favorite downtown side, was Dimitri. I was definitely surprised to see him; I rarely do since Dimitri's a bit of a vampire, only playing from late night into the wee hours of the morning. During those hours, the cops hassle him less.

Underground, Dimitri's a rare bird. Not only is he a night owl, he's impeccably clean-cut when performing, and that includes the subways. Believe me when I say, impeccable hygiene is rare in the system. His six foot something frame looks extra large when he plays, as he sits on this tiny, foldable stool, usually backed up against a pillar. He is always one hundred percent into his first love, his music. He reminds me somehow of a minstrel when playing the trains.

Dimitri *breathes* music, in the most intense way. He was

classically trained in Estonia from a very early age, and has known a life of guitar and music ever since, becoming versatile in almost any style you now throw at him. He is one of those musicians whose life mission is to strive towards mastery. Music absorbs almost every minute of his life.

When I heard Dimitri that one time at the audition years ago, it was clear, right then and there, his intense love and respect for his art. Whenever his hands touch his guitar, the world shuts down around him and he and his guitar become one. "You must make love to your guitar," he would say to me with his thick Russian accent whenever we'd hang out and jam together.

I stood behind the pillar, out of the way, listening to the beauty of his music. He elevated even the most common of popular cover tunes to an intricate musical level most have never heard played on a guitar before. I watched as person after person paid their respect with their dollars into his case. Finally, he took a break and sipped some water from the water bottle standing next to his stool. I approached and dropped a dollar into his case.

"Hey, Dimitri"

"Heidi, hey, long time no see. Listen, I have not seen you. Is that your guitar?" as he perused my gear stacked onto my dolly.

"Yeah, I'm looking for a spot."

"Well, I am done here now. If you want, you can have this one. Why do I never see you here?"

"Well, Dimitri, you're like a bat, you only come out at night, and I'm more of a daytime/rush hour person. So, I guess we just miss that way." I smiled. "But, yeah, I'd love to play here, but only if you're really finished. I can go somewhere else if you want to keep playing."

"I am done. I have made my money. I am done," he repeated. Then Dimitri leaned over his still open guitar case to place his coveted instrument gently inside as if it were a Stradivarius.

"Hey, so how's your friend Patrick doing? How'd his audition go, did he get the record deal? We should hang out again and swap songs. I had a really good time with you guys last time." Dimitri continued to look down at his case and stopped his packing.

"Umm...ummm...Patrick. Patrick...." He stopped again.

"What, Dimitri?" A chill suddenly ran through me.

"Patrick, he is...gone," Dimitri said, his head slowly raising up to look at me with more emotion than I'd ever seen emanate from Dimitri's eyes before.

"What do you mean, gone?"

"His mother told me, last month. She would not say very much, not about details, and I did not ask. But it was suicide. It is still inside me, you know. He was my friend. It is still hurting me. She brought me some of his things that I have now. But it is not the same, you know?" Dimitri's gaze lowered again to his guitar.

"Oh my God, Dimitri. He was your best friend."

"I know." And he stopped.

"I'm in shock. He had so much life and talent and..." I couldn't digest it any further. I had no way to put information like this in to any context that made sense there on the platforms. Then Dimitri spoke again, still looking at the ground, "I know the producer from the label who liked him and had him audition, told him he loved his music and his sound but he could not take him because he was too old. I know that hurt him. But I did not think that much. I do not know...I do not know..." Dimitri trailed off. Still frozen in that spot on the 59th Street platform, I leaned down over his stool and gave him a hug. "Listen, okay, I have to go now," Dimitri said as he rose off his stool and folded it up. His gear now completely packed and his stool tucked under his arm, he looked at me again: "It is good here tonight. You will do well."

"Thanks, Dimitri. Let me know if there's anything I can do."

"I am writing a song for him, "Breath of Life," it is almost done. I work on it every day. You will hear it."

"I'd like that. Take care, Dimitri. I'm so sorry about Patrick. Call if you want." I got lost again trying to catalogue the information just given to me while standing on the subway platform, and once again, gave up.

In a daze, I began to set up, feeling this was actually the very best place for me to be this evening. After receiving that news, I knew I'd be better off channeling all my confusion into music. I looked at my cell phone to check the time, and noticed the date— it was a year to the day that he, Dimitri, and I had spent that one creative night, making and talking music and eating Chinese food into the wee hours of Manhattan. And now he's gone. Patrick's story stabbed at me. He had struggled so much of his early life with drugs and addictions, and had finally cleaned himself up, putting all his talent and emotion into his music. Then, he'd finally been given a chance, a "break" as it were, only to be told, in essence, "Sorry, it's too late." That timeline itself was inconceivable to fathom. I wished to God at that moment that things were different. I wished that humanity was a bit less judgmental, and a bit more flexible in their expectations and their requirements of others, especially of those who are just giving, not taking, from the world. I played the entire night for Patrick—59th was his favorite platform. I played in his memory. I liked the feeling that two people he knew were gracing the platform back to back. I'm sure the both of us in his honour. And I'm sure he knew we were there.

Wednesday, July 11th, 2007

Remind Me...

You know those days when you wonder why you're doing what you do? Those days when you feel as if you're just going through the motions? Well, today, Wednesday, July 11th, was one of those days for me. Consequently, I ventured underground to find myself again. I had recently been knocked down by a spring cold of sorts, maybe because I heard from MUNY again: even with a full band, I was once again rejected. So I was definitely searching for my footing.

Still a bit wobbly from the bug, I set up, luckily, on my favorite Uptown ACE platform. As I sang, I felt at home.

"Hey"

Times, times like these
They make me weep
They bring me to my knees
Whoa, whoa, these days
What are we to do
Whoa they make me crazy
We gotta find something new
Whoa, whoa, these days

> *What are we to do*
> *Whoa they make me crazy*
> *We gotta find something new*
>
> *So won't you give a little help here*
> *To understand*
> *Why we're tearin' down this Promised Land*
> *A little help here*
> *To help us see*
> *What's hurting you*
> *Is killing me*

After a few tunes, however, my energy waned. I kept singing though, still searching for that feeling; that place where I'm completely at one with my music and can move another human being across a loud, dirty city subway platform. As my energy faded, the contributions in my guitar case dwindled. Donations run parallel to one's emotional input. I was in a semi self-conscious state of mind where I was wondering how I sounded. Rejection can to that to you. (Not the place you want to be when singing in front of hundreds of people.) I kept on wondering if I was getting to anyone at all. But of course, I know very well that if I'm busy wondering whether I'm getting through to anyone, I'm most likely not.

There I was, singing and constantly contemplating. That's when a tall, thin black man wearing a bright blue t-shirt and black pants let a dollar bill float into my case. I nodded a "Thank you," which I always attempt to do when a person makes a monetary contribution. However, unlike most people who donate a dollar, he stayed as I finished my song, then spoke: "Do you remember when you were five?"

This was a first. *I wonder if he's just all about Jesus?* was the first thing that popped into my head. It was my first thought because next to "I am a producer," the wandering Jesus cohort is the next largest that interrupts my singing down there. Liberally interspersed amongst the thousands of people who hear me every day, these religious missionaries silently slide up to my guitar case, place a dollar inside, and then inconspicuously whisper in my ear, "Jesus loves you" or "Are you saved?" I wasn't in the mood today for a long religious debate or to fend them off, so I suspiciously answered,

"Umm, yes?"

"You remember when you were five?"

Somehow I felt a bit more at ease in the face of the guy's questions. "You mean, when I was five, like before I had to pay rent?" I joked.

"Yes. Can you remember a specific memory?"

Now I was curious and a bit exposed, as if I was being given an assignment in acting class. "Yes. Yes, I do."

"Good. Sing from there." He smiled, walked toward the stairs, stopped, and added, "From one artist to another."

This time, I thought of when I was five and started singing from my swing set in my back yard.

> *So everybody say*
> *Hey!*
> *Everybody say*
> *Hey!*
> *Everybody say*
> *Hey, what we need is love*
>
> *Love rescue me in the morning*
> *Rescue me at night*
> *Love rescue me when I'm weepin'*
> *Lift me up to the light*
> *Love rescue me when the world is*
> *So dark and closing in*
> *Love rescue me*
> *Rescue all women and men*

And wouldn't you know it, the whole experience was so incredibly different. The sound felt easy, happy, and flowing, and the money followed.

The train pulled up toward the end of my song, and the man in the blue shirt got on. I was still singing, swinging on my swing set; each note was effortless as I visualized my innocent feet arching into the sky. I turned to catch a glimpse of him, hoping in some way to acknowledge his help. He was at the window in the train looking at me as I sang. The doors closed on the C train and with the same slow grace he used to drop that dollar bill in my case, he raised his hand, waved to me, and gave me a wink. He was grinning, realizing what he had done for me.

I smiled back as my hands were busy playing my guitar with all the joy of an innocent five-year-old. I laughed to myself as I finished out the song. That was amazing. He heard. He heard that I was not in the moment. He heard that I was singing outside of myself. I wished I'd gotten to ask him what kind of artist he was. Maybe in fact he was a teacher of the arts? With that kind of insight and ability to communicate, I'd have gone to see, hear, or watch whatever he was involved in.

Who would have guessed someone was listening so closely underneath the insanely busy sidewalks of Times Square? He had given me, in those two to three sentences, what I had forgotten: the gift of presence. He reminded me why I sing.

Monday, July 23rd, 2007

The Sticks

I got home today, after a super long day in the city, to a voice mail on my phone. And wouldn't you know, it was the rare voice message from none other but...One. Now, mind you, I don't think One has a phone of his own. So every time he leaves a message it's from a different pay phone number at some random location in Manhattan. Anyhow, as usual, it was happy and upbeat: "Yo, Heidi. What's up? Just checkin' in to see how things are goin' for ya. Listen, I just wanna let you know, I got the sticks. Yeah, that guy Ron, he gave 'em to me and I wanna thank you for 'em. Okay, I dig the bucket boy thing. You're crazy, girl. Oh and that smiley face. Thanks again and God Bless."

He got the sticks. It worked. Somehow, in this underground maze, the carrier pigeon setup worked. Go figure.

So now, at least we know the system works...just in case you ever feel like getting something to an subway musician at some point in time, just hand it over to someone who knows of someone who knows someone. It'll probably get there.

Wednesday, July 25th, 2007

Stand By Me

It took a few minutes for me to find my groove today. But I found it. Always a good feeling, and I settled right into it.

Soon after, a tall, black, smiling man came up to me. He had a guitar slung over his shoulder and said to me, "You know, I hear a lot of musicians down here and I have to say, your voice, your sound... it's got something special about it. I was standing over there," (he pointed to the pay phone on the side of the tracks) "talking to my friend, and I was thinking, 'I have never heard that song before, but I like it a lot, and that voice...' Anyhow, you have what I'd call 'The Spirit' in your sound."

"Thank you." These kinds of comments, the specific kind, can't help but make a singer smile.

"Really, it's something you can't put your finger on...indescribable. And later on, I was sitting on that bench and reading. I couldn't focus on my reading because your singing touched me so much, and I kept hearing different instruments—piano, drums, etcetera—with your song. You have...soul. You know that, don't you?"

"Wow, again, thank you. Well, at least I moved you. That's my goal down here. I figure you have to feel something to sing here, otherwise it's just contributing to the overall noise factor, you know? So, thank you for your kind words."

He topped the other compliments with, "Well, it's carrying a unique energy and you're definitely touching people." That made my day. Once again, this underground world lifted me up. It's ironic that all this light, listening, and kindness happens in one of the loudest, dingiest places in Manhattan. The guy introduced himself as James, a fellow musician, and we exchanged numbers for contacts and the like.

As we were talking, a marginally familiar woman approached.

"Hey, I never heard from you!" I looked at the smiling woman with a video camera in her hand, stumped, and then I remembered… it was Minor, Poet Minor, the "producer" with the TV show.

"Oh, man, I'm so sorry. You know, I get so many cards and folks coming up saying they are this and that and that, they'll do this and that for me, that I tend to not pay much attention anymore. But I do remember you, yes, and you did give me your card."

"Yeah, I can only imagine what comes your way down here." She held out another business card. "Listen, like I said before, I really like your sound, your talent, and would still like you to come on my show and sing if you want to."

I took her card and felt kind of bad now that I'd ignored the first card she gave me, since here she was standing right in front of me.

"I'd like to be on your show; I'll follow up this time, promise." And I once again took her card and handed her mine. She glanced at it briefly to get my name.

"No, Heidi, thank you! Look forward to having you on my show!" Then she went on her way, smiling to catch her train.

I finished up my set and James took my spot. As he was pulling out his guitar and chatting some more, his high E string popped. "Ah, my string broke."

"I have another one," I offered, as I began to unzip my guitar case.

"No, that's okay. I do as well, I just kind of like playing without it now and again, kind of changes things up to a modern/avant-garde sound, you know?" Guess he was going for a bit of a Phillip Glass thing there, not sure. All I know is I most definitely need my E string. As I was about to leave, he started in on "Stand by Me" by Ben E. King.

We sang a bit, others joined in. It was amazing. He had such a superb energy to his performing, as if he's with the people rather than there for them. A little bit like Ron, but more communal, since he was sitting on the side of the bench right with the commuters while he sang. It was a welcoming and inviting atmosphere and everyone felt immediately comfortable singing with him. It was somewhat magical: the jam that had begun with "Stand by Me" ended up going on for almost an hour, all without a high E string. People came, people went; they joined in and danced. I stayed for the whole community jam. I think we must have gone through every Motown hit known to man. It was magical to be able to make complete strangers into singing partners within seconds, and have the experience just keep spreading and continuing on its own energy.

I have to say, today was one of the most uplifting days I've had. Today the subways reminded me of the neighborhoods in New York and elsewhere, normally undesirable to the wealthy of society, where artists gather and create, inspire, and share ideas and their individual gifts of art. Today the subways reminded me of the East Village in Manhattan long ago, and Williamsburg, in Brooklyn, up until about a year ago, when these neighborhoods were full of artists living in places the wealthy would not dare step foot in, as they were deemed too dirty, scary, and dangerous. But in these neighborhoods, art flourished. Trends were created, concepts exchanged, voices heard, and ideas and artists born. Then the money moved in. Those with money have, time after time, after years of artists making these undesirable areas their homes, seen the possibilities and moved in. They and their developers come in, take over, and turn art into condos, songs into restaurants, theater and dance into "acceptable" buildings for "acceptable" people to live, work, and socialize in, in the way money deems "correct."

This day I realized that the subways are, in many ways, like those neighborhoods used to be. The one very unique aspect that the subways have over the now gentrified neighborhoods of New York City—and elsewhere in America—is that those with money will never wish to inhabit the subways by pushing us out and making it their home. Although, sometimes I actually do have frightening thoughts of some huge developer, someone like Donald Trump or some such, sweeping in and "cleaning up" the trains, and in doing so, erasing all trace of the art that's lived there for so long. Crazy, right? I know that seems kind of far-fetched at this point in time—I mean, who would ever consider such a place "valuable?"—but I've learned by watching it happen above ground, over and over again. Anything's possible, especially if money's at stake.

But, for now, this underground artists' colony remains and thrives (with the exception of the random raid by the cops), providing a freeing and unique environment in which to make art and move souls.

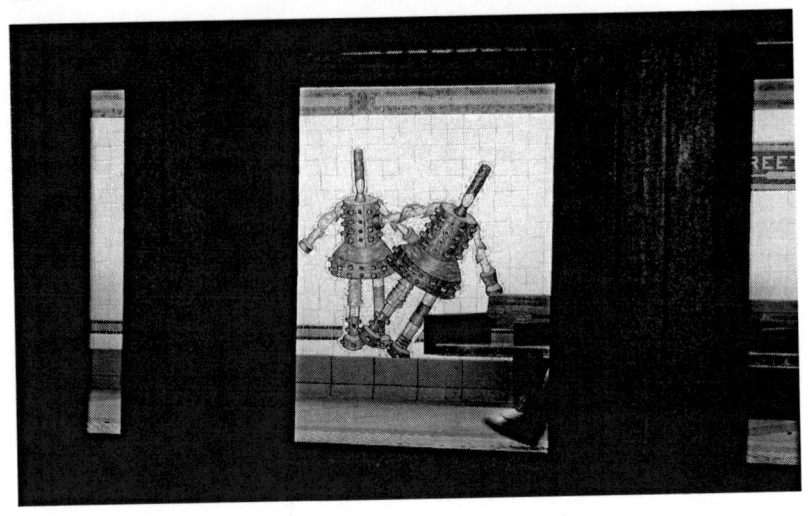

Monday, July 30th, 2007

The Drunken Prophet

"You...c'...sing," I heard a deep voice say, coming from the bench in front of me on the ACE at 59th Street. I looked up to see a large black man, oddly dressed, intoxicated, and sitting on one of the usual wooden benches. He was wearing too many clothes for a warm summer day in New York, and his shoes were half socks, half shoes, clown-like with some bright colours poking out one of the "sock shoes." He was leaning sideways, halfway falling off the bench and half holding on to it for dear life.

I'd been playing for about half an hour and was still feeling a bit "off." I was considering calling it a night, despite the great spot I'd landed. The man in blue would have, I'm sure, told me to think of when I was five or twelve, or hanging upside down from a tree or something, but no matter where my mind went, I still felt stuck. Although I was considering a premature exit, it bothered me because I had had a goal of getting past the evening rush hour to the point where the trains run less frequently, where I could really sing in peace. But, I felt vocally unsteady somehow. So after pushing out the last song, I regretfully started to pack up, when I heard another interjection from the drunk dude on the bench: "Yeah, you....ca...sing."

"What? I can't sing?"

"No..." He stumbled, searching for the next line of words. "No, you kin sing…you jist ain't singin'! I jist think yer afraid of yer own voice." He steadied his swaying body as he grasped the bench's armrest.

That comment just went right through to me. He was dead-on. This raging drunk dude had called me on myself. He had caught me not making art but "noise," as I call it when someone's just "singing" and not feeling. Even though I was conversing with a drunk, the competitive part of me rose up. I picked up my guitar, pulled the strap over my head, took some more water, put on my picks, determined to *make music*.

"This Kind Of Moment"

This kind of moment, this kind of moment
This kind of moment is a moment with you
This kind of moment can completely change a woman's mind
And baby it's completely changed my mind about you

Whoa you walked in, I turned around
And for some strange erratic reason, whoa! My heart hit the ground
I tried to speak, I lost my breath
I tried to move, but man I couldn't even take one step

I can't explain where this man came from, how he, in his intoxicated state, could hear what I was not doing, or was capable of, for that matter. I couldn't explain why I'd even decided to engage in this dialogue with him. But, without hesitation, I did. And oddly, from the moment I felt his comment as a challenge, my voice was back. I was *in* my music once again. I was in my voice, and the guitar case filled up quickly. This odd drunk had changed my day.

It was a need
It was a need and I couldn't get enough of what I'd seen
It was a trance, oh what a trance
And I couldn't help but notice how you looked in those pants

This kind of moment, this kind of moment
This kind of moment is a moment with you
This kind of moment can completely change a woman's mind

And baby it's completely changed my mind about you

Finally, after almost forty minutes of music, of comments, garble, and clapping from the bench (most of which I ignored, as I'd gotten my groove back and wanted to enjoy the performance), the drunk guy chose a train to board. I guess he'd decided his "job" there was done. He propped himself off the bench to try to stand. I was deathly afraid he'd just tip over and I'd have to call for help, but with much effort, he managed, somehow, to get himself upright and zigzagged toward the train's doors. Suddenly, he turned around and, standing in the frame of the train door, blew me a kiss. I nodded and smiled in response, at which point the guy decided a thank you "up close and personal" would be far more appropriate. *Oh nooooooo! No, no.* He staggered toward me and held out his hand. But a handshake, it turned out, would not suffice. He reached for my hand again, and for some strange reason, decided he just had to give my hand a kiss. *Oh my gosh. No.* I squirmed as I again obliged, figuring it was the only chance I had to get rid of my newfound motivational coach. The guy, apparently satisfied with the hand kiss, sashayed his way back toward the train. But just then, the doors closed. *Shoot!* The inebriated clown stumbled back just as the doors opened again. He stepped forward and they closed. Please. *Please open the doors, dear conductor person,* I begged in my mind. And just as I was thinking that: *Wham!* The doors slid open just the tiniest bit.

It seemed the female conductor had seen this whole last episode unfold in front of her. Doors opened, the drunk Svengali backed up; doors closed, the drunk guy approached. He just could not, for the life of him, seem to figure out how to time his stumble to the opening of the subway doors. Finally, the female conductor poked her head out of her window and verbally directed the stumbling maestro, "Wait 'til they open, *then* go inside!" He moved toward the now blissfully open train doors, but just as he was about to enter, he stopped, grabbed onto the car door, turned to me, flourished one hand into the air, and shouted, "*Sing!*" The conductor, thank God, had kept the doors open for his last bit of coaching. He tripped up the ledge of the still open car door, took one more step back to catch himself, and then heaved himself into the doorway, which at this point, lay only half way open. He stood there with the doors closing on him, squishing him for a second into a drunken frozen statue. Then the doors snapped open again, causing him to literally fall into the train car.

Once he was safely inside the doors, she gave me a little grin and a nod. Okay, this woman is now officially my hero.

Not long after the drunken exit, Ron stopped by the platform. He listened for a while and we chatted a bit. "So, I heard from MUNY, you know, Music Under New York, the folks with the banners?"

"Yeah, yeah, you go out for that?"

"Yeah, second year in a row. This year I went with five other musicians, crazy right? I mean they did such a phenomenal job, all on top of their game. The percussionist plays for *The Lion King*, among other Broadway shows; just a great bunch of guys, and very talented. Anyway, we did our thing, back in May. I haven't said much because I didn't want to stress out about it too much. But, I heard today."

"Yeah, what they'd say? You get it? I mean, they g-g-gotta accept you this time. I mean, you had a full band an' all."

"Yeah, you'd think, right? But, nope. I'm stumped on that program. I mean, I did it once on my own, it went well, but that was a no-go. Now this year, full band and still a no-go. I'm not sure what they're looking for. But you know what? I'm going back. I'm going to audition again next year. I mean, no reason not to if they'll accept my application again, right?"

"Baby, I'm sorry, I m-m-mean, that's ridiculous. Don't sweat it though, baby. You do fine down here. M-m-maybe even better down here than up there."

"I know, you're probably right. But at this point it'd be nice to get accepted, just to know I've gotten in. You know?"

"You will. Next year you will, I can feel it. Just do your thing, baby, and you'll be f-f-fine. I can tell that 'bout you. You'll be fine."

I played on, we chatted some more, and when I was done playing for the day, I asked him again if he would accept money for the items bought for me the other day.

"You sure?" he replied.

"Of course. You did me a huge favor. Here. It's your money, Ron." I counted out the bills from my case. He thanked me, more than willing to take the money today. It was a Monday. Always slow on Mondays.

I told Ron briefly about the drunken man on the bench and how he had flipped my day around. "The universe shows up in some odd outfits sometimes."

"It sure does. Kind of like a drunken prophet."

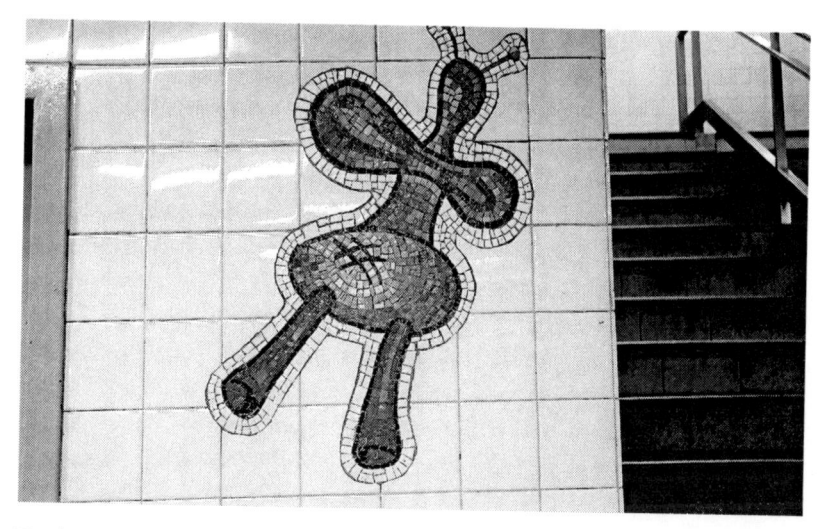

Friday, August 3rd, 2007

Miranda

It's been a stressful week, mainly financial in nature. The end of July and into August is often a super sluggish time for the city in general and particularly for freelancers and artists it seems. It seems the hotter it gets outside, the slower the country moves, including this fast paced city. This week has been brutally hot here, which has made sojourns underground even more challenging than usual. Normally, Friday is a lucrative and fun day to play underground. But today felt more like a Monday than a Friday. Most of that was due to the heat and, I suppose, the mindset it put all of the commuters in. It seems that once the temperature reaches over ninety degrees in Manhattan, people seem to get really pissed off. Add to it a trip to the steaming subways, and folks are fuming.

I headed uptown to check on the ACE at Times Square. In the good spot, there was a young man with a guitar, doing originals; no amp, just singing. He reminded me of myself when I first began. So brave and free. Cool. I asked him how long he might be.

"I just got here about fifteen minutes ago. I'd say maybe a few hours."
Ah, the search goes on.

Just then, Barry from the a cappella group, Made Over, came by. "What's up? You singin' today?"

"Yeah. I've been to two spots on the east side already and it seems as if this heat outside is just pissin' people off and they don't want to hear music. They don't want to hear anything, it seems. They just want to bitch when it's so hot underground."

"You should ride the trains like we do in the heat."

"What? You mean play on the train cars?"

I'd seen mariachi bands and break-dancers work the train cars themselves, but had not really considered doing so myself for more than a millisecond. Most likely because the platforms have treated me so well. But today, in this heat, I was almost swayed.

"Yeah, they're air conditioned, and you make good money. You should just pack yourself and your guitar and play the cars."

"Oh, I don't know. Don't the cops get on your case on the trains? And what about my guitar, I'd be scared it'd get smashed or something if the train lurches. How do you stand up and play guitar in those cars, anyhow? It takes all my concentration to do that without having to hold onto a guitar and sing!"

"You can do it. The dancers do, the Mariachi guys do. You'll see, after a while you get train legs."

"Train legs?"

"Yeah. You get used to the movement; you develop what ya call train legs. We usually work the NRW. We just get on at 42nd Street and ride it all the way to the end and back, and do that a few times and make our money." He paused for a minute, and I digested this new option being presented to me. An option that apparently included developing a whole new pair of train-specific skills. He continued, "But you don't wanna ride the old cars."

"The what?"

"The old cars, you wanna avoid them. You know, the ones that are rounded on the outside with all the seats going in one direction, they're loud. We call 'em tin cans. They're loud. You wanna stay away from the tin cans."

"Okay." I was still trying to picture myself singing on a train car and not quite getting there in my mind, although the thought of air conditioning on a day like today was really pushing me to expand my horizons. "I'll have to think on this some, Barry. But I still don't think I feel okay about playing my guitar on the train. If I lose it or it gets damaged, then I'm done and couldn't work."

"We just gotta get you a train guitar." Barry was never one to be out of useful ideas. "We'll get one, you'll see. The cars are it in the summer. You'll see." Wow, train legs. I guessed these were like sea legs but for the industrialized world. There was "train guitar," which seemed to be just an old guitar you didn't care about losing if it got smashed to bits on a train.

"It sounds like a whole new skill set to me. I'll think about it some more, Barry. Thanks. But, I should head back uptown now and see if 59th Street is open. I really need to sing today."

"I know, baby, I know. I'll catch ya later." He gave me an oversized hug from his six foot something frame.

I headed up to Columbus Circle to see what was open. All spots were free. *Yes!* I set up on the best one, the downtown side of the ACE. I looked at the crowd in front of me—everyone looked comatose from the oppressive heat. Even though no one said anything, I could still feel their heat-induced attitudes. It was a rough kind of heat and it permeated everyone's elemental attitude about life today. I began in on my repertoire. I sang, but today, instead of folks walking up and putting money in my case at a regular clip, they just stood there and stared blankly. They looked drugged. Every now and again, as a train would come by to take the next load of people from the platform, someone would say softly, so as not to expend too much energy, "That was beautiful." But still, for some reason, had no "umph" to search for their cash. It was the oddest thing. This happened over and over again: people would clap, compliment me, and walk on. They were just too hot to do any extraneous movements at all. Reaching for a wallet, into a pocket or a purse, was just too much action for such a hot day. Same phenomenon happens when it's too cold as well. People either get lethargic or frozen about moving, and that's all there is to it. On those days, you sing to robots. Robots who smile.

It was becoming comical. Well, as comical as it could be when my guitar case lay barren and I still had rent to pay. I played on, enjoying, as my audience did, the brief bursts of cold as each train pulled in, opened their doors, and blasted me with cold air. As this hot/cold cycle without income continued, I thought more and more about Barry's suggestion of playing those air-conditioned cars. Then, out of the corner of my eye, I caught the eye of a little girl wearing a bright pink sundress. She was just standing, staring, transfixed. I smiled at her. She, with a bit of hesitation, smiled a huge, partially toothless grin back at me. She had dark blond hair and very fair skin; she must have been about seven. Her folks were next to her, yet, not paying too much attention to the eye chatting. I continued to play, and a minute or two later I noticed the little girl walking toward me, carrying a dollar. She delicately approached my case and laid the dollar bill inside. I thanked her quietly and privately in the midst of my song. Then she, once again, flashed that brilliant toothless grin of hers as she scurried back to her folks.

I decided I'd sing for her and her alone. Everyone else on that platform was in their own summer stupor. The young girl in the pink dress seemed to be the only human awake on the platform today. Looking at her, you would think the temperature was perfect down there. You would think there was absolutely nothing wrong on the planet at that very moment. You'd think life, right there, in this instant, underground on a stifling ninety-some-odd degree day in New York City, was Heaven on earth. I sang for her.

Not one full song later, I opened my eyes and, to my surprise, right there in front of me, far from her folks, stood the little girl again. She was so brave. "What's your name?" I asked. She paused for a second and began to speak when a train whizzed by. She stopped and looked to her left briefly, indicating that she preferred responding once the clamor had subsided. The train passed and I went first, "I'm Heidi."

"Miranda," she squeaked.

"It's so nice to meet you, Miranda."

She smiled, "Your singing is pretty."

"Thank you, Miranda. Thank you for your kind words, they mean a lot."

She scurried back to her folks' side. I sang again. For Miranda, of course.

For some reason, this little girl felt no discomfort there today. While everyone else around her felt as if they just wanted to either kill or die, Miranda was oblivious to any distress in her surroundings. It made me wonder for a second just how much of what we feel is real, and how much is actually in our minds. I thought about that in relation to everyone sweltering on that platform, and also in relation to how my own life had felt to me this past week. I'm thinking now that it's really mostly all in our minds; that it's our perception of what is going on around us, versus what's actually going on, that makes all the difference in the world. I'm thinking now, after watching blissful Miranda surrounded by antagonistic commuters, that it's actually our state of mind about our surroundings, versus our actual surroundings, that matters the most. If that's the case, I have little to worry about: heat, money, or audiences. It all matters very little, unless, of course, we want it to.

Tuesday, August 21st, 2007

Reunions

"I haven't seen you in weeks, One!" I shouted as I got to the bottom of the ACE. The only communication I'd actually had with One recently was a few phone calls, saying, "Yo, Heidi, God bless, it's One. I've been thinkin' of you, just checkin' in," and thanking me for the sticks that Ron had relayed to him. So, to see him there with his cans definitely brought a big smile to my face.

We gave each other a hug (albeit sweaty on his part, from playing underground in the heat). Immediately, he held up the drum sticks I had had carrier-pigeoned to him via Ron. The note I had written to him on the sticks was almost all rubbed off from constant wear, but the words "Can-man," "Bucket-boy," and my signature remained close to the tip portion where his hands never go. After some chitchat, I guess he saw I was itching to play.

"You want this spot?" He paused for a second. "You can have it if you want."

"Oh, no. I mean, sure…but I can go to 59th, really…"

"No, girl, it's One here, don't I always take care of you?"

I grinned, argued no further, and he made space for me on the platform as I started to set up.

"So, how's your mom, Heidi?"

"She's doing good, One. Thanks for asking."

"So, what's goin' on in life above ground, Heidi? You stayin' outta trouble?"

"Yeah, One, things are good."

"Your friends know about One? You told them 'bout me?"

"I've told my friends above ground about all you guys here, yeah. They're intrigued mostly."

"Hey! Did you show your friends that picture you took of me?" he asked with uncertain curiosity.

"You know, I did."

"Well, what did they think of One?"

"They like your shades and they like your cans. That's what everyone comments on the most, One."

"Yeah, well, these here shades, they got their purpose. And my cans, well, they're my life; ya know, my rhythm."

He seemed to be on a roll today in referring to himself in the third person; don't even ask me why. "Do your tight friends know that One looks after their princess here in the subways?"

"I'm sure they know. And I'm sure they appreciate it greatly." One paused for a moment as I continued to set up. He then looked up and out poured more questions.

"How's your boyfriend?" I made the "slice the neck" sign with one finger, indicating it's kaput, over, done, finished. He disgustedly responded, "Why do people always do that?"

"What? Break up?" I was taken aback at his random and energetic outburst.

"No. Why do people always do that with their hand across their neck? Why don't they just say 'it's over?'"

I laughed. "I don't know, One...I don't know. Just easier to do the hand thing, I guess. But okay, yeah, it's over."

Again there was a slight pause as One thought for a second. "Aw, Heidi, I know you're a heartbreaker, I can tell that. What happened?"

"I don't really feel like goin' into the whole thing, One. It's complicated...usually is, right? But it's cool. It's over."

I was grateful to have the trains to help me make this transition to being solo again. I figured I've mastered the multiple changes here underground, so I'm sure I can handle this life transition, too. As tough as any breakup is, with the trains and the music as my muse, I was sure I'd be fine. Not wanting to rehash anything anymore in my mind or heart, I added, "Do you mind if we change the subject? I came to play today to kind of forget about all that stuff, ya know." After a moment of silence, One obliged me and changed the subject.

"You know, Heidi, I've noticed recently, there've been these new dudes, these musicians I've never seen before. They're new to the scene and all. But the thing is this…they stay for hours, sometimes six or eight. At least they say that's how long they're stayin' when I ask, you know? It's not right, in my book!"

"Well, One, I highly doubt anyone really stays that long. And if they do, I doubt they'll do that more than one time or so, don't you think?"

Then I remembered, "Well, except those one-stringed guys do actually stay forever, and they're always here. So, in a way, I agree. They're the only guys down here who do that, though. Why is that, One?"

"It's two!" One exclaimed, obviously disturbed by something I'd said, almost as much as the "finger across the neck" motion I'd made earlier. "Everyone thinks it's one, but it's two!"

"Two what?"

"Two strings!"

"Really? Wow, but it looks like one…"

"Yeah, but it's two and I get so tired of everyone sayin' it's one when it's two strings!"

"Okay, okay. It's two, One…but sometimes it really sounds like one."

He gleefully added, "You should hear the guy on the east side—he makes those two strings sound just like a violin."

"Wow, cool. I'll have to hear that. I'd really like to."

By this time I was set up and had begun in on my set. One, who had not, as of yet, packed up his gear, was still sitting facing me, resting on the edge of the wooden bench. What a picture that was: there I am, all set up to perform, facing north with my guitar around my neck and case out in front of me, and right beyond my case, not two feet away, was One, facing south, surrounded by his cans/buckets and grinning his grin behind those always dark twenty-four-seven secret sunglasses he wears.

To really do what I came for, to purge this breakup thing, I began straight in on "Step Back," the song inspired by the past breakup. One randomly decided to accompany me on his cans/buckets, facing me the entire time, giggling, as he could immediately tell what the tune was about. We're always in sync when we jam, even through the rhythmic changes, even though most of the tunes I play are originals that he's never played before.

"Step Back"

How could I think that you
Were fallin' too
When all this time
You were just playin'

But I believed
In what I'd seen
And everything
You had been sayin'
But I've come to see
That you're here with me
'Cause your nights were getting longer
But you're just bidin' time
With my heart and mind
Waitin' on the next thing to come along
I'm tellin' you to

Step back, step back

I could feel the song doing its job of balancing out my universe, verse by verse. While singing, I recalled the unappealing—but I have to say, pretty creative—"cake-and-eat-it-too" proposition my ex had presented to me, pressing the subject for weeks after the breakup. Each time his "See, I'll go and do this and this [subtext: her and her], and we can still be…" plan was presented, I'd give a flat-out "No," choosing to write a song instead. That's usually my therapy. That along with singing.

> *You wanna pick and*
> *Choose half, choose half*
> *The part of me you*
> *Wanna have*
> *While you're out havin' fun*
> *So keep on*
> *Walkin', walkin'*
> *Don't wanna hear you*
> *Talkin', talkin'*
> *I know you're*
> *Rockin' with another one*
>
> *Don't go and tell me*
> *Don't go and say*
> *I don't want to hear that you'll be back again someday*
> *Don't say you're sorry*
> *And don't' say a thing*
> *Just keep on walkin', walkin'*
> *Let do my thing, but*
>
> *Step back, step back*

Then, after a few jams, I had to be blunt. "Hey, One. I love the percussion, but I just don't make as much money when folks join in with me, and I need to make rent and stuff. So, can we jam another day?"

"Heidi, Heidi…okay…that's fine," One said, layering on a thick film of sarcasm. "No, it's okay, really, I understand. Do your thing and One will go and get stuff done outside the trains."

"Thanks, One." I watched him organize his buckets in preparation to head out to take care of "stuff."

"Bye, Heidi, and don't forget to breathe." One left, peering at me one last time out from behind those sunglasses of his.

I dug into my tunes, soaking up the spot I'd secured with all my being. Toward the end of my playing, I looked up to see the always-friendly Izzy approaching with a black beret perched on her head. Her long skirt waved back and forth around her acoustic guitar as she made her way down the stairs to the platform. "Hi," I said, always happy to see her friendly face. "Hey, I won't be that long, Izzy, if you want to play." I hoped she wanted it because there wasn't anyone I'd rather pass it on to in the world.

"Yeah. What time?"

"Thirty minutes, and I'll be done."

"I'll wait, okay?"

"Yeah, Izzy. Hey, I have an amplifier for you. It's my older one, the first one I bought, before this one," and I pointed to the larger one I now traveled with in the system. "It's small and I think it's light enough for you to carry, with your shoulder and all."

"For me? Why don't you sell it?"

"I could, but I want to give it to you, Izzy. I can meet you tomorrow at three if you want. Entrance to the ACE on 8th Avenue."

"I can do that. Thank you, dear."

"Great. Hope you can use it." And I went back to finish my set.

Thirty minutes later, it was time for the changing of the guard, I turned the coveted ACE over to deserving, soon to be amplified, Izzy.

Tuesday, September 4th, 2007

Journeys

It's the end of summer here in New York, and I've noticed an interesting phenomenon happens every year at this time. Toward the end of the summer, during the last few weeks of warm weather, hundreds of thousands of monarch butterflies descend on New York City. The delicate creatures take this intensely long journey each and every year southward for the winter. Their journey, I'm guessing, requires a stop, a rest. Often times, the rest spot they choose each year is along the Hudson River.

There are bushes, mostly rose hips that have been planted along the Hudson, separating the industrial West Side Highway from the mighty and ever-changing Hudson River. These phenomenal creatures often choose to alight on these bushes. It's odd to see. First one, then two, then dozens of monarchs alight on the beach plums planted all along the Hudson. It's even more amazing to think that there are thousands of rare monarchs right in front of you, just hanging out for a while, hoping not to be noticed, smack in the middle of Manhattan. Of course, for anything to go unnoticed in this city is kind of tough—even these creatures have a bit of a hard time. During my run today, I noticed a homeless man had somehow captured not one, but an entire collection of these helpless creatures in each hand, their wings struggling between his fingertips, and was loudly raffling them off to passers-by. Given that everyone passing him was also surrounded by thousands of the exact same butterflies, I'm not quite sure what he thought the "hook" was, but he obviously was very committed to his gig. Ah, that good old American capitalistic spirit, it never fails to amaze. I swear, absolutely nothing is sacred in this city.

I'm mentioning these beautiful creatures (the ones not being raffled off, at least) and the timing and path of their migration because, in a way, they have paralleled the journey I'm experiencing through the subways. This annual and lengthy migration of these delicate insects represents a change in the circle and evolution of life. Oddly, coincidentally or not, at the same time as the monarchs' migration south, this change seems to be also occurring in my life as well. I've been offered a publishing opportunity for *The Subway Diaries*. Although I'm not sure it's the right fit for the book, or whether I'll take it, it's nudged me to make the decision to in fact publish the *Diaries*. Making this switch into publishing mode is a big change from where I began, which was writing just for me. This is another morphing process. And although it ups the game a bit in that I'm now working with a photographer, publisher, editor, and designers...the journey remains basically the same for me. The only difference is that I'm now accompanied by others who are as much a part of my adventures underground as I.

These butterflies also parallel my enthusiasm for my newfound world underground. Somehow, no matter how many times I see them, they elicit the same response in me: that child-like enthusiasm, that desire to shout "Look, look, look!" that I'm sure I had the very first time I saw them floating gracefully in the air, catching wind. It's funny how I've found the same exact feeling of pure, unadulterated happiness and joy underground.

Today, I saw not only their journey, but also my own journey. The streets of New York are one of the most unlikely environments for the delicate monarch butterfly to alight, and yet, in droves, they do. Their beauty exists, perched *en masse* amongst the skyscrapers and traffic, much like the beauty that emanates from the musicians and artists far underground in the dark and dingy subways.

Thursday, September 13th, 2007

Let's Be Candid

I'm now traveling the underground some days with Jennifer, one of the photographers for *The Subway Diaries* and its website. Along with Jennifer, two other photographers, Henning and Diana Mejia, also shoot for *The Subway Diaries* as well as a talented collection of other photographers who've joined in on the underground bandwagon along the way.

Jennifer's a young, pretty, bright twenty-something girl who is driven and has an outstanding work ethic. Today she accompanied me, just to get a sense for how the subways feel from my perspective. We met at 43rd Street and 9th Avenue and walked over together to the entrance of the ACE. Jennifer and I lugged our respective gear down the stairs and I approached the Bob Marley Guy, who was on a break. "Excuse me, do you know how much longer you might be?"

Keeping his headphones on the whole time, he answered in his thick Caribbean accent, "About a half an hour more."

"I'll wait then, if it's okay."

He pointed to the side of the staircase. "You have to stand back there." He wanted me to stand by the wall so I wouldn't distract folks from giving him donations. I wasn't offended at all for being told to remove myself from the stage area; I'm used to that routine.

With that information, Jennifer and I decided to hang out for a bit, and she would shoot randomly while we were waiting for the spot. "Can I get some shots of him?" She pointed to the reggae guy and jiggled her camera, as if still waiting for permission from me.

"I'm sure it's fine, but you may want to ask first, just out of courtesy." She asked and he didn't seem to mind at all. He was actually pretty oblivious to most everything with those headphones on. Being photographed didn't upset this particular performer's pre-recorded mojo one bit.

Not more than four minutes into our standing off-stage, Izzy wandered down onto the platform. She began to approach the reggae guy and then spotted me standing in the corner, as per my instructions. She immediately detoured from him and came over to me. Just then, Jennifer wandered back over with her camera, grinning because she was already getting a kick out of the whole scene. I introduced Izzy to Jen and vice versa. They exchanged hellos, and both seemed genuinely glad to meet each other. "You taking pictures?" Izzy asked of Jen.

"Yeah, I was just shooting that guy. He's a hoot!"

"There's days when I sometimes want to shoot him, you know, when his stuff is in the stage area and he's over there just hangin' out, resting. Basically, no one's using the spot and it's just a waste. But then, I think 'no, I'd definitely be arrested,'" Izzy answered, more than adding to Jennifer's initiation experience.

While we three waited for our reggae friend to finish, we chatted. As Izzy started talking, Jennifer began taking random shots. Using the gathering and photo shoot as her "soap box," Izzy thought this was a good time to vent about our current President Bush. She went on for a good ten minutes about how much she disliked him, his views, and "the whole war thing that he's gotten us into." Izzy was really not happy with the way the country is being run at the moment and made sure Jennifer and I knew it in no uncertain terms. She suddenly smiled, with a history written upon her aged face. "When a woman or black man becomes president, well then, that'll be the day! Now that'll be a wonderful day!"

After politics, Izzy moved straight on to religion. The religion topic, I think, might have been spurred on by me mentioning to Jennifer that I would love to capture the Mad Man of Manhattan. Then Izzy piped right in, "Well, I know what's wrong with him. He reads the Bible too much. That's what happens to people when they read the bible too much. They go crazy…just like that man. It's not good for you to read the Bible that much. It confuses your brain, and that's what happens. Same with that president of ours, he's crazy cuz he reads the Bible too much." Izzy was perhaps even more adamant about the Bible subject than U.S. politics. But, to her, at this particular time in history they were obviously intricately intertwined. She became more and more animated and spoke bluntly, making sure we "got it"— her point and all. And we most definitely did. She seems to have a diagnosis and solution for just about any problem you throw at the woman. I think Izzy should run for office.

Despite the captivating conversation, Jennifer, Izzy, and I were getting antsy, wondering when the Reggae Guy might be wrapping it up on the platform. His repertoire today consisted of not three, but two songs…over and over. I couldn't figure out why he'd leave out the third tune of his repertoire. Was he just not in "good voice," as the opera singers like to say? Or did that one tune get somehow messed up on his recording, leaving him only with the two remaining Marley tunes to sing and sing again.

"Why doesn't he move now? It's been more than half an hour,." Izzy huffed, furrowing her brow. She then confessed, "I like reggae an awful lot, especially Bob Marley, but I just can't seem to sing or play it. And the crazy thing is that…" She flapped her arms about as she blurted out, "I'm from Trinidad!" Izzy was obviously seriously bothered by the fact that she was from the Caribbean, yet hadn't a hint of her culture's music in her, or rather, coming out of her. From her contorted face, it was clear she'd been wondering about this lacking musical gene most of her adult life, having to make do with her trademark version of "Killing Me Softly with His Song" by Charles Fox and Norman Gimbel, and other U.S. standards.

We turned our attention once more to our "two-song wonder" as Izzy abruptly announced she was going to look for a place elsewhere. "I may go the 123."

"Be careful, the cops are rough over there," I warned, recalling my psycho cop from a few months back.

Izzy nodded in agreement, "I know. I've gotten two tickets there before. So what time are you playing 'til?"

"Come back in an hour. I may be done then, if this guy leaves soon like he said. I'm not planning a long set today."

"Okay." She hoisted her guitar onto her shoulder.

"Hey, Izzy, maybe Jennifer would like to go with you and take some photos...if that's okay with you?"

"Sure, she can come."

Jennifer thought that was a great idea since I hadn't begun playing yet and she'd already snapped just about as much of Reggae Guy as she could. We agreed she'd find her way back in half an hour or so, when I, God willing, had taken over for "Mr. Bob Marley." The two set off toward the stairs. While passing our two-hit wonder, Izzy walked right up next to him, leaned in, and boldly said, "She's *waiting*, you know!" He nodded a slight nod in perfect time to the reggae beat playing on his headphones. Man, she's fearless. But you know what? It worked. Jennifer and Izzy were not even at the top of the stairs when Reggae Guy turned around and silently motioned to me that the spot was now mine. *Go Izzy.* I still think she should run for office. Can you imagine, Izzy in politics? She'd be great. She'd cut to the chase, tell it like it is, no holds barred, and she'd come up a solution that she'd be completely committed to. She'd get things done. She is exactly what doesn't happen now in politics and what's so desperately needed. I'd love to put her in some executive office for one day and see what happens. You know those politicians would never be the same after a day with Izzy. Anyway, I'd vote for her.

I set up and started in on my music. Not fifteen minutes into my set, Danny moseyed by and unabashedly shared, "I've just been up at 59th Street. I did okay. Did good." He grinned to let me know he cleaned up, as usual, as he dropped me a dollar. Danny always gives me a dollar. Not because he wants my spot, it's just what he does. Out of courtesy, I suppose. Danny made himself at home and started to chat with me in between my tunes. It's what he does, chews the fat after his gig and before his dinner. You could set your clock to Danny with his routine. He's refreshingly predictable. His predictability is like the rising of the sun and setting of the moon. Without realizing it, it grounds you. If it were not to happen one day, you'd really be thrown.

"So, Danny, it was cool seeing you above ground the other night at 59th. I usually only see you underground. I really like your stories. You know, the ones about your life." (Danny and I bumped into one another above ground, and he was as chatty above as he is below. Perhaps more, if that's actually possible.) I swear, Danny could have his own museum with an audio tour to go with it—narrated, of course, by Danny himself, since no one tells those stories like Danny does. I've told friends about Danny and they always ask if he's really telling the truth. I have no idea, of course. All I know is that he is sharply consistent with his narrative. Every story easily repeated, every fact in its place, every single time it's relayed. So my hunch is, yes, he's the real deal, to the bone. That man has had one heck of a life.

"Yeah, I was goin' to play. You caught me at the circle."

"Well, I love hearing about your life in music."

"Yeah, I've got some livin' on me, that's for sure." Danny paused briefly, jumping right back on script, "I'm gonna have some good food for dinner."

"Really? What are you planning on having, Danny?"

"I'm gonna get this smoked sausage, it's from this deli on my way home. I get it all the time." He'd obviously been thinking about this particular meal for the last hour. He was on a mission regarding that dinner.

"Hey, Danny, you know it'd be really cool if you could stick around for a bit. My photographer, Jennifer, is here, and I'd really love it if she could get some shots of you!"

There was a slight pause as Danny grinned at the thought of having his photo taken. He then looked down at his lap and said quietly, "Sure, I can do that."

"Cool. You know, I got some great shots of you, just with my camera phone yesterday. I'll get you copies. I promise."

"Thanks."

"Yeah, I shared them with some of my friends and told them all about your voice, Danny. They were very impressed."

Then he threw me that "Thank you, I know" grin again, the one I've come to enjoy seeing when I throw him compliments. I started re-tuning my guitar. "So, you did good today, Danny?"

"Yep, I made me some dead presidents," Danny said matter-of-factly.

"Dead presidents?"

"Yeah, dead presidents." He pointed to my guitar case. "Them dead presidents are where it's at. Ya gotta have them presidents or you're not gettin' nowhere. Dead presidents…they open doors."

"So, Danny, what's your favorite dead president?"

Danny stopped for a minute to think, "Jackson, I like Jackson. And Lincoln's okay, too."

"Yeah, I hear that, Danny. George is kinda "so-so" these days."

"Yeah, George ain't even popular these days. I like Lincoln. I tell you, without them dead presidents, you can't do nothin'. Like if you meet a girl, you can't take her nowhere without them dead presidents. Ya need 'em." Then Danny stopped for a minute and looked down at the platform. "Unless you're one of them movie star types."

"Movie star?"

"Yeah, you know them guys with that low voice, they talk…" and he lowered his soft tenor speaking voice to a louder, low, growly one, "like this…you know, they got that voice, that talkin' voice that girls love. Then you're okay, you don't need the dead presidents so much."

"Oh, I don't know about that, Danny, that kinda voice isn't all that. Not all girls fall for that voice, believe me. So, you gotta have dead presidents to get girls? Is that what you're saying?"

"Yup. That's how you get the girls. Unless you got that movie star voice an' all."

"So, you only sing for the girls?"

"Yup."

"Well, what about the guys on the platforms?"

"They're there. But I sing to the girls," Danny explained, as if it was a given that girls were the only reason to do anything. I grinned as he continued, "Girls, girls are like…" Danny paused. "They're like church, ya know? You know when everyone gets up and prays and sings and gets all spiritual-like. Girls are like that."

"Wow, girls are like church—well, there's a TV advertisement in the making, Danny. You could bottle and sell that phrase." Danny laughed and glanced at my case.

"You're doin' pretty good there yourself with them dead presidents."

"I think you've brought me good luck, Danny." As I sang, I wondered some more about Danny. I could just see him in his heyday. He's a huge flirt now, I can only imagine him as a young musician in New York City, developing and honing those skills on girl after girl that he'd meet along his tours. I could just see him at clubs, scoping out the room before his gig started, choosing his female target for the night, playing his gig—probably focusing on her the entire time as he does on the subway platforms still—singing to her and only her, all night long. Then when his gig was done, he'd make his approach. (His approach being the cap on the deal, which he'd be fine-tuning with each and every conquest). Yes, I'm sure Danny was the definition of a player or ladies' man back in his day. I bet the choosing, the musical massaging and capture of a girl, was as much an art form to Danny as was his singing.

My singing, which doesn't, however, involve the intentional "capture" of men, was feeling really good, and just about half an hour later I saw the unlikely pair of Jennifer and Izzy walking toward me. I wrapped up my song and asked Izzy where they had gone, and why they were back so soon. "There wasn't no good spot," Izzy replied.

"Shoot. Well, I'm not going to be that much longer, Izzy, and then this one's yours."

"Yeah, but I got to show Jennifer some places," she said turning to Jennifer for endorsement.

"Yeah, she showed me shortcuts to everywhere and everything. I never even knew half these places were there before," Jennifer concurred.

"Cool." I'd thrown Jennifer right into an odd new world, to say the least, yet she seemed happy and relaxed absorbing the flow underground. Wanting everyone to know each other, and being the only one who knew the entire crowd, I made the introductions. When I introduced Danny and Izzy, I wondered if prior to this any of the performers knew each other by name. I'm finding most times, the answer is no. But I'm also finding that it doesn't really matter. They don't seem to need names in most cases. I'm finding that they know each other by face and description only, and that seems to be enough underground. Sometimes I feel funny when I do the whole introduction thing, since they have co-existed for years—sometimes decades—without needing to know names, and there I am, making it seem so important. But that's just my way, and so now they've a name to go with the face they've known for years, and that I figured couldn't hurt any. I started singing again as Jennifer photographed Izzy and Danny as they sat on the bench to listen. Those guys are my most favorite audience members.

After ten or fifteen minutes of music, photos, and the requisite chitchatting, Danny announced, "I gotta go get my smoked sausage for my dinner on my way home." I've never seen Danny stray this far off schedule since I've known him. I was honoured that he'd delayed his "Groundhog Day" dinner itinerary for Jen and me.

He pulled himself up by balancing himself between the handle of his metal cart and the arm of the wooden bench.

"Bye, Danny," I said, as he sauntered toward the train doors, pushing his cart.

"Bye, darlin'." And he gave a nod to Jennifer and Izzy as the train doors closed.

"I'm going to do one more tune here, Izzy, then it's yours."

"I'll take shots of that and then I'm going to head off for the evening," Jennifer added.

I finished my last tune and packed up. Seamlessly, Izzy moved her gear over and tuned up her guitar. She placed her metal harmonica holder around her neck, reapplied her trademark red lipstick, and put out her bucket. Jennifer moved in to take a few shots of Izzy. I don't think either of us was prepared for the closet "ham" that was lurking inside of our beret-topped friend. It was clear after about three minutes that "candid" was not in Izzy's contract. Izzy always turned her face straight on to the camera, which Jennifer was trying her best to "secretly" move around Izzy, to catch her off guard, just once even. Well, from what I observed, there was less than zero chance of Izzy being caught off guard in a photo when she was performing. From my vantage point, which wasn't one of stifled hysterics, there was no chance on earth that Jennifer was going to get a candid shot out of Izzy. Izzy hit poses and contortions I'd never seen before in a sixty-year-old holding an acoustic guitar. Heck, I'd never seen them in a twenty-year-old, for that matter. Jennifer would sneak up behind Izzy. Izzy would keep her body in the same direction and twist her head around like a doll, so as to continue to face the lens. At one point, Jennifer tried so hard to capture an "unplanned" Izzy that she backed up to the platform's edge. I was absolutely sure she was about to tumble backward onto the tracks, but just as I was about to shout to her, she safely stepped forward, toward the center of the platform. Safely on the platform, Jennifer bent down to her knees to get an upward angle of our Trinidadian guitar and harmonica player, figuring there was no way Izzy could control that shot. But even that was a bust—Izzy bent right down with her, guitar in hand, face never leaving the lens, her knees as close to the ground as any rock star (or aerobics instructor for that matter). It looked like musical photo shoot gone *Saturday Night Live*. At that point, Jennifer, now also laughing, gave up. Even the audience was giggling.

Her song over, and apparently having had enough of the "capture the camera" game, Izzy announced bluntly but, of course, diplomatically: "Okay, you can go now." Guess the photo shoot was over. Izzy's candor and spunk rank up there with Danny's predictability and flirting skills. Both of them, one of a kind.

We said our goodbyes, each put a dollar in her bucket, and left Izzy to her art. Jennifer and I wandered up to the mezzanine and chatted about the afternoon. "I really had no idea that this whole system of playing, and acquiring spots, and ways of interacting existed among the musicians who play the subways. I really had no clue...until today," Jennifer concluded.

"It's wild, right?"

"It is. And I really would have had no idea how friendly everyone is down there unless I'd gone with you today. I mean, I think people kind of make things up about subway musicians, or just assume stuff. I just saw them before as random people, with really no connection to one another. And you know, I never really thought whether they were nice or not. I'm definitely going to look at the musicians underground in a completely different light after today. I'm honestly glad to have seen this world through your eyes, Heidi. These shots will be great!"

She "gets" it...I thought to myself. I definitely chose the right photographer for this world.

Friday, September 21st, 2007

Rental Fee on the ACE

"Where you goin'?" One asked, as I wandered to the edge of the platform where the A train stops, not wanting to interrupt his gigging. I'd been away for a few days due to some recording projects I'd been asked to do, but definitely needed to center myself again on the platforms.

As I stood there, leaning on my guitar head, I answered, "I think 59th Street, 'cause you're playing here. Sorry not to say hey, but you seemed so in to your sound, I didn't want to interrupt."

"Well, wait a minute. Do you want the spot until seven-thirty or so?"

It was six p.m. and still rush hour. "Well, sure." I figured that some time at the ACE was better than no time anywhere else. Friday night is a prime night for performing underground. People are so glad the week's over that they're almost always in a good mood. It's the polar opposite to playing a Monday. Plus, most theaters are dark Mondays and on Fridays all the theaters are in full swing, sharing their large weekend audiences with the musicians underground. So, all in all, Fridays are great nights to sing.

"Yeah, I only need to make eight dollars," One declared. *What?* I thought. *Eight dollars?* Okay, this must have something to do with his "other" life, although eight bucks is some pretty measly hush money. I have no idea why eight bucks was his magic number for this Friday, but I didn't argue, I just accepted the deal, sans questions, but with one request: "Hey, One, can I take a picture of you with my camera? The last ones I took were with my cell and they're not that good."

"Heidi, Heidi, Heidi… what 'cha takin' pictures for? I don't look good today."

"One. You look the same today as you do every day…what are you talking about?"

"Heidi…awwww…you're like Pavarotti."

"You mean the paparazzi, not Pavarotti!" I said in hysterics.

"Yeah, yeah, yeah." One grinned. "Paparazzi, Pavarotti…it's all the same. Heidi, what are you taking these photos for, anyhow?"

"You know, my book."

"What do you mean, your book?"

"You know. I told you about it. *The Subway Diaries*, about all this stuff, all you guys and all." I motioned around the train platforms. "You're in it, as well."

"What?" One said as he sat up straight from his usual hunched over position. "What do you mean, I'm in it?"

"I told you, One, there's a whole chapter just for you."

"What's it called?"

"Ummm—*One*," I said sarcastically.

"Heidi, Heidi, Heidi…what cha doin'? Goin' puttin' me in a book for. You're gonna change my life, Heidi."

"Well, I can take it out, One, or call it something else."

"What would you call it?"

"Well, I could call it 'Two.'" I joked, messing with him.

"Is it on the web?"

"Well, it's been on the web in pieces for a bit, until it goes to print, yeah."

After a moment, One resumed his normal stance, hunched over his plastic paint cans, with a moment of introspection. Suddenly he sat upright and declared his discovery: "Oh my gosh! Now I know why all these odd things have been happening to me!"

"What do you mean, 'odd things?'"

"Just this week, I was walking through the train stations up there..." and he pointed up toward the landing, "and some guy came up to me and said, 'I know you...I know you...42nd Street!' And he handed me a dollar bill! Heidi, so you're gonna make me famous...you silly girl." He seemed half excited at the thought that people were recognizing him, and half a bit quivery that this was happening without him doing a thing. He grinned and moved to the side, relinquishing his spot for the next hour or so.

I sang, feeling a bit odd having One there as a participatory on-looker since I'd not been on the platforms for a number of days, and I normally like my space solo for the first few tunes, at least when it comes to people I know. I'm odd that way— strangers are okay, people I know are a tougher audience. So when I've been away for a bit, I like the audience to be one hundred percent stranger. But that luxury was not granted, as One parked himself directly to my right and had already started right in on his "breathe, focus—focus, breathe" mantra.

"On The Inside"

Whoa I've been livin' out on the edge of insanity
Whoa I've been knockin' for someone to let me in
Whoa I've been searchin' most everywhere for the key
So I can step right up, I can know the truth, I can finally begin

Not long after I began, I noticed Izzy slowly coming down the stairs and wandering over to where One was parked, sitting on his cans, which were doing double-duty as his chair. Izzy approached with a dollar in hand.

"No, Izzy," I said. "Don't give me anything...really."

Izzy looked a bit confused, as this is the normal protocol and polite thing to do, especially if a musician wants to play the spot next. "Give it to One, he's the one who gave me the spot, and he needs to make eight bucks tonight, so now he only needs to make seven." Izzy, slightly confused, but willing, handed the dollar to One, who took it. "You look cute today, Izzy. I like your sparkly pin." I nodded in her direction. Izzy was dressed in light blue flannel pants that looked suspiciously like pajama bottoms and a sky blue matching top, with a sparkly pin resting on the neckline. Somehow, pajama bottoms or not, the outfit suited her. Izzy grinned bashfully.

"Thank you."

One let out a very audible sigh. "Only girls would notice these things."

"Thank you for the amplifier, dear. I'm getting used to it at home first before trying it here. It's very nice though. I like it. You sure you don't want to sell it?"

"No Izzy, it's yours. I'm glad you like it, enjoy it."

We discussed her options of platforms, and Izzy announced that she was going to go elsewhere, although she wasn't quite sure where yet. "How long you think you're gonna be?"

"Probably not that long. As long as this holds out, I guess." I held up my water bottle and jiggled it, showing it was almost empty.

"You have to freeze it," Izzy, true-to-form, explained as she began in on her "theory of transporting water to play the subways." She explained to me: I should always put my water bottle in the freezer the night before, and then I'll have a full, cold bottle of water all day for singing. She walked over and pulled a newspaper- and tin foil-wrapped bottle out of her bag and asked me for my almost empty bottle. Izzy took both bottles, walked over to the train tracks, bent over the edge of the platform (I guess so as not to spill and water on the platform, which to me seemed more than amusing, given that everything else known to man is on the platforms already) and began pouring half of her bottle into mine. Izzy came back over and handed me my now almost full bottle of water, and began to describe in detail her method of insulation for gigging underground. She held up her water bottle, which at this point had half of the wrapping torn off, exposing the many layers of "Izzy insulation" beneath.

"See. You have to first fill your bottle and freeze it. Then you have to first wrap it in tin foil and then in newspaper, to keep it cold for your day. Then you put it in a plastic bag so it don't sweat all over your gear. See?" She held up her bottle as demonstration. It was the Izzy infomercial for her "Super Duper Water Transporter."

Izzy put her special water bottle back into her backpack, zipped it back up, swung her guitar onto her shoulder, and shouted, "Good luck, sweetie," as she left the scene.

Rental Fee on the ACE

Again, I began playing, all the while hearing intermittent comments from One to my right: "Breathe, focus, focus, breathe." And of course, every time I heard him tonight, I'd lose focus for a second and forget to breathe properly. This was mostly due to the fact that what I really needed was some "alone" time on the platform. But I never let him know.

Like clockwork, Danny arrived off the A train and, as could be predicted, he sat right in front of me and listened. As always, he smoothly dropped a dollar in my case. I always protest and he always says, "That's okay, darlin', God bless." I went ahead and introduced Danny to One. Both musicians nodded and exchanged mumbled heys, probably not caring at all, but still I do the introductions anyway.

"Hey, Danny, I got some really cool photos of you the other day." Danny grinned.

"Is he in the book, too?" One asked.

"Yeah, of course, One."

"Well, does he have a whole chapter, too?"

"Yes, One, he does. It's called "Danny Boy"—surprise, surprise." Then for the first time, I noticed a twinge of jealously in the small "humph" that passed from One's mouth as he digested this new information.

"You still changin' my life, Heidi…an' I'm not sure if I'm ready for it. You know, fame an' all."

"Aw, One, you just let me know and I'll take you out of the book in a heartbeat. Just say the word, okay?" There was no response as he mulled over his options.

After about fifteen to twenty minutes (his normal resting period while listening to my music), Danny announced it was time for him to get the dinner d'jour. Tonight, fried chicken was on the menu. Right after his menu announcement, two NYPD cops passed us, causing Danny and One to focus immediately on the cement floor, as if by looking at the ground, they'd become invisible.

The cops got on the train and all eyes were free to roam again. Danny got up for the next train. While walking past me, he held out his hand for a "middle five"; I grabbed it. "See you later, Danny." Grrr, I dislike the tension that cops bring. I really do. I guess I should have been more concerned about myself since I was the one performing, but the threat they pose oozed out of both One and

Danny, and that bothered me, overshadowing any fear I had for myself. It hurt me to see their programmed responses that must have developed over years of harassment. I was, however, grateful that the two cops just left and didn't bother any of us.

"Bye, darlin'."

I started my song, after which One randomly shouted over the hum of the trains, "Hey, Heidi!"

"What?"

"Do you believe in God? You know, in religion and God and stuff?" he now shouted over the train that had just pulled in.

"Yes, I suppose, but not the organized kind, more the spiritual kind," I semi-shouted back, still kind of wanting to be "solo" on the platform today, to ground myself. (Although it was becoming more than apparent that was *not* going to happen tonight.)

"Not the 'organized kind?'" he repeated, still way too loud, given that we had, oh, say a hundred other people listening.

"Yeah, I really don't go for much of anything that's organized."

"Ah," One said, still quite loudly, "So you're a 'wild child.'"

"No, One. I'm just a…a free spirit, I guess."

"A what? A freak?"

"No!" I shouted back, not at all wanting to be misunderstood on a subway platform. "I'm a free spirit! Not a freak! A free spirit, One!"

At that point I noticed it was seven-thirty and offered One the seven dollars that he still needed to earn that night if I could stay for another half an hour or so, maybe even in peace. One accepted, readily announcing he had to scoot uptown to "take care of some stuff." I wasn't at all surprised, but grateful I'd just bought myself a bit of "alone" time. I figured eight bucks was a pretty good rental fee for the Uptown ACE on a Friday night. I love One, but tonight I really needed to feel my singing. I paid my rent, and it was well worth it.

Wednesday, September 26th, 2007

The Powers That Be

I'm not sure there will be any entries this week, except this one...

This week, the United Nations is in session here in New York City. Today I'd planned to meet with Jennifer underground for some more photos. Just as I was headed outside with my gear, my phone rang and it was Jen. "Hey," she said. "Listen, I've already traveled to four or five stations on three different lines to shoot musicians on the way to meet you, and I didn't see anyone playing, not a one!"

"What? Why?"

"I guess it's the whole United Nations thing. I mean, I saw a few guys on drums get booted by cops down at Union Square, and then I saw Izzy get booted before she'd even really set up."

"That's crazy!"

"Yeah, I finally got to the ACE and heard a little bit of drumming. I followed it and saw the exact same guys who had just gotten kicked out of Union Square setting up on the Uptown ACE. I went down there to try to take a few shots, and not a minute later, the cops showed up and shut them down *again*. So I just left. I thought I'd call you to fill you in and save you the trip."

"Damn! And I was really lookin' forward to singing and getting some shots with you today!"

"Yeah, you should have seen those drummers. They were pissed. I mean it was like just fifteen minutes earlier they'd been all set up at Union Square when they got shut down, then they set everything up again and kicked off all over again."

"This sucks," I mumbled. So the U.N. seems to be antithetical to musicians performing in the subways. "Whatever..." I'm sure that'd be Dimitri's response at this point.

"Yeah, I know. I really wanted to get shots today as well. I even went up to the cops on the ACE and asked them if musicians were allowed to play today and all I got was a big fat 'No! Not today.' So, anyway, I thought I'd let you know."

I was so bummed. Not only did I realize I'd have to do extraordinarily well underground the next three days to pay my bills, but Jennifer and I also have to get these shots done.

We set a "rain date" and hung up. I decided instead to do some contract work I needed to do regarding my songs that have just been placed in a movie. I called the present attorney I'd hired (at great expense) to discuss what needed to be done. He and I went through some options and then, at the very end of the conversation, he informed me that all of the money (equivalent, honestly, to my firstborn, in my financial world) I'd given him as retainer was gone, used up, kaput! He said he had even gone over the twelve hundred dollars I had given him. "Heidi, I've been very generous with you in not charging you that extra hour."

Here I'd just asked a question about the music I've hired him to represent. It'd finally been placed in a film, he goes through my choices for contracts, and I was about to make a choice, when he announces, "Ooops, time's up! Sorry!" Geez! I felt like I was in a Monty Python skit! It reminded me of the one about the cheese shop, where the guy walks in wanting to buy a piece of cheese. He asks the owner about this cheese and that cheese and the shop owner goes into great detail about every cheese on the list. And yet, each and every one the customer chooses, the cheese guy is flat out of. I felt like that. I felt like the poor cheese guy, but with a bit more at stake. And in my skit, I wasn't laughing, I was pissed.

So, there I was, speechless on the phone for the second time this morning. I had been all set to have the music I've written and worked so hard on, secured in the closing credit in this heartfelt film which was just about to do a film festival tour, and I'm now left with no viable way to protect any of my art, to keep it safe, and to keep my interests in check while taking advantage of this opportunity.

Today, I was also sadly reminded that once again, it's often the case that the attorneys make the money in the music industry, not the artists themselves. I also discovered, in doing the math, that even if I could come up with another retainer fee for the lawyer, ironically, the earnings from the song placement in the movie would've equaled exactly the attorney's fee requested just to write the contract. It would be a complete wash for me...the artist, the creator, the soul behind what has generated the income to begin with. All of it would go to the person whose business is based on writing up contracts to protect against distrust. Their business is based on a sort of "law of distrust." I couldn't live that way. I'm sure I'll be contemplating all of this for a while, but more importantly, I'm thinking of a way to get back underground, where I feel completely protected, as soon as possible. Back underground where trust rules.

Wednesday, October 10th, 2007

Abraham, The Peace of Time

~AM~

My day began with a relatively ugly trip uptown to a morning meeting with, yes, more lawyers. At this point, as you can probably guess, I'm not a huge fan of lawyers, and wish to God I could do without. But the more involved art gets, the more it seems these guys get their hands into things. Ugh. On top of the lawyer maze, I'm trying my best to digest all the branches of this book and album thing, and all that they involve. I mean, it's all great stuff: book being published, album being recorded, music in films…those are all great things that I love and am grateful for. It's just that the flip side is I spend less time underground and more time, well, making this stuff happen. So, sometimes I miss my balance, that balance usually felt on the platforms. I'll get it back, though. I have faith.

I walked to the Uptown A train without my guitar, with the anticipation of another "exciting" legal meeting rumbling inside me. While waiting on the platform, leaning on a pillar, I was, for the first time in a long while, actually only an observer underground. I hid in the stairwell wings and because I didn't feel chitchatty today, I secretly watched my friendly Bob Marley singer sing his tunes, since he had the stage this morning. He was back to his standard three song cycle; that third tune added a little variety to my wait. After his first song, he rested by the stairwell just in front of where I was standing. I figured he might not realize it was me without my equipment. He turned around and looked at me for a second, headphones on, waited a beat and then blurted out with that thick Trinidadian accent of his, "Where's your guitar?"

"It's not with me. I have to go uptown for a meeting." I scrunched up my nose, letting him know I didn't want to go.

"Oh," he said softly, headphones still on, and looked down at his shoes, as he remained leaning on the railing. "Where are the pictures?" he suddenly asked, his head popping up again.

"Oh, my photographer has them. It takes a bit of time to get them, but I will get them for you, I promise."

"It takes a long time?"

"Yeah, it kind of does." I wished I could have pulled out a photo to give to him right then and there. It would have made me feel more a part of and less "the observer" this morning. "Hey, what's your name?" All this time I have spoken with this man, but I never knew his name and I wanted to know.

"Abraham."

"Abraham. Nice to meet you, Abraham." He lifted only his eyes up this time, keeping his head bowed toward the cement platform, and grinned ever so slightly. Silence fell between us as the loud trains whizzed past.

Finally, he looked me in the eyes: "What about that CD?" I'd told both him and Izzy about everything I'm working on, but was surprised he'd remembered that.

"It's coming along," I said quickly, as I wasn't really feeling like going into all the crazy details of trying to get a CD out on zero money.

"When do you go in the studio?"

"I've been in the studio, and will be again; just takes money, you know?" I was trying to answer as best I could without going into the drama of "CD on no money and lawyers now owning all I had to begin with" world. Another awkward moment passed until Abraham's curiosity got the best of him, or perhaps he was just trying to fill in the silence. Although, from watching him all these years, just standing and resting without a sound on the platform, silence and Abraham seem to be close friends.

"How many songs you have?"

"Oh, thirty, forty…maybe more."

"On the album?"

"Oh, no, ten or twelve on the album. But we may split it up into two EPs. You know, six and six."

"Ah." He bowed his head once again in contemplation.

"But, don't worry," I jumped in, if for no other reason than to reassure myself. "My album *will* get completed and you'll get to hear it, Abraham."

Abraham raised his head again, "Okay. I want to hear it. Thirty songs?"

"Yeah, but, honestly, I haven't written in so long, Abraham…and I just know there's music inside me, waiting to come out. I can feel it so often. And I just don't feel myself when I don't have the time to write. I really miss it." Enter my Type A, artistic self. This combination in me is in part, I suppose, the instigator and source of some of my greatest accomplishments. But it's also the source of, at times, some pretty prickly internal conflict. That endless flow of creativity mixed with thoughts of what I'm not doing while I'm doing something else often kind of gets to me. I can say for sure, though, that the two times I feel truly at peace and am not worried about stuff I'm "not doing" are when I'm performing and when I'm songwriting. That's when I'm centered, and at peace. Maybe that's how you know your calling, your passion: when that sense of peace hits. Other times, while working, I often feel squirmy with an uneasy, kind of "fish out of water" feeling. It's the artist's dilemma, I suppose. Or maybe it's just a "Heidi dilemma." It's okay, either way, I'll own it.

As I was thinking about how I hadn't written a song in a while, and of course feeling squirmy about it, Abraham, without judgment, pressure, or expectation, softly stated, "Take your time." How'd he know? How did this guy, who in all the time I'd been underground, I'd barely spoken to, know exactly what to say right then?

Those three words instantly gave me permission to breathe. They magically took me out of myself and brought me back to now. Those three words—"take your time"— and even more so, perhaps, the energy with which they were uttered, suddenly made me feel completely alright about my path and the process and timing of all things truly worthwhile. Abraham spoke these words as if they were a truth. A truth that, in New York City and in the year 2007, I'll admit, no one seems to have the luxury of feeling very often. Those three words changed my day. I often wish I'd pushed "Record" on my phone or something, just so I could play the words back when needed. I've said it to myself often enough, but I don't buy it coming from me. But when Abraham said it with that "sit in the sun, have a margarita, don't worry, be happy" energy of his, it really did the trick.

Just then I heard the familiar rumble of the Uptown A approaching (since, by now, I can pretty much tell the sound of almost any train before it even reaches the platform). Sure enough, directly following that rumble, the A train came screaming out from the dark tunnel and pulled to a stop. I wished I could've just stayed on that platform and played my music, but instead I walked toward the car door. I turned and said goodbye to Abraham. He nodded his "headphone nod" back at me. Then, I leaned out a bit from the train door and said in a stage whisper of sorts, "Wish me luck."

"Good luck," he said.

And just like that, that former ugly feeling I had regarding my trip uptown no longer felt quite so ugly to me.

~ PM ~

After my detour from life uptown to see the lawyer, I headed back home, immediately grabbing my guitar and amp. Even though I was completely exhausted from the first part of the day, I'd promised myself some underground time, to balance it all out. I headed back to the trains and lucky for me, the first spot I checked out was empty. I set up and started in. People were responding, even though the rush hour trains were frequent and loud.

"Have I Lost My Way"

Have I lost my way
Comin' 'round this bend
Am I leading with my heart and not my head, my friend

I'm standin' on the edge
I didn't think I could fly
But each time I fall, you catch me with your eyes
You catch me with your eyes
With your eyes

And this might be my time to fly
And you might be my golden mile
I know this just might be a turn in the road
But it just, it just might be love
Whoa, oh, oh, it just, it just might be love

While I was singing, I perused the crowd, as I tend to do, looking for interesting people to watch, I noticed a middle-aged man sitting at the very end of the bench closest to me. He kept turning his head half way toward me, putting his hand in his pocket and pulling out his wallet. Every time I stopped after completing a tune or because of a very loud train going by, his wallet would go right back into his pocket again. This "wallet in, wallet out" scenario continued over and over for about four cycles. Each time I would sing, the wallet came out. Each time I stopped, the wallet went back in. I felt as if I (or perhaps he) was in the middle of some social experiment or something. What was he doing?

As this pattern continued, I began to look more closely and noticed that the bill he started to pull out each time was a five. That's so sweet; he must be shy and doesn't want to interrupt me. I guess he wants to either buy my selections CD for five bucks or he wants to give it to me just for singing. Either way, I thought it was a sweet gesture he was contemplating on his part.

Finally, his train pulled up. The man got up and walked over to my case. He looked me in the eye and held up the five-dollar bill while I was singing. I nodded, both in thanks and as an "okay" toward the CD if he wished to take one. Then the guy performed a first on the platforms: he bent down and started to unabashedly make change for himself out of the cash in my case. *All that "mish-mash" for change!* I mean, lots of folks make change, but they always do it so because they don't have a one and it's the only way they can leave a tip. But this guy, no, he just wanted change, and I guess to save himself a trip to the bank. And from his lead up, he wanted change with a quick exit so he wouldn't look like a fool for more than the few seconds it took to hop on that train. The guy timed it just so…just so that he was able to grab the five ones, fan them out, wave them in front of me so that I could see he was not (really) stealing and hop on the train. Had I been quicker on my feet, I could've pretended he was waving them in my face for me and innocently snatched all five out of his hand, saying "Thank you" with a smile just as he walked away. Sure, I'll be your bank today, be my guest. I thought to myself. What nerve! Being wholeheartedly unimpressed with the "quick change artist," I sang on, the feeling of having been slightly scammed quickly replaced by the positive feedback being given by the large number of folks who seemed to be genuinely digging my music.

Another guy hopped off a train soon after my banking customer left, turned toward me, and immediately reached in his pocket. I could tell he had pulled out money, but that he was having trouble finding ones. Frustrated, he stuffed the jumbled bills back into his pocket. As he started to walk past me, I was at the very end of my tune, the best part where it builds. With that, he backpedaled to me and, with an air of "Oh, whatever…!" he threw a twenty into my case. Okay, so that definitely made up for crazy change guy. This guy, we like. He obviously does his banking somewhere other than the A train.

I wrapped up not long after that generous donation, since as I'd accomplished my goal of replacing the inauspicious start to my day with going underground, regrouping, and, per usual, touching a little "crazy." The "crazy" factor never fails to stop by in one form or another when I sing. But I can promise you, I'm never bored when I sing the trains.

And thanks to Abraham, I went to sleep easily that night. For the first time in a long while, I felt the peace of time.

Thursday, October 18th, 2007

Connections & Candy Apples

I trudged up the stairs to the downtown side at 59th Street, all other locations I had checked being filled. Even though it was late, sitting right there was one of the Asian two-stringed instrument guys. He had his background CD going and was bowing back and forth, back and forth to Karen Carpenter's "Rainy Days and Mondays." I asked him when he might be done. With a furrowed brow, he curtly announced, "Nine!"

"Thank you." I decided to wait, since it was a good spot and now not that far from nine.

While I was waiting, a woman sat down next to me. Her shirt said "Big Apple Circus" and she smelled just like cotton candy, candy apples, and popcorn all mixed together. Sitting next to her, with those aromas, I could almost hear the ringmaster. I asked her if she worked for the circus, not having ever known anyone who did. She said she did, admitted how tired she was, that she had been on her feet since nine that morning, and that her head hurt from having eaten so much cotton candy. My stomach turned at the thought. As we were talking, a train pulled up, the car doors opened, and a homeless man stumbled in from the platform and collapsed in the car. He was kind of like my Drunken Prophet buddy, but this guy obviously needed help. A woman, dressed like she had a serious corporate job, in her business suit, skirt, jacket, and all, without missing a beat, helped him to his feet. "God bless her," said the woman next to me.

"Amazing. You know, I see everything down here." Then I thought about it for a second. "Well, not everything, but a good chunk of life goes by you while you're down here, that's for darn sure."

"You play down here?" she asked.

"Yeah. I do and I love it. I'm just waiting for this guy..." And I pointed to our neighbor to our right, "to wrap it up so I can sing."

"Well, that's cool. Yeah, I'm sure you see a lot down here, but I bet I've got you beat in having seen stuff," the woman said, playfully challenging me.

"What do you mean?"

"I've lost almost my entire family to drugs." Whoa, that was an abrupt change of pace, especially coming from someone I just sat down next to.

"Oh my God. Your entire family?" I thought to myself for a moment about the enormity of that statement. It was having a tough time sinking in. "What's your name?"

"Annie. Well, it's actually Annabelle, but that just sounds like a doll's name, so I go by Annie."

"Nice to meet you, Annie, I'm Heidi."

Then Annie went through the list of those she'd lost in her family: her two brothers, her mother, her son, her father... and the list seemed to just go on and on. I was shocked and saddened at the same time. She seemed glad to be able to tell someone, though. I was glad to listen. We talked on, she filling in the details of each family member's passing and comparing upbringings. She asked about my style of music. I opened my guitar case, rummaged around, and pulled out a CD. "Here."

"Oh, no, I don't have any money."

"No, don't worry, it's for you." I figured perhaps she might like to hear some music when she finally got home and "de-circused" herself.

"Thank you. You know, sometimes I get so stressed out that I go into my own world and I just shut the door and turn up the music really, really loud. It makes me feel better." I wasn't sure if my music would be her kind of music, but I was glad she had it to listen to anyway.

Nine finally rolled around, and it appeared that the Asian guy had gotten a second wind since, despite my glances in his direction, he didn't seem to be budging one bit. If Izzy were here, I know she'd get him to move. Oh, Izzy, where are you when I need you? Annie was still sitting next to me, due to an oddly non-existent A train. She glanced at her watch, down the tracks, and then to the guy still playing his two strings. "Do you want me to tell him he has to leave now? I mean it's nine and he said he would let you sing. Plus, I want to hear you sing!" Oh my God, it's an Izzy surrogate. I love it. But somehow, after hearing her story, I didn't think I wanted to burden her with having to hold a stubborn musician to their word. It can be a hassle. That's why, in these cases, I usually just move.

"No, thanks very much. That's okay, I'll go to another spot or maybe just go home. I've really enjoyed talking with you, though." I stood to go. I have to say, it's rare for a musician to not keep their word underground. But I'm not one to argue on this subject. He knows as well as I do how important his word is to another musician. I preferred to move on.

"Thanks for the CD, I'll e-mail you. I've really enjoyed talking with you too, Heidi," Annie said as she stashed the CD in her bag and I stood to go.

"Likewise, I liked chatting with you, Annie. Hope your train shows up soon!" And I hopped on the Downtown C back to Times Square.

I have to say, even though I didn't get to sing, oddly, I still ended up with that grounded feeling. Probably because I got to really connect with someone and share my music with her, even though it wasn't live, but through my CD. And ultimately, "connecting" is why I go.

Saturday, October 20th, 2007

That Subway Face

Today was the day that I got to sing for Poet Minor on her show *Different Voices* on Time Warner TV. We finally got it together and coordinated the date, time, and show material. She's the creator, director, and host of her show. She does it all. Over these past few months, though, our conversations regarding scheduling and the format of the show, I've really gotten to know Minor. I have come to learn that she is one of the most energetic and upbeat souls I have ever met. So personable is her personality that I feel as if I'm doing a TV show with an old friend I've known forever. That's a great feeling. I believe, as I get to know her better, she is as passionate about what she does as I am about what I do. That element in and of itself is the foundation for a very cool friendship.

Twelve thirty was show time at the TV studio, even though anything prior to three for me to be singing seems way too early. I'd wrangled a fiddle player friend of mine to come along and accompany on some tunes, just to make it more fun and interesting. My fiddle player and I arrived, set up, did sound check, and played the show. Amazingly, I didn't fall asleep. As we were breaking down with the crew, one of the studio technicians asked Minor, the host, how she had found me. "Well, I was in the subway at 42nd Street,"

Minor said, "and, you know, I had my Subway Face on."

"Oh, yeah, girl…you gotta have your Subway Face on," the technician responded, "or down there, you may not get out alive!"

"Yeah, nothin' gets through my Subway Face. Except Heidi. She somehow got through. She seemed so comfortable down there, doing what you know she loves to do. Plus, she can sing! Yeah, I heard her and she got straight through my Subway Face. Anyhow, that's how we met, and that's why she's on the show!"

"Go, Heidi!" the crewmember said to me. I smiled.

I left the studio, did some shots with a studio photographer, changed out of my heels into my much more comfortable subway shoes, and headed under. I felt a strong need to be "home" after being in that studio with all the cameras, monitors, and mics. Although I'd had a blast working with Minor and her crew, and was supremely grateful for the gig, I needed to touch people live, in real time, again.

Minor's right: the musicians I know are happy and grateful to be able to perform and share what we do on a daily basis, and make a living at it. And by doing so, we hopefully break through just a few of those "Subway Faces."

Thursday, October 25th, 2007

Truth

It's turned colder in New York City, and the damp fifty-degree day was a challenging one to trudge through above ground. But it somehow made the warmth of the subways all that more appealing.

I scooted underground around three thirty p.m., and headed straight to the Uptown ACE, where Annette had the spot. We said our quick hellos, I dropped a dollar in her bag, and she got back to work.

Finally after an hour of "spot-shopping," I landed on the Downtown ACE at 59th Street, my second most favorite location to play. Just as I was about to take my guitar off the cart, I heard a walkie-talkie and looked up to see two police officers standing at the edge of the platform. Ahhhhh...This is why there's no music here... Shoot! I stood in the coveted spot for a few minutes to see if the cops were waiting for the train along with the rest of the people on the platform, or doing a sweep of some sort. But, the trains came and went and the two cops remained. Finally, after they did their thing—going back and forth across the platform, checking inside the open train doors every time a train pulled up—I decided I'd be bold. "If I set up here," and I pointed to the spot between the two trash cans, which is "the" spot on that platform, "are you going to tell me to take it all down again?" I asked one of the two cops, once the train had pulled out of the station.

The cop looked at me and paused for a moment. "Well, I won't, but my lieutenant over there..." and she pointed across the cement to a cop standing at the platform's edge, "He may give you some trouble. He's the guy in the white shirt." I looked over to the lieutenant, who was appearing all "super official" with the constant babble coming from his always-on-full-volume walkie-talkie. I wondered if I'd mess up his mission by singing. But then she added, "But we're not going to be here much longer. You may want to wait about fifteen minutes or so and we should be gone."

"Alright, thanks! I can do that." So I stuck my earphones in and stood right there, trying my best to stay inconspicuous even though train after train came and went, and I remained—not just on the platform but steadfastly on the spot, so I wouldn't risk losing it. I kept my head down, ala One and Danny, thinking somehow that this might make me invisible enough to avoid any questioning by Mr. Lieutenant Guy. I just really didn't want to be shooed away before I'd even gotten started. As I was standing there, keeping a super-low profile, I thought, "This is nuts, I have to do all this nonsense, pretending I'm not going to sing for twenty minutes, just so in twenty minutes I can sing...it's crazy." But I remained, putting faith in the female cop informant.

Ten minutes passed, fifteen minutes passed, eighteen minutes passed, and twenty minutes arrived. I looked up and around the platform, to check on the all-clear, only to be surprised that I was now surrounded by five times the number of men in blue, all with their guns and billy clubs, walkies blaring. It was as if a sea of blue lemmings had just invaded my stage. Oh, this is not going in the right direction at all. It's turned into a friggin' cop convention. What were they all here for? Were they going to stay the whole night and hold their annual meeting at 59th Street or something? I kept my head bowed lower, hoping my ingenious, learned "camouflage" would hold. Finally, after a few more minutes, I took one headphone from my ear, heard no more walkie-talkies and looked up. No cops. I took a few steps toward the edge of the platform and looked down as far as I could...still no cops. Yes. Excellent. I'd done it! I'd waited it out and now the platform was mine. I was still a bit tentative, yet pretty darn ecstatic nonetheless. I guess that 59th Street must have been their final meeting place before they headed back to either change duties or change shifts. Honestly, I didn't really care as long as I got to sing.

I unpacked and set up. I began to play. The platform was super busy and the energy felt really good today, at least now that the cop convoy had pulled out. In the beginning, I sang a fun, up-tempo tune that almost always makes folks clap and dance, then moved to a ballad I'd written, the one that was placed in the film I'd gone through all the contract nonsense for. The film was about New Orleans and the Katrina victims. It felt good to have a song of mine in a film that hopefully would do some good and perhaps open some eyes. It also soothes me to sing it. And after all that cop stuff, I felt the need for a bit of soothing.

"Lay Me Down With Your Hands"

Lay me down
With your hands
So I might sleep like a child

Stay beside me
When I wake
So I might walk and might run wild

When I seek, you give direction
When I ask, you lend a hand
And when I turn and look behind me
You remind me who I am

When I got to an instrumental interlude, I looked up for a second. In that second, I saw, of all the people, my ex. He was just there, standing at the edge of the train platform, as if frozen. I'd never in my life seen the look I saw today in his eyes. He wasn't moving, smiling, waving…he was frozen, as if his feet were super-glued to the platform, his eyes riveted on me. The sadness I saw in his eyes cut to my core. I'd never seen that look ever before from him. The instrumental over, I went back to the vocal line of my song, our eyes catching each other's more than looking away.

> *Come, surround me*
> *With your arms*
> *Guide me safely toward the dawn*
>
> *Touch me gently*
> *When I stir*
> *Lift me higher, make me strong*

I sang while my ex stood there, frozen, now with tears welling up in his big brown eyes. The impending tears caused him to look away and bring his sleeve up in an attempt to erase the evidence. Suddenly, the steely grey doubled-breasted suit seemed to dwarf him as his tears overshadowed his corporate exterior. With the noise of the approaching train, he looked down the tracks to see what train was coming, then back at me one last time, and suddenly he made a beeline for my case. Head still bowed to hide his tear-filled eyes, he dropped a twenty into my case and jumped onto the train faster than I'd seen anyone do in all my years underground. The speed with that money reminded me of the slight-of-hand beggar woman at Bryant Park, but in reverse. As I began to sing again, I wondered what was going through his mind. Why was he caught so off guard and so unabashedly sad…and in public? Was he regretting, wishing, missing in some way? Or maybe he'd just had a *really* bad day. It was odd, though, to see him so vulnerable in such a public space. I felt badly for him, how could I not. We'd been as close as two human beings could be when we were together. My instinct was to help, but I knew that even if I'd stopped in the middle of my song, there was nothing I could do as he stood there, his eyes pouring his heart out while simultaneously shutting me out. I could do nothing. I just let him go. I closed my eyes and got completely lost in the song.

> *When I seek, you give direction*
> *When I ask, you lend a hand*
> *And when I turn and look behind me*
> *You remind me who I am*
>
> *When I turn and look behind me*
> *You remind me who I am*

> *Lay me down*
> *With your hands*
> *So I might sleep like a child*

I needed to thoroughly immerse my soul after all I'd gone through—first with cops and now with my ex silently spilling his heart and seriously confusing mine. I bathed in the lyrics, allowing them to wash over me completely as I sang. Like my first day underground, and many days since, complete abandon took over. I gave in fully to the sound, rhythm, and feel of the music, noticing nothing else around me, feeling almost as if I'd left my body and mind on the platform while I sang. And similar to so many days in this cement world beneath, despite all that had preceded that moment, everything fell away and I felt free.

Soon, people started to come up and give money. When I was done, I opened my eyes and the entire platform erupted in applause, followed by a woman who came running up to me and said, "Where is that song from?"

"It's mine. I wrote it. I write all my own music. So, the stuff that I play, the tunes you've never heard before, I probably wrote."

"Wow," she said, "those are the best lyrics. Simply beautiful!"

Behind her was a young girl, now revealed, staring at me, somewhat mesmerized. Just staring. "Do you have more? I'd like to hear more, please."

Although the song I'd sung was one I thought the least likely to gather a crowd and applause on a New York City subway platform (due to it being very slow and almost spiritual in nature), it seems to move every time. But today, I believe the truth came, not just in the song itself, but also through the delivery. I believe whatever leaves you when you sing in earnest on those platforms is what then leaves space for your truth to come through your music. I have as yet to figure out what that "thing" is that disappears when you sing underground. But what I do now know is that what is left is a pure honesty in art. I have no idea who or how many people in that crowd put a dollar in my case, but what I do know is that what they gave me was of far more value, money definitely not being in same category as truth.

Today I thought more deeply about what makes truth so. I wondered why choosing to be out of one's physical body, and even slightly out of one's mind, brings that person somehow closer to the truth. Perhaps it really is connected somehow to that same "something" I experienced dropping away that first day in the trains. Today I purposely left my physical body for a moment when I sang. I had to, given all that had just gone on prior, just to utter a single note. And in doing so, I was able to—despite everything that happened previously—sing that truth. By getting out of my head completely, I was able to touch others, perhaps even more strongly than at any other time I could remember. It almost appeared as if the stronger the opposing forces are that are working against you, the greater the truth is reached in one's art, one's passion. I began to compare in my mind these experiences I have with music and truth with others that take one out of oneself for a moment: when one is in love, or moved by a piece of art, literature, a poem, a dance, a piece of music, or even by a phenomenon of nature, like an extraordinarily memorable sunset. They all have a common thread: they remove you from the familiar and tangible, and place you above that, in a place where you feel free and unfettered, moved and almost weightless. I wonder now if all these experiences have similar effects on one's being because they actually all represent truths in their own right. Or put another way, perhaps experiencing that feeling of being taken away, taken out of oneself, is actually a very good marker of a truth manifested. Of course, every out of mind and body, being moved, experience is different and subjective. But that feeling, that feeling of being moved, is common to all and I now wonder if perhaps we should all practice being out of our minds, just a little, on a regular basis. Not think so much, just feel. Perhaps by doing so, we'd all walk a little lighter.

Saturday, October 27th, 2007

Tryin' Out My Train Legs

Especially after the last few emotionally tough roller coaster days, and after searching for a spot for what seemed like forever, I felt lucky to have found a platform to play on. I was planning on continuing on for a few hours to make my bills, when, just one hour in, a tall cop walked by, waved his arm and tilted his head, quickly telling me to move on. *Oh, give me a break.* I was more than bummed. I'd fought so hard for this opportunity to play and he was taking it away with one snap of his head.

As this wordless encounter was occurring, I looked up at a tall, elderly man dressed in a suit and tie, holding his briefcase at his side, who'd been listening to me for the past fifteen or so minutes. When I was prematurely stopped, he just shook his head. I noticed, as I packed, that he had such a disappointed look on his face. "That's not fair," the stranger said.

"No, I agree, it's not. It's not at all."

"Seems kind of like a waste of manpower, if you ask me," the man added.

"Agreed. One hundred percent agreed. You don't have to convince me any. But it happens so often I'm getting used to it, unfortunately."

I'll say it again: there's this very powerful, unspoken dialogue that goes on between performer and listener underground. It's a nod of a head, a smile, a kiss placed on a dollar bill before it lands in the case, or a hand placed over the heart prior to donating money. All these gestures say more than any bills or even words could ever express. Who knows, the silent gestures may be just a by-product of all the noise that surrounds us down here. Maybe these little nods, smiles, thumbs up, and kisses blown are because any words would be most likely drowned out by the cacophony underground. Whatever the reason, this rather intimate exchange between musician and artist is part of why I love the trains so much. I love how close we are down here and how we communicate, most often, completely without words.

I packed up without any contesting and walked toward the train door. Just as I was leaving, a tall, thin black man wheeling an electric keyboard in a small grocery cart, accompanied by a shorter woman holding a yellow bucket, asked me in disbelief, "You leaving?"

"Cops."

"Oh." Just hearing that was enough– they both jumped on the waiting train as if they were running from the scene of a crime.

The train started to pull away with me, the tall man who'd given me the compassionate word and the keyboard player and the woman with her bucket cradled in her arms.

Just as the train started on its journey, the keyboard player gracefully, in one motion, laid his very large keyboard across the small grocery cart, sat on a foldable stool against the train doors, and had began to play. So, he does the platforms and the trains, too, just like Barry. But instead of train legs, he's got a train seat. That, it seemed, would be even tougher than the leg thing, I thought to myself as the car lurched and swayed side to side, rounding corner after corner as it screamed through the dark tunnels of the system. He wasn't about to let some cop stop him from his music. I love the resourcefulness. Excellent. The woman, still cradling her yellow bucket, leaned against the opposite set of sliding doors (obviously using her train legs) and started to sing. She had an easy, soulful voice, right out of the Motown era, and together they started playing and singing "Dancin' in the Street" by Martha & The Vandellas.

The whole mood of the car lifted. I could see the tall, compassionate man change, his former disappointment being replaced with a smile as the music got to him. I love seeing that happen, with my music or another's. It's magic. I really wanted to get to my dollars to give to the musicians. But my dollars were at the bottom of my gig bag, which was zipped tight and bungee-corded twice to my cart. The car was swaying back and forth so much that even contemplating undoing my gear for a dollar seemed ludicrous. So I started singing along. The duet didn't seem to mind me making them a trio as the vocalist and I switched off on pieces of the verses. Then something wonderful happened. Little by little, a few more people joined in humming, singing, or clapping along with the familiar tune. With the energy on the train, I started to feel revitalized. Soon the entire train was singing the song, and the once dreary, chaotic ride became a train full of joy and exuberance. Then the compassionate man leaned in amidst the singing and whispered to me, "You know what defines a culture, don't you?"

"Ah, I'm not sure," I responded, still trying to keep my balance in the moving car.

"Two things: music and food. We got half of it goin' on right here."

"Yeah, add a pizza and a Corona and it'd be complete!" I grinned back, wondering if he somehow knew the Heartbeat guy.

I had to really try to keep my balance on the crowded train while we sang. But I did try to let go for a minute and just stand, unattended, while I sang. And you know what? I could see how this is possible. I could actually feel the balance, anticipating the movement of the train, unattended. I could actually feel my "train legs." As the train slowed to a stop, the keyboard player flipped his instrument upright and the woman passed her yellow bucket around, accompanied by, "Thank you for your donations. Thank you for your donations." And then they moved through the doors to the next car.

After singing on a train with what felt like half of New York, I certainly felt as if I'd gotten my feet wet enough to brave the train cars on my own, somewhere down the road. I'd definitely have to tell Barry I might actually be okay with the train thing. I now know how it works—sing one song, pass the hat, move cars, sing another song, pass the hat, move cars. All that was missing was that disposable guitar. In the cold of winter or blistering heat of summer (or when the cops get really bad on the platforms), I'll now keep the cars in the back of my mind as an option. Although, I'll be perfectly honest, I think I'd prefer keeping my music and stunt work separate for now. At least until I gather a solid collection of "stunt guitars" to subject to the experiment.

Now at 42nd Street, the compassionate man looked me straight in the eye and said, "Good luck."

"Thanks. I'm going to find another spot to sing, and I'll try not to get in to trouble." He smiled and we both went our separate ways on the platform. I was sure someone was at 42nd Street on the Uptown ACE. Even if Annette had finished for the evening, chances are that the spot was filled within minutes of her leaving. But I went anyway, dodging the now heavy rush hour flow of foot traffic in the subway tunnels as quickly as I could while dragging my amp and guitar behind me. I scurried down to the platform and was surprised to find Annette, just standing there, gear all packed... just standing in the spot. "You want the spot?"

"Yeah," I said, "Sure. Are you done?"

"I have to go to the bathroom, so you can have it."

"I'll stay if you want and hold it for you while you go." Given that Annette and others have done this for me numerous times, I have zero qualms about doing the same. I mean a bathroom or water rescue can make or break an evening sometimes. Really.

"No, you play," she said. "How long you think you'll be? Two hours?"

"No, maybe one. I've already played some up at 59th, 'til the cops came." And I made a face.

"Oh, yeah? Well, you play and I'll come back in a while when you're done. It's perfect timing! I could use a break anyway." She was apparently pleased to both get a much-needed break and have a secure prime spot to come back to once she was revived. For me, I was just grateful to slip into a great location, so close to home. How lucky was I? I mean, honestly, what are the chances?

I set up. The acoustics being different at 42nd Street than 59th, it took me a few minutes to get my auditory bearings, but find them I did, and I played on. I had a great audience. One twenty-something guy sat down, removed his earphones, and listened for half an hour, buying my CD and chitchatting in between tunes. Having someone remove their earphones and actually keep them off is a trick these days underground. I heard that before the iPod, it wasn't such a contest. But now there's a lot to compete with down here. So when real life wins out over the pre-recorded, it's very cool.

About twenty minutes in, Annette came by, dropped a dollar in my case, and said, "The spot is yours."

"Really?"

"Yeah, girl, it's yours, I'm done. Enjoy yourself, I'm going home." With that, she stood to the side of me to wait for the Uptown A train. I began in on "Walk on Through the Rain," my "perseverance" song, figuring it fit the tone of my night. I sang it, channeling everything that had gone on earlier tonight inside of me through the words, melody, and rhythm of the song.

> *When I feel the weight at the end of the day*
> *I close my eyes, I hit my knees and pray*
> *I feel the weight at the end of the day*
> *I close my eyes...my eyes*
> *I walk on through the rain*
> *I walk on through the rain*
> *I walk on through, walk on through*
> *I walk on through, walk on through*
> *I walk on through the rain*

Afterward, Annette started clapping, and then my friendly platform people joined in, as well, clapping, singing, dancing, and of course, donating...the whole nine yards. There's that truth thing again, I thought. It just moves people, no way around it.

I turned to Annette. She was smiling, grooving, and then she began to sing the chorus from the tune right back at me, but in her own, unique, "Annette" style: "Walk on through, walk on through...yeah yeah yeah!" She sang and danced, smiling at me the whole time. "I like that 'walk on through' part...Yeah! That's what we do down here, girl. I like that! We walk on through, yes we do."

Sunday, November 11th, 2007

The Cold & Cracks in the Economy

The fall-to-winter transition here happens in stages. First, there's the compulsory addition of sweaters and long-sleeved shirts (which is bad enough for someone like me who really lives for warm weather and its accompanying wardrobe). Then there's the need for full-fledged coats, hats, scarves, mittens, and anything else you can dig up to make the winter tolerable. We're creeping up on that second stage rapidly here in the city. Well, it's probably actually arrived (the *real* cold, that is), but I'm just too stubborn to seriously acknowledge its existence until my first day of real frozen pain. Then it sinks in for the season. Don't even ask…maybe it's a genetic thing, but I'm the only one in my entire family, immediate or extended, who can't stand the cold. And I'm the only one who was born and spent my earliest years in the South, so maybe it's a nature versus nurture thing. You know, environment versus genetics. Maybe where you're born determines your body's thermostat for life. Who knows? What I do know is I really only tolerate temperatures sixty degrees and over. Below that, I'm shivering. So, being the warm weather creature I am, I'm experiencing my pretty normal time delay in the "appropriate-dressing" department— I'm really not prepared, mentally or physically, for winter's assault on my underdressed body. I've been playing in a shirt and sweatshirt up until now, but today that definitely wasn't enough clothing for long

The Cold & Cracks in the Economy

stretches of time on an icebox of a subway platform.

It's not just that I like the warm weather. I can't *move* in winter clothes; I always feel kind of trapped. And add trying to get a guitar strap over a huge, down winter coat and then play lovely music, not to mention finding my guitar strings when my guitar is pushed so far out in front of my body…it just feels impossible. I'd tried to avoid the "Michelin Man" look as long as possible, but I could tell I was going to have to give in sooner rather than later. Winter was inevitable.

The stations were far calmer than usual today. Maybe it was the cold, but maybe it's what's going on in New York City and probably across the U.S. to various degrees. At the moment, the Big Apple is experiencing something that's having a huge impact on the commerce: not only is there a screenwriters strike, which, if it continues, will effect the entire film and television industry in the city, but there's also a stagehands strike, so most of the Broadway and Off-Broadway shows are closed. This particular strike impacts the city in so many ways, from restaurants to hotels to shopping venues, all the way down to parking garages and the like. The list of trickle down is endless, and it effects almost every commercial area of the city. That being said, the traffic is way off underground, especially on Sundays, when the after-theater crowd pours out of Broadway's Sunday matinee shows. There are some underground performers who wait for an hour or more in the afternoon just to secure the late night after-theater crowd. But it's different now with the strike. I'm not seeing the crowds that normally pour through the Times Square station at the end of every Broadway show. The traffic is still there, of course, it's New York, but it's far spottier than usual. So, yeah, we're part of the trickledown, it seems.

This, I fear, may be just the beginning of things to come in our economy. But, I am of the opinion that the gulf between those who have a lot and the rest has widened about as far as it can before cracks begin to appear. Union strikes, in my opinion, are prime examples of those cracks. I've thought about this for a while, as I watch the U.S. economy change, and the dollar continue to weaken. I've even thought of making a sign for my guitar case saying something like "Euros and Foreign Currency Welcome." I'll think about that one for a while, though, and see how things turn. I just figure, if some foreign tourist has a bunch of Euros or foreign currency in his pocket along with some greenbacks, personally I'd rather have the Euros at this point.

So, the fastest city in the world is in a holding pattern, a "wait and see" mode. As we enter the normally lucrative holiday season, it could mean some real devastation for the city's revenue. We'll just have to see. But let me say here, as an artist, I completely support both the Writers Guild and the stagehands union in their strikes. The entertainment industry is no longer made up of a large number of independent companies, studios, independently owned theaters, and television stations; almost the entire industry is now in the hands of a very few players. For the workers in the entertainment industry to have any say in securing their livelihoods in this environment, against these huge conglomerates, they must strike or I guarantee you they'll be ignored, and they and their families will suffer greatly. The timing of the strike was not random: staging a strike at the height of the Christmas Season will have much more impact than at any other time of the year, giving the striking workers the leverage, the most bang for their buck. It's unfortunate that there's such an imbalance of power and earnings that this must happen. But I understand why they are doing what they're doing, and I support them wholeheartedly.

Back to the cold. Annette, looking all sharp, had the Uptown ACE and there was a decent crowd on the platform, for a Sunday night with no Broadway shows. A few stations still hold their own in a time like this: the Uptown ACE and the 123 Times Square being two. Thank God. I asked Annette if she'd just begun. She had, but was only going to be there for one more set. Then I could have the spot if I wanted. She motioned her finger for me to come closer.

"Listen, Ron...You know Ron, right?"

"Yeah."

"Well, there is a chance he may come back, but us girls, we need to stick together. So you can have the spot, and if he comes back after I leave...you never saw me, okay?" Annette and I are two of a very few females on the platforms. She knows as well as I, it takes bravery and it's more challenging to be a woman underground than a man. So I really appreciated her looking out for me like that.

"Okay. But if he comes back before you leave, then we lose."

"No baby, you lose. I don't lose anything...I'll have already played."

I grinned, "Yeah. You're right, I lose. But Ron, he always takes care of us. He'll be okay with it, I'm sure." I stepped to the side to hang out and enjoy her music until she was wrapped.

"Do you mind if I take some shots of you, Annette?" I rummaged through my guitar case to find my recently donated camera. "They won't be as good as my photographer's, but I don't have any of you and I'd like some for the book and website."

"Sure, girl, as long as you give me copies."

"Of course, I'll get you copies! I've actually spent the whole weekend burning DVDs of photos for all the guys down here. I'll burn you one, too." I took as many shots as I could and then stood back and listened to Annette. She sounded amazing today. Dead-on.

"Thanks for your donations," she'd say. "And I have CDs here for sale, they're ten dollars." She'd reach into her gig bag, grab a CD, and hold it up, "And every time you buy a CD it helps to keep me in the studio recording, so thank you for your donations everyone." The consummate performer, her sales pitch continued. Annette's been working on her album bit by bit with her earnings from the underground. And now, four years later, she's almost done. She smoothly works that tidbit into her dialogue these days: she is so proud of what she's about to release. And rightly so. You can see it in her eyes and body language as she dances to her tunes. She can barely keep the excitement inside. I know how much work goes into what she's doing. I'm so proud of her. As I'd been waiting in that winter wind tunnel of the ACE, I fast became frozen to the bone. As Danny says, "That ACE, it's one of the coldest platforms in the city come winter," and he's right. I stood there with my guitar, shivering, and wondered if I could even play once the spot was mine. I was unsure if I would thaw out enough to play, since my entire body had begun to shake. Okay, I get it. Winter's here. I have to dress for it for real now. Winter, you win. Shoot.

Finally, Annette wrapped up and I took over the spot. Just as the changing of the guards was taking place, Ron sauntered up, looking rightly confused. Annette finished with, "Well, you guys will work it out, I know you will," as she rolled her gear to the side and waited for her approaching train.

"Do you mind if a play a bit, Ron?" I asked. "I'm truly only going to be forty-five minutes at the most. I'm already absolutely frozen!" In his constant kindness, Ron was completely agreeable with my request.

"I'll go play the downtown side, babe, and come back in forty-five to check in."

Honestly, I didn't last long. The special guitar picks I'd bought to help me play in the sweaty heat of summer were doing me absolutely no good now with frozen fingers. I couldn't feel a thing. My hopes that I'd warm up once I began to play and sing were fading fast, as I could barely keep the pick between my numb digits for an entire song. Man. I definitely need a better cold weather setup. As I was doing my best to maneuver my fingers through each frozen tune, I saw a large white guy coming toward me. He was large in the way a football player is large, and casually dressed in jeans and a sweatshirt. He came up very close to me, much closer than anyone but someone I know very well would do. I was surprised and took a step back. "Listen," he said as he pulled down the neck of his sweatshirt, temporarily stretching it out of shape to reveal a police badge. "Listen..." I felt my heart sink. "You gotta..." It sank again. "Move your stuff closer together. You're takin' up too much space and it's rush hour. Move your stuff closer together."

"Uh, okay," I said, barely able to get those words out of my mouth 'cause I was in shock, having thought, of course, I was going to be booted or worse. "Yeah, okay," I repeated, still stunned and sounding like a broken recording. Then the guy was gone, continuing with his platform beat. Wait...what's going on? Why the change of heart? *Who knows*, I thought as I moved my gear. *It's all so random.* But the undercover linebacker was certainly a breath of fresh air, bright light amidst all the cracks. Happily, I scooted my stuff into a tighter circle, thereby taking up less space on the platform, as instructed.

I sang, shivered, and sang. Just as I was wondering if I could pull

off a few more tunes, I saw across the platform the front wheels of a square grocery cart being gingerly guided down the concrete steps with a "gu-thump, gu-thump" rhythm and sound. I knew that rhythm. I knew that sound. And once the cart had landed on the platform and the driver was fully in view, I was right: it was Danny. Before he was even completely visible, a huge grin flowed over my face. And about a minute later, when he was finally at the bottom of the stairs and could look up, a grin of equal magnitude spilled over his. He pushed his cart over to where I was singing. The seats were all taken on the back-to-back benches, so I watched as he pulled out his handy-dandy fold-a-stool and sat right down in front of all the others seated in the benches for a visit/concert with me. *I love him!*
"I'm frozen, Danny," I half whispered and shared just with him.
"Don't you have your tracks yet?" he asked.
"What?"
"Yeah, your CD. Ya gotta have your tracks on CD for the winter so you don't get your fingers cold." He began mimicking playing guitar on his stomach. "You know, when you play your gee-tar," he said in an emphasized Southern accent. "Ya want your tunes on a CD so your fingers don't get cold playin' gee-tar."
"Ah. That's a good idea! But, no, I don't have tracks."
"Ya gotta get your tracks for the winter, darlin'. I know this keys player who did that so he could keep his fingers warm." He looked at me, giving me a "You know?" kind of nod and grin. "Yeah, you're right Danny. It's a good idea. You're right, because my fingers hurt!"
Danny looked out to the train rails for a moment. "Broadway-Nassau's where you gotta go in the winter; it's a whole lot warmer than the ACE." He spoke as if he was sharing a common known fact that he had read in some guidebook about New York City.
"Really?" I absorb everything Danny has to say about the subways. The same goes for Annette, Ron, and Izzy. They've been here much longer, and I'm honoured when they share these valuable pieces of information with me. Deciding to change the subject to try to get my mind off the cold, I jumped in proudly with, "I finished my new song!" I'd played Danny some of this new tune of mine last time I saw him and I'd promised him I'd share the whole thing with him once it was complete. When Danny, One, Rob, or Izzy show up, it's as if we're in my living room and all of Times Square just happens to be

there, somewhere in the background. The comfort level is such that for some reason, I seem to have absolutely no qualms about pulling out a half-written song, a work in progress as it were, and playing just as far as I've written so my friends can hear it and give feedback. I feel so comfortable underground that I can sing a true work under construction, stop half way through for my friend's feedback, and not care or even notice in the least the hundred or so other people also there on the subway platform. The commuters must think I'm crazy—starting songs, stopping songs, discussing a verse, a bridge, a chorus, arrangements, etcetera—all while standing, amplified, in the middle of Times Square. But honestly, I don't really notice. None of us do, really. It's no different, I suppose, from Danny bursting out in into a random a cappella line from "Oh Sole Mio" by Eduardo di Capua in honour of Luciano Pavarotti's passing this past September. He was great; he jumped straight from the end of his last R&B tune into this little snippet of opera, and then announced, "That, ladies 'n' gentlemen, is in honour of the late, great Pavarotti. Yes it is, ladies and gentleman. Pavarotti, the greatest tenor ever." Danny was obviously a huge fan, and I'm sure Pavarotti would have been proud to hear this particular tribute. The platform loved it, that's for sure.

"Lemme hear it," Danny jumped in at the announcement of my latest creation.

"It's really rough still, Danny; I've not played it for anyone yet." As I started in on my test market for Danny, and a good chunk of Manhattan as well, I felt oddly comfortable. Even though I knew the song would abruptly stop since it was only half done, having Danny there as my real audience made me feel one hundred percent safe to test it out. I started in on its rhythmic intro, hitting my guitar body with the palm of my hand, using my guitar as a percussive instrument.

"It Goes Back To You"

Whoever said
It would be easier
To tell you I'm leavin' you
And start anew

Whoever told me

That it would be better this way
When I don't hear your voice each day
What can I do

Whoa and the days are getting longer
And the nights are getting' stronger
And every time I stop
It goes back to you
Whoa
Every time I stop
It goes back to you

The first two verses and chorus over, I looked for Danny's reaction.

"Good. Good. I can hear it arranged: voices, harmonies, instruments. Good tune."

I was relieved I'd finally sung the new tune in progress for another human being. It always solidifies a piece of art once you let it out for the first time, even in its creation. The new song demo made me forget momentarily about my frozen body, but the cold rushed back once it was over. I sang one more song, as that's all my fingers and shivering self would allow, and motioned for Ron, who by that time was standing to the side, to come on over and take the spot. "My fingers are cold," I said to him as I began to pack up.

"Okay, baby. You need to dress warmer."

"I know, I know!" Maybe for this year, at least I'll be more appropriately layered for the underground. Today, it turned out, was my one painful day to really drive home the season. Despite my annual prayers to the contrary, winter actually does happen every year. Darn. Before I'd completely zipped up my bag, I remembered: "Hey, Danny, I have something for you." And I pulled out the DVD of his photos and handed it to him.

"I can see them on a computer?" he asked with anticipation.

"Yeah, or you can go to the drugstore and print copies, whatever you want, but they're yours." He seemed genuinely touched, and put the DVD in his cart overstuffed with musical gear. "Go ahead and play, Ron. I'm so done here. Thanks so much for the minutes."

"Well...I'll wait 'til..."

"Wait 'til what?" I looked around. "Oh! You want us to move...

we're in your way! You need to be right here. I forgot. Sorry."

"Well...yeah," Ron said, ever polite.

I caught on: Danny's "port-a-seat" and my dolly were still in his spot, his spot being right up at the benches. Since Ron plays without an amp, he needs to be right up close to his audience. His system is perfect for how he performs. Poor Ron, he'd been so generous in handing me the uptown to begin with, and Danny and I were still taking up his stage area.

"C'mon Danny, we have to move so Ron can play." Danny and I stepped to the side and Ron laid his guitar case on the ground, abutting the edge of the back-to-back benches where he always places it.

"Okay, y'all," he started in addressing the crowd, "I know, you're thinkin'. Y'all are thinkin'...'oh no...he's gonna play that guitar'... And you know what? You're right! With all them crazy Broadway strikes just shuttin' down Broadway, well, at least ya got me! At least ya got Ron ta keep y'all entertained 'til those lights come back up on Broadway." And he loudly banged out a few really harsh dissonant chords, just to wake everyone up, segueing directly into his lovely guitar playing and smooth-toned, soulful and pure rendition of "Lean On Me" by Bill Withers. I patted Ron a goodbye on the shoulder so I wouldn't interrupt him. "Be careful, baby."

"Thanks."

I gave Danny a hug, jumped up and down a few times to de-ice my now numb feet, and scurried out of the station, knowing it was going to be a very cold walk home.

Monday, December 31st, 2007

Rockin' The Port

A new program has just begun as a test market for the holiday season in nearby Port Authority, called "Tunes in the Terminal." I'd been asked to play, and jumped at the gig. I've been completely MIA for the past six weeks working on the book and album. I have to say, that during this process, I've missed the underground more than I can express. Vicariously reliving it through the writing was an okay second, but the real thing is always better. The thought of playing inside the warmth of Port Authority seemed a luxury in the winter months, compared to the bone-numbing temperatures of the subways. (Especially for cold-blooded me.) I was booked on the twenty-ninth of December and I pulled myself away from the book and album to do the gig. It went well. The space was lovely, it was warm, no interruptions, except for the random loud speakers announcing the bus arrivals, and there was both a bathroom and water access. Relative luxury. After my first gig there, I was offered one more gig, at the very last minute, for New Year's Eve. Why not? Why the heck not? I live right next to Port Authority, it lies right on top of Times Square, and Times Square *is* New Year's Eve...so at the very least it's got to be an entertaining evening.

I arrived at Port Authority around five thirty on the thirty-first and checked in with the main operations office. They were going to just wave me in, but I firmly requested a badge/permit since I knew that the place would be swarming with cops and there was no way I was going to be hassled after being asked to sing there on New Year's Eve. I know the drill by now. The operations manager wrangled a pass that was good for the rest of 2007. "Perfect. That's all I need it for," I said and I wheeled my gear out to the main concourse.

Port Authority is the main bus terminal of New York City, sitting right on top of the Times Square subway system, smack in the middle of Manhattan. All outgoing and incoming buses arrive and depart from Port Authority, traveling to all parts of the country. "The Port" also consists of two buildings; one houses most of the bus terminals and a myriad of shops and fast food restaurants, looking much like a mini-mall—New York-style—while the other is somewhat less commercial, more vacant and utilitarian in its demeanor. I requested to be placed smack in the middle of the "mall" portion of the main terminal, figuring I'd get the best view of most of the New Year's Eve humanity (and insanity) from that vantage point.

I set up and started in on my tunes. I graduated to a real microphone and microphone stand, which I'd borrowed from my musician neighbor, taking the place of my tiny, inconspicuous clip-on microphone that I usually use underground. I use the tiny one simply to avoid attracting the attention of cops. But I had a pass in The Port, so I could use a real setup, plus the space was so large that I found the little inconspicuous clip-on didn't really cut it acoustically. I set everything up, tested the new-fangled real mic, and began. It took me a tune or two to get the vibe/acoustics of the space, as well as the sound and feel of the new mic under my belt, but once I did it felt wonderful and so free to know I was actually allowed to be there and that no one would kick me out.

"Rock With Me"

Sometimes you feel like it's all done
Before you begin the day
And sometimes you wake to a cold sun

Rockin' The Port

> *Even though it's the middle of May*
> *And sometimes it feels like you're all alone*
> *And all that was up goes down*
> *But let the rhythm and the music take you to the floor*
> *It'll pick you up and turn you around*

Not five songs in, I heard a voice behind me say, "Excuse me, miss?" I turned around to see a cop standing behind me.

"Yes?" I said, this time in complete composure.

"Have you been given permission to play here?"

"Yup, I sure have!" I whipped out my handy-dandy badge as proof.

"Okay, I'm sorry to bother you, Miss. Good luck."

"Thanks." I went back to my playing. As I played on, it began to sink in…I'm in Port Authority Bus Terminal, probably the second busiest place in the city, commuter-wise, next to Times Square on New Years Eve, and I'm getting to sing…this *is* fantastic.

I sang on, absorbing the acoustics and the serious people-watching. There were crowds of locals, those from Jersey, and tourists, all coming to join the other million or so people in Times Square for the festivities. There were spangled hats, wacky glasses displaying "2008" in large writing, costumes, wigs, high heels, high boots, feathers, spandex, leather, patent leather…It was like Mardi Gras and Halloween all mixed together, but with everyone wearing large down coats over their wardrobe. It was one jolly crowd. They were all super friendly and chatty, and many stayed on for twenty minutes or longer just to listen on their way out to Times Square. It was kind of a gatekeeper spot I'd landed. To me it was superb.

I got a million "Happy New Year's" smiles, and a good number of "dead presidents," along with the other unusual New Years items in my case. Many days I discover I get jewelry, small books, weird trinkets, boxes with stuff inside, and tons of crazy notes on various pieces of paper with offers that really belong in the "Adult Services" section on Craig's List. It's like a bizarre kind of Christmas when I go through the notes and cards left in my case. They're very entertaining. My guitar case becomes a trippy treasure chest of sorts by the end of a gigging week. I was looking forward to exploring the entrails of my case later on this special night for crazy 'n' bizarre collectables of 2007.

In between tunes, I looked up to see a very tall black man pushing a baby carriage, walking toward me. I'd seen this man before but couldn't recall how I'd known him. Then it struck me: top of the carriage was perched an enormous black box. The "coffin"...it was "Tell Me Off" on the move. The box looked so huge, I swear you'd have thought it was a Manhattan studio apartment as it loomed over the tiny blue baby carriage it was balancing on. As he passed, I heard him say, "That was beautiful."

"Thank you. Hey, you're Tell Me Off For A Dollar, right?" The man smiled, showing his white, white teeth against his dark skin. "Hey, so what's in the box? I meant to ask you last time." There was a slight pause with no response, so I quickly withdrew my inquiry by saying, "Or, should I not ask?"

"Oh, no, you can ask," the man said slowly with his low voice. "It's just ...there's really not much in it."

"Really? Well, what's in there?" I decided to let my curious self win out over the little voice in the back of my mind that kept on saying, "Shut up, Heidi. It could really be a body!"

"Well, really, not much...just an inner tube, a bucket, and my sign." Tell Me Off reassured my inquisitive mind.

"Really? That's it? That's all that's in that huge box! Why is it so big then?" I mean, the box must have been six feet by four feet and hand painted the blackest of black.

"Well, I found it, so I keep it. I kind of like it now."

"So, is the sign your "TELL ME OFF FOR $2" sign? I asked as I retuned my guitar.

"Oh, it's changed. It used to be two dollars, but I had to lower my price, now it's a dollar. Now it says "TELL ME OFF FOR $1."

Wow, recession hits every industry, doesn't it? Now might be a good time for that "I Accept Foreign Currency" sign. "Hey, so, where are you usually? I want my photographer to get a better shot of you, if that's okay."

"Yeah, sure. I'm usually in the tunnel." We went through the exact location/"business address" so that my photographer might have a fighting chance of finding Tell Me Off. "But I don't come out every day."

"I know, that's fine, we'll try to find you."

"Okay." A slight grin passed over his face at the thought of another photo shoot as he turned to grab the handle of the powder blue baby carriage carrying his now infamous black box. He leaned into his luggage to start it moving.

"Happy New Year!" I shouted, as Tell Me Off threw me a grin. I wondered where Tell Me Off and his odd collection of belongings lived, how many takers and how much he made in a typical day being "told off." I kind of doubted he was one of the eccentric rich who beg. I think those guys travel light, and carrying a coffin around all the time is definitely not traveling light. Well, my questions would have to wait for another day, as it was New Year's Eve and I had some singing to do.

"Happy New Year," Tell Me Off mumbled in his slow, low tone. The man and his carriage regained momentum. As I started playing again, I began thinking that just seeing "Tell me off for a dollar"... or two dollars...or whatever the economy will bear...made me miss the trains. I'm really looking forward to the warmer weather and hope the cops have settled down a bit once I go back.

> *Come on and rock with it, baby*
> *Move with it, baby*
> *Come on boogie with it, baby*
> *Baby, rock on*
> *Come on and slide with it, darlin'*
> *Keep the rhythm goin'*
> *Can't you hear the music callin'*
> *Baby, rock on*
> *Baby*

After about two hours of singing, I needed a break. It was odd. I'd been so conditioned not being able to get water, or go to the bathroom, without giving up my spot, that I held out until the last possible moment. Finally, I was so parched that I packed up and actually did go to get water, reminding myself absolutely no one was going to grab my spot while I was away since I was the only one gigging at Port Authority tonight. Leisurely I came back to set up again, revived and ready to sing. About twenty minutes into my second set of tunes, a group of cops passed by, apparently herding a group of day laborers to a location that was near but, luckily, not in front of my guitar case. The cops seemed to have the whole situation under control until one of the day laborers indicated he had something else on his mind. Drunkenly tripping left and right, the guy dug into his pocket and pulled out a dollar. He mumbled something to the cop and waved the dollar in his face. "Okay, okay…" the cop said as the guy stumbled toward my case. He missed the target once, but managed to bend over, barely finding his dollar, the wayward one finally making it into the case. One it hit the target, he turned back to his two buddies, who were still completely surrounded by police officers. The officers began to herd them once again, but this mini herd had a different plan in mind. Apparently the first of the stumbling drunkards had started a domino effect, because one by one each of the three drunken men silently pulled out their respective, mangled dollars, waved them in the cops' faces, and stumbled towards my case to drop in their donations. The cops' faces during this show were almost more entertaining than what the laborers were doing. The fact that the entire comical scene was being performed in complete pantomime, combined with the fact that the cops played the straight guys while the drunk laborers played the clowns, made it even more amusing and oddly similar to a Three Stooges episode. Finally, all three intoxicated, vaudevillian knock-offs had completed their donations, "Okay, okay, you guys, let's go now," one of the cops said as the other cops stepped up and began the herding of Larry, Curly, and Moe once again. The traveling show shuffled off.

 As I played, I noticed that Port Authority seemed to be a haven for these immigrant day laborers. These Hispanic immigrant men, most likely illegal, but some legal, hang out in the Port Authority Bus Terminal at night. Many are the "other half" of the mother and child DVD bootlegger teams who work the subway tunnels. These are the men who, for very little money, build the skyscrapers that go up at lightening speed in and around the five boroughs of New York. Some build the office buildings, the condos, and the apartment buildings of New York City. Others work on the smaller, privately-owned brownstones and small tenement-style walk-ups. They're the men, hired by huge developers to turn their visions into a reality, at very low cost. They work from seven am onward, six days a week, drink until they don't even know their own name, and then crash at this bus station. These men are at various stages of intoxication, while wandering back and forth in the Port Authority, sometimes congregating, other times involving themselves in distractions on their own—such as fiddling with the pay phones, bumping into travelers, hanging in the restrooms, napping on the floor and the like, but working to build our cities and towns. Then they wake up and start all over again. The hope is, I suppose, to somehow through this routine, build a better life for themselves in America. To me it looks like an endless cycle of labor and alcohol. The hypocrisy is, of course, how we in America use or employ these men, both legal and illegal, to build our cities and towns, all while building massive walls and barriers to block their entry. These men make the developers rich. And of course, the laborers themselves will never be able to inhabit one of the high rises they build because they are too expensive. I feel, having seen the mother and child bootlegger teams and now the male counterpart in the day laborers, that there needs to be some humanity in the cycle.

The motley crowd continued to listen and drop dollars, wishing me a "Happy New Year," when I noticed a couple standing in front of me, a little ways back. They'd been standing there for a while talking. Then they walked over and gave me a thumbs up as they dropped a few fives in my case. "Where's your agent?" the man asked. "How come he didn't get you a gig for tonight?"

I smiled, "I don't have an agent. This is my gig, and honestly, I like it here. It's better than you'd think." The couple looked down at my case full of money and nodded, wide-eyed in agreement, as they walked out to join the night's festivities.

I noticed as the night wore on that there seemed to be an inordinate number of folks who had the need to shake my hand. Don't get me wrong, I appreciate everyone's support and friendly nature. But when the last guy came up and said he had seen me many times, loved my music, shook my hand, then admitted, "I've been homeless for over ten years," I hesitated. I'm not a squirmy person, but after shaking ten to twenty random hands in a three-hour time period, representing all socioeconomic backgrounds…I felt a strong need to be able to clean them off. Note to self, bring hand sanitizer!

I went back to singing; sold some CDs, guzzled my water, and made a good chunk of change, enough actually to tide me over for a while. I wanted to stay all night, I truly did, but after four hours, I'd almost run out of steam.

Finally, completely tapped out, I reluctantly packed up my belongings and, feeling fatigued, I stumbled as I hauled my gear off the raised portion of the mezzanine and pulled it downstairs to back exit of the Port Authority. I tried to use the exit that puts me within one block of my apartment but it was barricaded up in preparation for the conclusion of the New Year's Celebration. Shoot! Normally I wouldn't care which exit I used to leave Port Authority, but this night…it mattered. There were over one million people out there in Times Square, there was no way I was going to be able to lug my gear through that crowd to get home…no way on earth. As I contemplated my limited options, I noticed, in the barricaded, coveted hallway, a dozen or so cops—all in full riot gear, each one carrying a machine gun—walking straight toward me. Okay. I'm going to ask…

"Excuse me?" I asked a fully armed cop reaching the barricade.

"The exit's closed," he said in a "Darth Vader" muffled voice through his plastic visor.

"I know, but I wanted to ask how crazy it is out there…I just finished working here and I have to get home with this stuff."

"Where are you trying to get?" another cop asked in the same "Vader voice."

"Right over there." I pointed down the hallway, directly behind them. "I live in that direction."

"You have to go to the other…" the first cop curtly started to explain again, but was immediately interrupted by his superior.

"Let her through," the head cop said. "Tell anyone who stops you that McGreery said it's okay."

"Thank you so much!" I quickly took full advantage of the offer without questioning it in the least. The first cop who'd told me the walkway was closed manned the barricade and tensed up as he reluctantly moved it aside to let me through, obviously not happy at being upstaged. He gave me a look expressing a sentiment that is usually accompanied by The Finger…*Well, Happy New Year to you too!* I mumbled to myself, wondering if this masked member of law enforcement was somehow related to my nemesis from the 123. They sure had some genetically similar characteristics in the personality department. (I mean, you never know, right?) I slipped through as quickly as possible with my gear, figuring these cops with their machine guns probably had better things to do than let random chicks with guitars through obviously off-limit barricades. I rolled my cart down the now empty hallway and was met by a man walking toward me, "I'm James, I work in the operations office. You sounded good tonight."

"Thanks."

"Are you trying to get out this exit?"

"Yeah, McGreery said it was okay." I said, proudly using my code word for my exit.

"Follow me, I'll let you out."

James and I walked the corridor and down the escalator to the street level. As he pulled out his ring of keys to unlock the door, a mob of people, apparently attempting to enter Port Authority to take buses home, had plastered themselves against the glass doors. A relatively lengthy conversation ensued through the locked glass doors between James and the mob of quite angry commuters who had apparently not been able to gain access to their buses for quite a while, due to the crowds. "You have to go around!" James shouted, and motioned through the glass.

"We've tried, the other cops won't let us!" a number of folks in the crowd clamored and banged on the doors.

"Go around, to the opposite side, there is an entrance on 8th Avenue," James attempted to explain again with words and hand gestures, only to get more angry responses from the crowd.

"We've tried!" they yelled back in unison. "We have to get our buses!" This dialogue went on for a while until finally James was somehow able to sneak the door open and create a path just wide enough for me to slip through into the angry crowd. I was scared to be let out into it, fearing for my life and gear alike, but knew if I could make it into the street, I'd be scot-free for the rest of my walk home.

"Bye, James!" I shouted as the door snapped shut and the drunken, heated, and frustrated crowd swallowed me up.

"Bye, Heidi. Be safe and Happy New Year!"

"Happy New Year!" I shouted. As the crowd pushed hard against me and my gear, I was forced to start walking at its pre-determined pace.

Wow, that was a switch, having an "escort" to see me safely out the back door, accompanied by compliments on the music, versus "being escorted" off a platform or ticketed for breaking some new rule, the rule always unbeknownst to me. A dichotomy, yes, but a most welcome one. It was about eleven forty-five p.m. by the time I got out onto the streets of the city. Times Square was absolutely pulsating with the energy of a million people, all waiting to explode with a strike of a clock.

After dodging numerous revelers, I finally entered my building and recapped some of the night's adventure to the guard at the front desk. I went upstairs feeling kick-started and completely rejuvenated after my five-week writing hiatus. That first "Rockin' The Port" experience made for one amazing New Year's Eve in New York City, and a most definite positive start to 2008.

Since then, The Port has become a regular gig for me. And I've actually embraced it wholeheartedly, as I get to stay warm during the cold winter months in New York City. I'm now there regularly on Fridays in front of the thousands of commuters, tourists, and workers who pass through. It's given me the chance to sing with a real microphone and amplifier without the fear of being ticketed or arrested, thereby allowing me to put all my energies into the music and people who pass by. It's actually taken some getting used to, to not have to stop for train sounds. Odd, eh? During this time, some very cool things have occurred as well.

I've begun re-working and re-recording my tracks and album material with a producer who is both very talented and quite real, both factors appreciated and refreshing. I'm being pushed farther than I ever could have imagined in this process. And since the changes are still new, getting up in front of one to two thousand people every week to try these changes out can be a trip, to say the least.

I've also been approached by Woodstock Music Convention to showcase for them in the summer. They had scouted me out on MySpace, actually. But as I was playing last week in The Port, a woman came up to me and said she recognized my voice she'd heard online, from across the terminal. She then introduced herself as part of Woodstock and reiterated they were excited to have me there this summer. It's amazing who one runs into while making art.

Finally, this past week I brought with me the two new purchases I had to make to for the space to work for me, since I've gotten more than a few comments on the lack of volume. One purchase was a more powerful amplifier; the second, a microphone of my own, since I had been borrowing one prior to this. The amplifier's actually bright yellow, which is quite indicative of how immune I feel in relation to the authorities in The Port. Underground, that would be a complete "come and get me" colour for the cops (although I'll be using it there as well, of course), as well as a mic and a mic stand. I was now "legit" with my Port ID, and I won't lie to you when I say that the feeling of being immune to the authorities was a good one.

Thursday, May 1st, 2008

MUNY, Take Three

I've been singing all winter and spring, splitting my time between The Port, where I get some "cop free" time, and the underground. It's great having two steady music gigs, that's rare for any musician. Amidst the two gigs that have kept me steadily singing, I once again sent in my application to MUNY for the third time. It's becoming an annual tradition at this point: get application, fill it out, submit it, get invited to audition, audition, rinse, repeat…

This year I decided to do the solo thing again. If organizing five other musicians had warranted better results, I'd have done a repeat of that plan, but the results being the same, I decided to go back to "plan A," the simpler one, and go out solo again, guitar in hand.

The location was different this year, still in Grand Central, but upstairs on a balcony overlooking the entire station. Once again, everyone there was super friendly. At this point it's become an annual reunion of sorts, since they all know me so well. I can see why the musicians themselves volunteer though, it's a fun environment. They all wished me "good luck," promising "third time's a charm."

I went in front of the semi-circle of judges, guitar in hand, hearing Ron's encouraging words in my head: "You'll get it this time, baby; third time's the charm. You'll be okay. You're always okay."

I'd had chosen a favorite, Bill Withers' "Use Me Up," and one

MUNY, Take Three

of my originals, "Step Back," to audition with this year. This year, however, felt somehow different, not just location-wise, not just because I'd auditioned twice earlier, but different from the inside out. As I was announced and just before I stepped in front of the semi-circle of judges, I got that jittery thing that sometimes happens before an audition of any kind. I felt "off kilter." I took a deep breath as I looked at the thirty panelists and then remembered that tall man in the blue shirt, and what he'd said to me a while back that'd brought me right back to my center: "Do you remember when you were five?" As I stepped out into the semi-circle, I bowed my head and remembered. I was five, and higher and higher I swung in my mind as I struck the first chord on my guitar. Suddenly, a supreme calm washed over me; that calm I get, now so effortlessly in the trains, was there with me at the audition.

I breezed through the first song as effortlessly as any performance I can recall. The first song completed, I re-set my capo for my second tune while the judges and onlookers were clapping. At the rhythmic and syncopated intro to my second tune, "Step Back," I kept a close hold on that "when I was five" energy. As I sang, I could see the judges and other musicians moving and tapping their feet. I dove into the tune, and once again felt one hundred percent in the music, making the entire audition an easy and effortless experience.

Once the song was done and the clapping took over, I spotted a conga player waiting in the wings to audition next and "remember, you're the heartbeat of New York. You're the heartbeat" washed over me. I looked around at all the musicians in the crowd, the judges (all of whom were musicians themselves), and those waiting to step out and express themselves musically to the semi-circle, and it was clear, the conga player was right: we are all the heartbeat of New York. We are all the heartbeat. I was proud to be part of this group.

After the audition, I walked off the stage and into the hands of the requisite reporters. That part is always a blur to me, the random questions asked of me after I sing from reporters and film crews from all over the world. But this time the audition felt sharp and clear to me. It also felt slower and calmer than in previous years, as if time had slowed down while I sang. It didn't rush by as fast, even though the time allotted was exactly the same.

After the "event," I did what I always do now after a MUNY

audition: scoot back underground to sing and wait to hear the verdict, this time for '08. As I was leaving Grand Central to enter the subway, I saw out of the corner of my eye a lone figure, a tall, thin black man, wearing a blue-grey shirt, just standing at the corner of the audition hall, leaning on a marble column. I stared. Was this the same guy from the A train? Could this be "remember when you were five?" I stared at the man, not one hundred percent sure it was him since I'd only seen him once and couldn't figure out why he'd be here at the audition. Then the man threw me a quick wink and a nod, and walked behind the column and out of sight. Suddenly, that same sense of magic and wonder that hit me the first day when the random soul took me to "the spot" at 59th Street washed over my body once again. I stood frozen for an instant and went back to my second home underground.

Friday, August 15th, 2008

Changes & That Pursuit of Happiness

I've been back underground now for the past three months. You know me, once the cold lifts, I'm good to go. In between working some more on my album and putting the finishing touches on the book, I've just received some pretty cool, as well as some pretty odd, news.

The good news is that this year, finally, I got word that I was accepted into MUNY. Yeah! Guess my friends were right, third time was "the charm." Now part of, "Music Under New York," I have a permit and a banner. I'm a "Banner Person." I know One's going to have a field day with that one. Once a Banner Person, always a Banner Person though, so that's one more performance option I now have, and one more layer of semi-protection from the cops.

This is going to feel so odd now, though. Going from all these years of being on my own and finding my own way without any support or any overseeing body, to now being booked in specific spots at specific times in the trains. What a concept. But most importantly, now I'll not be harassed as often by the cops when I sing, and that's going to feel very, very odd, but very cool.

For these past three years, I've been performing solo, without anyone telling where or when to be anywhere. That's a huge appeal for me. It's an enormous sense of freedom to come and go at will when I need to for financial, spiritual, or artistic reasons.

However, with that freedom has come the daily tension I and others experience involving most often random and seemingly unlawful law enforcement. The latter aspect is tough. I'm feeling that now is a really good time for that banner and permit. I get my first few bookings in a few weeks. I'm excited.

Alongside the good news of getting accepted into MUNY, a very odd thing has occurred underground this spring. For the first time, Madison Square Garden (MSG) has decided to do a reality show of the underground, the prize being a performance at one of their large MSG venues. Never in my wildest dreams did I think that would happen. The Donald, perhaps, but MSG and a reality show? Anyhow, their new MSG program is called *Soundtracks* and they've asked me to audition to compete for the eight remaining spots left after they fill the first eight with musicians discovered through random scouts underground. My feelings have been mixed about the show because these are my friends they are asking me to compete against. These are the exact people who stand by each another day after day, week after week, year after year in all weather and against all odds. I know a number of the underground musicians feel the same. We are family. Most reality shows pit strangers against strangers, not family against family. Somehow, this feels a bit "off" and I'm not sure they realize the potential ramifications for us. I'm not sure, however, as I see it unfold, that they even care.

Finally, I decided to be included, and worked overtime to help as many of my friends get into the MSG program as I could. The irony of course is that it was mostly web-based and the underground is not web-based, it's people-based. Most, if not all, of my friends had no way to apply. I spent many nights setting up MySpace pages for Ron and others. Remembering what Danny had said to me when we first met about wishing to play a huge venue just one more time, I called the producer of the show and arranged for Danny to come with me to audition, since Danny had no web way for MSG to pre-screen and include him otherwise.

The auditions were held downtown during a brutally hot summer day in the city. I searched around the crowd of musicians for Danny and found him with his cart, calmly sitting like the Southerner he is, underneath the only tent in the area, fanning himself with an information sheet, grinning that unmistakable "Danny grin" of his.

I introduced Danny to the producer and filled out the appropriate forms for both of us. We sat and waited, and waited, Danny telling jokes and recounting his musical history for all to hear, thereby keeping it light. I finally got to sing, followed by a brief interview about my music and *The Subway Diaries*. But they left no time for Danny. I felt so badly. I was crushed. This man had been cleared by the producer, had come all the way down, sat in the heat for hours, and they found no time for him to do what he does so well, sing. Not even one song? He'd have blown them away. And I so wanted him to have a shot at playing a large venue again. I was fuming on his behalf, but Danny, on the other hand, seemed almost un-phased.

I realized, as Danny and I walked away from the audition site to grab coffee at McDonald's, he's one of those "lucky" ones, the one's that "have everything" and know it. It seems to me that so many underground carry this air of having everything, regardless of what it is they actually do or do not materially possess. Danny's definitely one of those souls. He's got what most people above ground search for their entire lives—through work, alcohol, climbing corporate ladders, money—and often never find. Those people may, in fact, walk by and look upon a subway musician with pity or even disdain, not realizing that the very musician they're judging may have everything they are still searching for. The unflappable contentedness that I've found to be so pervasive underground is not based on possessions or recognition, fame or fortune (all that which MSG was offering up at that audition today). This happiness is real and strong. It comes from the inside, never bought or superimposed from the outside, never decided on by someone else's judgments, never left to change with someone else's words, only worn with a light. This kind of happiness that I observe so often in my artist friends underground is that of someone who has found and owns their world and their sense of self, completely. They own their own happiness so well, that nothing outside of them can touch them. I've found it's that element alone which is perhaps the one "prerequisite" that equips a human to play the trains. If you don't have it when you go under, you develop it. You develop it in order to stay. If you don't, you leave. And to be honest with you, it's the greatest life lesson, the greatest gift a person could ever hope to gain in a lifetime. If you've found that which makes you happy, you have everything.

Danny and I continued to walk over to the nearby McDonald's to enjoy the air conditioning for a bit and chat about music. We found a table, and after getting his coffee, Danny rustled through his cart, pulled out an old cassette player, rummaged a bit more, and pulled out an unmarked cassette or two, and began to demo his past and present tunes that he'd written, no headphones, the tape recorder blaring fearlessly in the middle of the McDonald's. I guess to Danny, one place is just like another when it comes to making and showcasing music. Needless to say, we made a few friends at McDonald's that hot summer afternoon. Danny, surrounded by quite a crowd, played his tape player and sang his original tunes, interspersed with stories of his hometown in South Carolina, making sure everyone knew, of course, that we were, in fact related. In between the music and the genealogy he'd intersperse random tidbits about the history of the Blues. It was like a talking, breathing, and very animated version of the Smithsonian's Museum of Natural History was visiting McDonalds. Those at McDonald's though, seemed to be eating it up (no pun intended).

He finally wrapped up his impromptu performance and we went to the train, me with my guitar and amp, he pushing his cart filled with everything. "Let me know when they call you, Danny," I said as we went out separate directions on the ACE. "Remember, the producer promised he'd fit you in tomorrow or the next day, and I want to make sure he does."

"I will, baby. I will."

They never called Danny to sing. I even contacted the producer to let him know how long Danny had waited, how much he'd looked forward to singing, and what a perfect representation of the underground he was. He apologized and said merely that they ended up with less time than anticipated and everything got backed up. I just wished they would have at least called him to tell him that themselves.

The show went on. They put us on TV and the judges made their choices (no audience call ins for this one, just internet voting). Once it was over I felt a sense of relief that MSG was finally gone from the trains. It's tough to put into words how it felt to suddenly have life-size posters plastered everywhere on the subway walls about us competing against one another. It felt somehow counterintuitive, somewhat exploitative, and overly commercialized. It felt odd to have this made-up, pre-fabricated "media blitz" imposed on this completely truthful world that exists, and has existed for decades quite happily without the need for any of that to make it "successful." The truth of the trains is almost a polar opposite to the flash and burn of something like MSG. Most of subway talent seemed to agree. It's funny, now that it's over it feels as if it was just the tiniest of disruptions in the much larger rhythm of the underground. It's almost as if we "tolerated" their intrusion for a minute, and once gone, we got back to our world and our art, uninterrupted only, of course, by our ever present crew of "officer friendlies."

Unfortunately MSG has stated that they'll be back again this coming year. Personally, I hope not. But either way, I know now that regardless of what swoops into the underground and threatens to change the culture of the subways, be it Walkmans in the '80s, iPods in 2001, Madison Square Garden and their *Soundtracks* reality show in 2008, or the impending ability to use cell phones underground, the subways and its musicians will remain a constant. And for that I'm thankful.

"The MSG fiasco" (The winner's perspective)

The organizers of MSG's Soundtracks *told everyone from the beginning that the prize for the winner would be a full performance, opening up for a major act at one of their venues. Never was it mentioned that the offer would end up being two songs during a halftime show, which would be unpaid, in front of a sports crowd that would be using that halftime to make phone calls, run to the rest rooms or food bars, and generally talk amongst themselves. By the way, as part of the show, I already played at a halftime and got paid to do so... so what makes this a prize? Nothing. It's a total insult and cannot be tolerated.*

Playing during a halftime is not a true showcase, it's filler, and no one really pays attention. I've been there. I've done it, and its glorified busking. Unfortunately, from what I've been told since being on the show, I shouldn't be surprised by anything MSG does to promote themselves.

We were used. You know the saying... 'You screw me over once, shame on you... do it twice, shame on me.'

~ Dorian Spencer, Winner, 2008 MSG *Soundtracks*

So, it seems our initial instinct was correct: it was not about the subways, the people, their stories. It was about MSG furthering themselves. How unfortunate when people use a community like that. How strong of Dorian to stop the insanity.

Sunday, January 4th, 2009

Thinking Back, Looking Forward

    It's funny, this book didn't start out as a book at all. It started out as a diary. It began simply as something that needed to be written each night when I returned home from the trains. In fact, no matter how late I'd get home at night from the underground, the writing happened. So I in no way started down this road to "write a book"—quite the opposite, in fact. But like most art that comes through me in my life, the book seems to have a heartbeat of its own, leaving me in the role of the vehicle, the voice, the medium. So here I am, basically along for the ride, and the ride is changing direction. Change is great. I do, however, miss the underground when I'm not there, but put my trust in the direction the art pulls.

    As I reflect on the past four years I've spent underground, I realize it's the natural ending of *The Subway Diaries*, this portion at least. One now has a fancy new drum set, allowing him to alternate between his first love, the cans, and the new drum set to accompany his vocals. Annette has finally, after four years, completed her album, which is doing very well in Europe and Asia. Ron finally got to France, at the kind invitation of his loyal listeners, to explore another country and do some busking. In conjunction with his daily subway gig, Danny's playing in clubs and bars in and around Manhattan with his new *Geechee Band*. All of this happens like clockwork, except, of course, if he's locked himself in or out of his apartment. Then all bets are off. He's asked me to join in on his above ground gigs, and I'm seriously considering the offer. It'd be an honour, and I'm sure a blast, to share a stage with Danny. Izzy's finally made peace with the little amplifier I gave her and she's sounding sharp underground. She alternates between acoustic and amplified as her shoulder allows. Abraham still continues with "No Woman, No Cry" (There's something calming about the constants in life). And I'm still cheerily greeted every now and again by the "white rabbit," Simon himself, and stumble on the distinctive sounds of Sam The Sax Man as I pass through the Bryant Park Tunnel. I run into Alex as I exit or enter at 59th Street every so often, and catch her up on the latest goings-on in my life, both above and below ground— the life that, I always remind her, she was most instrumental in helping me create. Poet Minor and I have ended up great friends and are creating a show to air on her network, revolving around the underground, this journey, and the music. Mad Man, still hopping mad, seems to have made his peace with me somehow (maybe word from above?), so he allows me to sing the NRW now and again, without spastic visits from his mad, hopping, barefooted self. I seem to pass "Tell Me Off" more above ground than under these days, which always throws me, as above ground he seems to travel light, and without his "coffin" and sign, I often don't even recognize him. But each time we pass and I'm clueless, he stops and stands right in front of me, unmoving, staring right down at me until it clicks who he is. He moves on only after I've given a hello in acknowledgment. He's quite adamant about the "hello" thing, so I'm trying to be quicker on the uptake there. And finally, Dimitri is back and forth from the trains to the globe these days. Now that his citizenship is all in line, he's free to roam, and does so frequently. His newfound freedom allows him to fly off, busk and do gigs in other countries, as we'd both spoken of doing.

Well, I knew it was definitely time to wrap the book when the following began to happen above ground. I knew I'd walk down the street and, at least once or twice a week, someone or other would randomly shout, "Hey, where you been? We miss your singin'. Where you been?" Or, "I've missed you underground, when are you comin' back to sing for us?" and other variations on that theme. It's odd when that happens in the middle of New York. Rarely do I know or recognize the people who are asking, I see so many underground. But I do know it's my cue to get back under.

Finally, with the book now off to press and album finally completed, I'm back playing both the subways and multiple gigs above ground these days (imagine that—*me* comin' up for air!). All this interspersed with voiceover and stunt work.

I've been spending my "off" time planning my voyage—my voyage to see the world, book and album in hand. That goal has been front and center for years, since before Dimitri and I even began speaking about it. We spoke of meeting up here and there in Europe with our music once we were both free to travel. He's there and I'm now ready to fly, so I guess we'll have to see how that new adventure works out.

While I look back to where I began a few years ago and observe where I am today, many thoughts and emotions come to mind. But three aspects stand out above all the rest:

First, while this underground world represents all that is unimportant and trivial to the society above, it's still intact, just as it was four years ago when I took my first step onto that platform at 59th Street. And yet, the world resting on the pavement above, with Times Square as a microcosm, has collapsed. In all their decades of posturing about what they held as all important and of value—money, possessions, status, climbing corporate ladders, survival of the fittest, and so on—"They" with a capital "T" and their world have now imploded on themselves, as markets crash; dollars, yen, and Euros devalue; and thousands of people's lives are now being uprooted forever. Meanwhile, this underground culture which functions on an opposite set of premises—love, compassion, trust, and kindness, which, for the most part, are considered valueless and disposable by society as a whole—thrives. This underground culture remains unchanged. Amidst all the chaos and dissolution above, the underground community's commitment to art and humanity, ticks on as if nothing's changed. In fact, in that world, nothing has, and for that I'm grateful. I'm grateful and honoured to be a part of such a culture.

My second observation is of a personal nature: it's about my art, my music. I haven't spoken much about my own music along this journey, as it's seemed unimportant as compared to the adventures

I've encountered underground. But, as I've been in the studio recording the last of my album, it's suddenly hit me how my musical style has changed over these four years. It's changed not only in a way that's now in line with my soul, but that's oddly quite in line with much of the subway culture itself. My sound began as a straight folk sound four years ago, still pretty "trapped in that box." But as I played day in and day out, there arose this gnawing from inside, this unsettledness from within. I felt as if I wasn't being true to myself musically, as if I was in a box that my life, up to this point, had "expected" me to be in. And without protest, I'd obliged and stayed there for years. But now at the completion of the book and album, my sound finally feels in line with my soul. I don't really like talking in musical categories—you know, more boxes and all—but for the purpose of describing the change, I'll give it a try. It's changed. It's changed from straight folk, to a more soul/blues/rock-based sound. What it's called doesn't really matter. What matters is that it's now right in line and growing with who I am. As I sat in the recording studio listening to tracks last week, I couldn't help wonder, which was which? Is it that soul is my truth and the subways just happen to support that? (Much of the music underground is close harmony, soul and blues singers, a cappella gospel groups, R&B, and the like). Or, in fact, have the subways had such a great influence on me that this is now the result? I feel strongly that where I am musically is my truth. I also feel as if one of the major reasons I feel so at home in the trains is because it fits my musical truth. It's the trains that have allowed me to find that truth.

Freedom is actually the subject of my third and final observation in the closing of this book. Because of the complete freedom underground I've been allowed to grow and discover things about myself as an artist and more importantly about life that I don't think I would've been able to do in any other context. Over these past four years, I've figured out what that "thing" was that disappeared from me that first day underground, allowing me to sing with complete abandon. That "thing" that for quite a while had remained a mystery to me, was in part why I kept coming back. That thing was ego (or left brain, same thing). To sing that first note in the trains, you have to drop your ego completely. In leaving your ego and all its judgment, criticism, opinions, thoughts aside, you're left only with your art, and its expression in its purest form. That's why the sense of freedom, that's why the sense of abandon and contentedness. I know now that freedom is what replaces ego when ego leaves you. In the trains, I've been as close to truth and spirit as I've ever been in my life. Now I understand why. Now I understand why I said to Ron what I did that day on the ACE: "Sometimes I feel as if I could die right here and be happy." Without ego, you're a hundred percent free, you're a hundred percent present, and therefore you're a hundred percent happy.

Originally, I'd not have chosen the circumstances that brought me underground; not the accident, nor the degree to which I was alone throughout the process. But now, as I look back, I don't think I'd have changed a thing. Because of what happened, I'm both physically and emotionally stronger, and the path I was led down has taught me more about life than I'd have ever learned had things happened differently. Because of what occurred, I discovered the subways, and they in turn helped me to discover myself. The subways have been a place where I can, without question or interruption, freely discover, grow, and be myself as an artist. Before the trains I belonged to someone and something else and I'd never even really been in a place where I'd felt free to be me without judgment. They, the trains, have given me the greatest gift I could hope for. They've given me my truth.

Some may view the subways as being dark, as I, in fact did that first moment on the platform at 59th Street. Now, however, I see them as pure light. In fact, I go there to feel that light. Others may judge the performers underground with pity and/or disdain, even while they are being entertained. In my mind, they are to be commended in their unabashed pursuit of their passions, and deserve the highest praise for remaining true to their souls. If everyone were to get even a taste of what I've been so lucky to have experienced over the past four years, they'd be lucky indeed. I am and will be eternally grateful to this phenomenal community of musicians underground and all it's taught me about music, art, humanity, and life. Now, however, I know I need to tour, as I feel a strong pull to see the world and experience different musical cultures, with my album and *The Subway Diaries* in hand. But it's always a bittersweet transition for me whenever I take from my "train time" to play or be somewhere else. The connection to the subways will always be a huge part of who I am, and I know that whenever I'm not touring and playing elsewhere, I'll be underground, as it's the one place on this planet, so far, that I know, without a doubt, that I am free. I can only hope that everyone gets the chance to, through whatever route they take, discover their own truth, their passion, whatever that may be. After all, it's the one thing in "the journey" that really matters.

It's funny how when you least expect it, life throws you a curve— a curve that pulls out a strength you never knew you had, a strength that changes you forever.

Oh, give me somethin' I can breathe with
Somethin' I believe in
So I can see
There's a brighter day
There's a brighter day

Give me somethin' I can walk with
That you and I can talk with
And we won't stop 'cause
There's a brighter day
There's a brighter day

~ Be good to each other. See you underground ~

Post Script with Officer Halitosis & Let's Make a Deal

Heeding the call of the underground, I finally got back under, excited to see my friends, to get back into the routine, and do what makes me happy.

I went straight to my first choice, the Uptown ACE at Times Square. Miraculously, no one was there. As I stood up after plugging in all my gear, Annette showed up to my left: "You just starting?"

"Yeah. I'll be about an hour, hour and a half, tops. First day back after a while."

"I hear that. Ok, so I'll come back at six thirty. You'll be here, right? I'm gonna go up to 59th Street 'till then. Just make sure you're here, though. Ok? I'll be back at six thirty."

"Yeah, that's fine. See you then." And Annette dropped a dollar into my case as I started in on my first tune. It felt good. I was glad to be back.

I was about an hour into singing when I smelled a pungent body odor that practically bowled me over. I finished my tune and took a moment to see where the obvious lack of deodorant was coming from; oddly, I could see no one of suspicion. Normally the smell and the "perpetrator" are pretty obvious. But this time, the source remained elusive. So I figured whoever it was must have already come and gone, and the odor was just their "gift" to the ACE. I turned my head back to my case and noticed three cops coming toward me: two women, both on the short side, looking oddly alike, and a tall man who walked with the swagger of a pimp. As they got closer, I realized the smell was the male cop. Damn, was this part of his MO? I thought as I tried hard not to breathe too much. Was this part of his intimidation tactic? If so, I've gotta say, it was kind of working. It was such a disconnect though, as he seemed like any other NYC Transit cop at first glance. He was tall, black, and almost looked as if he could have been a basketball player or other athlete. But the punch he packed had nothing to do with sports. I'd never have guessed from the visual that he didn't know how to bathe or use deodorant. It's a surprise every minute, down under.

"Do you have an ID?"

In order to escape the odor, I bent down to platform level and rummaged around as long as seemed reasonable to give him what

I had. All I had with me was my insurance card, as I'd cleaned out my wallet at home, leaving all my stuff there, and somehow that was still stuck in there. "Here." I reluctantly stood up to face the cop and his BO.

"You know you're not allowed to play here, right?" he asked, as his breath suddenly hit me harder than his underarm odor. Every plosive and "h" made me feel as if I was going to hurl.

"No, I didn't know," I said, wondering what exactly he was talking about. Did he mean the amp? Had things gotten really tight in the trains while I was MIA, writing and recording? Then I realized as I handed him my insurance card that my new business card for the book had come out too, and was stuck to the back. Oh, shit! I thought. Now I'm done. I mean, there's a picture of me in the subway, train whizzing by with my guitar in hand, and the card reads "The Subway Diaries." If they go on the website I'm cooked, as it opens with talk of cops. Oddly, however, all he said was, "This all you have?"

"Yes," I responded, now, honestly, getting kind of scared as to what they were going to do with me. "What's your date of birth?" he asked. I told him and the guy actually took out a ballpoint pen and wrote on my card. My jaw dropped and my mind began to race. Hey, that's my personal property there you're defacing, scribbling on, and running your pen back and forth over to try and make the ink start. What are you doing? What's going on here?

The stinky male cop handed my cards to one of the female cops, who started up the stairs to who knows where, my documents in hand. My moment of comparatively "fresh" air I was breathing while my head was turned away from Officer Halitosis, was, however, short-lived. "Are there any warrants out for your arrest?" My arrest? A warrant for my arrest? Are you crazy? Look at me, I'm singing! Once again, my mind went crazy as I stood silent, sweating, everyone staring at me, and his breath killing me word by word. But somehow, I knew deep inside this was not a person I could protest to without getting deeper into whatever it was I happened to have stumbled into.

"Ummm...no!" I said quietly but emphatically back, trying to figure out through osmosis or some non-verbal communication what the heck was going on. But all I kept getting was harassment and stench.

"Well, we're checking now," and he motioned up the stairs where the female cop had taken my now destroyed insurance card and business card, which I was still sure would get me into some real trouble. "And if there is a warrant out, we're putting you in jail," the stinky officer continued. What? What? What? My mind went fast again. Jail? What? Me? For what? No! Jail? Are you kidding me? But I just stood silent, clenching my teeth, as all these thoughts went racing through my head, clambering to have a voice. Everyone was staring. The entire platform. I wondered what they were wondering. I wondered if they thought I was some secret criminal who'd been posing as a busker for all these years and now the cops had posed some kind of "sting" operation and had finally closed in, right there in front of their eyes on the Uptown ACE. I wondered if they thought that, or if any of them actually knew what we go through day in and day out just to sing.

"Where do you live?" Officer Halitosis said, once again torturing me with every expelled breath. I didn't want to tell him. He concerned me, frightened me, and my instinct was not to tell him my address. So, I made something up. "East side or west side?" Again, I made it up. "What's your apartment number?" We're just standing here for God's sake, you're not filling out any forms, what do you need my apartment number for? Again, I blurted out a made up apartment, glad now that I had as there seemed zero reason for him to ask any of this while we're waiting to see if there were any warrants out on me, and if I should be arrested or not.

"C'mon, we'll go upstairs." I grabbed hold of my dolly and began to wheel it toward the bottom of the cement staircase as everyone on the platform continued to stare silently. "Here, I'll help you," he leaned in and said, completely out of character, as I began to lug it up the first step.

"No," I said curtly back and leaned away from him, grabbing my gear with both arms. "No. No, thank you. I have it," I repeated.

"Let me help you."

"You two make a great team, you know that?" he said to the two female officers as the one with the documents pulled out her pad and a pen. "We got ten of these guys today and only one got away. You really make a great team." Ten? Ten?! You guys got ten musicians? Don't you have anything better to do in the New York City subway system than harass, ticket, and arrest musicians? I looked

Post Script with Officer Halitosis & Let's Make a Deal

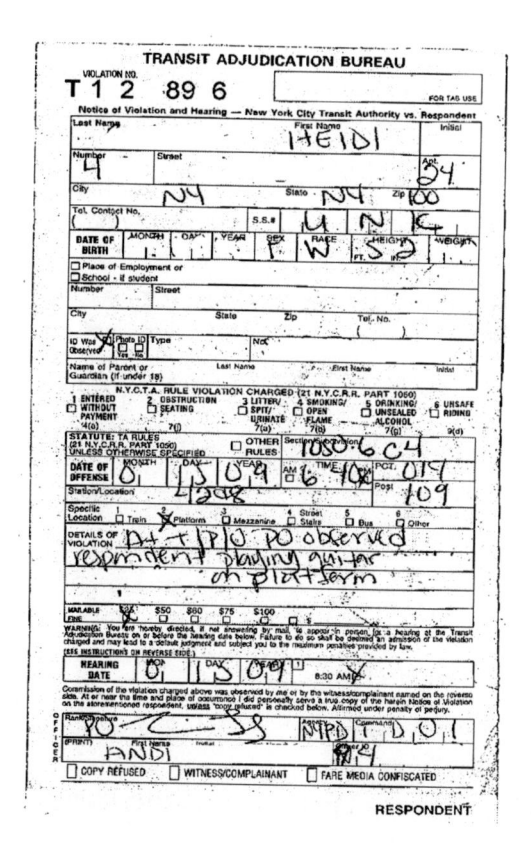

down at my watch. It was six forty-five—Annette never came back. She always comes back, even just to say she's going home and not going to sing. She always comes back. I knew then she was spending the night in jail. My heart sank and I began to boil inside. Just then, the female with my cards walked over and started to write on her pad. I've got to get out of this, I thought. I'd gotten out of the only other real "jam" I'd stumbled into a few years back with some tears and a bit of acting, but I was spent today and completely dehydrated from the heat, so no matter how I tried, I just couldn't cry. I tried. I scrunched up my eyes a number of times in an attempt to get out of this, this whatever the heck was going on, but no-go. Nothing. I was too dehydrated to cry. Wow, never had that happen, I thought as I stood there, leaning on my guitar, sweating. I'll start to just shake a bit and see what flies from that. "You better take some deep breaths, girl, 'cause we can't have you passin' out or nothin'." Right, you can harass me, you can accuse me of being a felon, you can deface my personal property, but no, "we" can't have me passing out, now can "we?" I kept on shaking, kind of getting into the rhythm of it all. "So, what do you have? You got some kinda disorder or somethin'?" the cop with the pen asked. I just kept looking down and shook my head. "Is it gout?" Gout? Where on earth did she pull that one out from? Wow, I didn't even know gout makes you shake. Ya learn something new every day, I guess. I'll have to Google that when I get home. I shook my head again. "Is it, is it gastroenteritis?" Again, this cop's got some inside information on "conditions" that I've been completely in the dark about. But, hey, good guess. She must be a frustrated quack physician. Thank God for all of us she's wielding a pen, not a scalpel. Although the gun on her side was creepin' me out as she continued to reveal her true, intellectual colours. (Or, should I say, the lack thereof.) I shook my head again, floored that she was pursuing this information, which had nothing to do with anything cop-related. And one would think she'd be concentrating on getting me out of there as quickly as possible—if something was truly going on with me, of course—not prying into what was making me shake and shiver. But no, she continued with the medical inquisition. "Is it, is it, is it..." She was obviously really trying hard to figure this one out. "Is it..." and she leaned in over her pad and pen and whispered, "Is it H1M1? You know, the 'pig flu?'" Ok, I wanted to "H1M1/Pig Flu" this woman straight to Jersey at that point. What a nutcase. God, how I wanted to at least correct the "M-N" thing for the baton-wielding wannabe diagnostician. But I didn't, I held my tongue. Barely. Damn, where is my tape recorder when I need it? Just then, the stinky one who was, gratefully, not within smelling distance but off to the side chatting with the other female officer, shouted, "What's your address again?" Weirded out, I looked up, trying to remember to keep on shaking just enough while racking my brain to remember what I'd said to him down on the platform so I'd be consistent. "Yeah, yeah, what's your apartment number?" Why this again? What's this obsession with where I live? Somehow, I pulled out the same fake address I'd given him on the platform and repeated it to him again, all the while shaking. Man, this is a lot of work to get out of a $50 ticket, or worse, it seemed. That act in

Post Script with Officer Halitosis & Let's Make a Deal

and of itself concerned me, though. What did he want with my address and apartment number? He wasn't the one writing the ticket, yet he had to know. That freaked me out. Then the female cop finally spoke: "Ok, so, all you have to do is pay this ticket here to this address." She handed me what was left of my two cards and pointed to the amount of $25 and the address. Yes! I'd gotten it down from $50 to $25 with the shaking/gout/gastroenteritis/H1N1 thing. I grabbed the handle of my cart and scurried toward the iron maiden that lets me out onto Eighth Avenue. Ok, that was not a good "Welcome Back," in my book. Something's afoot and I've got to figure it out. This is my work, this is my home, and this is my family they're messing with. After Sunday's ticket it took a number of days for me to get my courage up to go back under, believe you me. That whole "Is there a warrant" episode really knocked some air out of me. I decided to try the east side, since the last cop had asked where else I play and I'd told him 59th. I didn't want to run into him again, and in four and a half years I have never had a problem on the east side. I got to Lexington and 53rd, and an acoustic guitarist who didn't speak very good English was just wrapping up. I asked if he'd had any cop problems, he said no, and I took his spot. About ten minutes in, a homeless-looking guy wandered right over near me, in between the same two columns as me, and proceeded to set up about fifty or so books all over the platform. Immediately, a woman tripped over an oversized Bible, almost falling and smashing her face into the platform. She gave the used bookseller a look as if to say "WTF?" and he gave her the exact same look back, as if this place was his rightful storefront. Not wishing to compete with his portable bookstore, nor be witness to any serious injuries on the platform, I packed up and moved down the platform to sing.

I finally felt "settled" and the only disturbance for the next twenty minutes was the bookseller, who had randomly decided to sing/yell a capella while he sold his used literature. I sang on, then a short cop with a rather "Officer Friendly" look to him wandered over to me. "You know you're not allowed to play here, right?"

"No," I said, as I always do. Oh my God, not again...

"Do you have an ID?" And you know what? This time I didn't. Not a hint of an ID on me. Imagine that. How silly of me, right?

"Nothing?" he asked again.

"Nope, sorry. All I have is my MetroCard."

"Where do you live?" Not this again. Please. This time I just said the west side and left it at that, hoping he would as well. "How long have you lived in the city for?"

"About three years," I said randomly.

"And you don't have an ID?" he inquired. "You've been here that long and you don't have an ID? You planning on getting one?" I nodded my head yes, going with his whole concept that I just haven't gotten around to getting one yet. "So, this is what you do for a living, or something else?" the cop continued.

"I do a lot of stuff, mostly in the arts," I said, staying as vague as possible. The cop looked at my guitar case.

"Well you're not doing too well there today, now are you?" Well, if you guys would just leave me alone, stop harassing me, ticketing me, threatening to arrest me, and let me sing, I'd be doing plenty well, thank you very much… is what I wanted to say. But instead, I said, "I'm doing ok…" and left the rest unsaid.

"So, what kind of music you play?" Are we off the harass me, threaten me, ticket me, arrest me thing and moving on to the "let's get to know each other" stage or what? I thought to myself as his formerly serious face sported a bar grin.

"Ummm… it's kind of soulful, bluesy… it's a mixture." I shortened the explanation, desperately wanting to sing and not make chitchat with a Transit cop.

"You play in and around in the city?"

"Yeah, I do, but honestly, I prefer the trains." The cop paused for a minute and looked down.

"You know, I should write you a ticket. But if you give me your card and promise you'll let me backstage at one of your shows, you can pack up. I'll pass on it today." You've got to be kidding me. You're asking me to trade you my phone number in exchange for not writing me a ticket? You want to make a deal? I bent down, letting my hand pass right over the colorful Subway Diaries cards that have my phone number on it, and pulled out one of my old cards that just say "Heidi" and have a web address. I stood up and handed it to the pick-up cop. He took the card, looked at it, then looked down at the colorful ones lying in my case, but said nothing.

"So…" I ventured in bravely as I packed up, "How come no one can play anymore down here?"

"It's a space issue. Platforms too crowded. And that's just common sense," the cop lectured while we stood on a virtually empty platform, as if I needed somehow to be schooled.

"Well, how come that guy before me didn't get a ticket? I asked him and he said he'd seen no cops and no one bothered him."

"Oh, I'd have easily thrown him in jail, he just didn't speak English well enough." Really, if you don't speak English, they let you go? Well, I'm going to have to brush up on my foreign accents then, aren't I...

"Nice try, though," the cop said, as if this response made any sense at all, his bar grin getting larger all the time. I was going to bring up the homeless bookseller who continued to wail on the other side of the pillar, taking up more space than thirty musicians ever could, but I decided to quit while I was ahead. I was not scared this time. Not in the least. I made careful mental note of his name and badge number, and turned to wait for my train. As I waited, I took out a pen and one of my CD covers to write down the information. Unfortunately, the pen was out of ink, so I put both items away and pulled out my cell to make a note to myself on my phone.

"Did you get it right?"

"What?" I said, matter-of-factly, as I turned around to see Officer Flirty standing behind me.

"My badge number. I figured you were writing it down"

"No." I said calmly. "I'm just checking a text from my boyfriend." Lying but hoping to kill two birds with one stone, the birds being him leaving me the heck alone, both now and forever. It seemed to work, as both believed me and stuttered, "Oh, oh, ok..." and sheepishly walked away, backward at first, then forward to the opposite side of the platform.

I've since found out I'm not the only one experiencing an escalated amount of unwarranted harassment underground. It's been happening in excess over the past few months. Numerous musicians have been ticketed, arrested, and harassed all in the name of "cleaning up New York." So as I write this, we, the subway musicians, have finally banded together (not a small feat I must say, gathering together a bunch of gypsies) and, with the help of an organization called City Lore, are pushing back at both the MTA and the City on this nonsense.

It's more than our work down there: It's our community. It's our family. It's precious to us, and I believe that without the musicians, the otherwise dark and dingy New York City subways would hold far less charm and wonder to those passing through, either commuting as residents or as tourists to this city. To many, the art and music of the underground is an integral part of the fabric of New York City. To aggressively stomp out music and art and curb our freedom of speech won't fly. It can't fly. I'll admit, I'm at times saddened and miss my world more than I can put into words. The extreme silence of the Subways hurts me so that now days I find myself walking everywhere, avoiding traveling underground at all costs. As platform after vacant platform only serves to remind me of the world that I love and that's given me so much. My hope is that with the support we're getting—from each other, the public, and the media—the music will, in fact continue to live underground. Let's just hope this book doesn't end up in the Smithsonian Institution as a document of what "used to be" in the Subways of New York City, but instead is a window to the residents of the city and of the world to most a colourful and phenomenal community that deserves to survive, thrive and continue, in turn, to give back to the world in it's unique, magical way.

A Few Notes

This Diary has been written over a period of four and a half years, chronicling my adventures as a musician underground in the New York City subways. The chapters are conglomerates (as diaries often are) of my experiences and observations over many days and nights spent underground. The contents of the Diary are all written to the best of my memory. Eight names in the book: Alex, Dimitri, Patrick, Simon, H&R Realty, Rodriguez, McGreery, and Bojangles have been changed to protect their privacy or because I simply could not find them in the system in time to have them look over the release form (an odd quirk of the Underground). Finally, all songs/lyrics in book are originals. (c) Heidi Kole 2009 Bohemiantherapy Music LLC ASCAP.

Biography

Heidi, originally from DC, often called a Renaissance woman, is a singer/songwriter, stunt person for film/TV, actress, dancer, voiceover artist, and author. Her songwriting credits to date include songs that hold both opening and closing credit spots in a number of films. Heidi lives in New York City, where she writes and performs her music, and continues to be an avid absorber of life, both above and underground, in and around NYC, the U.S., and the globe.

Photo Credits

Jennifer Thomas: Pages 1, 26, 36, 40, 70, 83, 91, 95, 99, 112, 126, 128, 136, 145, 151, 166, 171, 193, 233, 242 and 253.
Henning P. Fischer: Pages 5, 11, 13, 16, 20, 46, 55, 77, 87, 116, 142, 162, 176, 199, 202, 208, 211, 213 and 224.
Harvey Manger-Weil: Pages 8, 31, 61, 118, 153, 157, 219 and 225.
Diana Meija: Pages 104, 109, 131, 135, 244, 247 and 251.
Damian George Wampler: Pages 53, 121 and 125.
Heidi Kole: Pages 73 and 103.
Tolga Adanali: Page 78.
Leo Cumings: Page 182.
Amy Rowe: Page 161.
Gary Scott: Page 184.

Special Thanks

City Dwellers (for Costas and Maro) (2002) © Mark Hadjipateras, 28th Street, NRW lines, New York City Transit. Commissioned and owned by Metropolitan Transportation Authority Arts for Transit (pages 70, 95, 99, 126, 166 and 171) and Times Square Times: 35 Times (2005) © Toby Buonagurio, Times Square–42nd Street, ACE, NQRW, S, 123 and 7 lines, New York City Transit. Memories of Twenty-Third Street (2002) © Keith Godard 23rd Street, NRW lines. Commissioned and owned by Metropolitan Transportation Authority Arts for Transit (pages 26, 83, 99, 145, 233 and 242) and the New York MTA for use in this book.